Keep Your Cat Healthy
the Natural Way

Also by the Author

Keep Your Pet Healthy the Natural Way
Healing the Mind the Natural Way
Keep Your Dog Healthy the Natural Way (Forthcoming)

Keep Your Cat Healthy
the Natural Way

Pat Lazarus

Fawcett Books
The Ballantine Publishing Group • New York

A Fawcett Book
Published by The Ballantine Publishing Group

www.randomhouse.com/BB/

LIBRARY OF CONGRESS CATALOGING-IN-PUBLICATION DATA
Lazarus, Pat.
    Keep your cat healthy the natural way / Pat Lazarus. —1st ed.
        p.   cm.
    ISBN 0-449-00513-5 (alk. paper)
    1. Cats—Diseases—Alternative treatment.   2. Cats—Food.
3. Cats—Health.   4. Holistic veterinary medicine.   I. Title.
SF985.L29   1999
636.8'08955—dc21   98-34704

Cover design by Barbara Leff
Cover photo courtesy of FPG International
Text design: BTD / Sabrina Bowers

Manufactured in the United States of America

First Edition: January 1999
10   9   8   7   6   5   4   3   2   1

This book is dedicated to the people who shared my strong desire to give new information to the public that can give shiny, healthy, and long lives to our cat companions—and who worked with me to make this book possible.

Acknowledgments

Obviously I owe the very existence of this book to the many holistic veterinarians who freely gave of their time and expertise in interviews with me, in sending published material, and in checking the manuscript word for word for accuracy.

Those veterinarians are, in alphabetical order, Nino Aloro, D.V.M., of Virginia; Sheldon Altman, D.V.M., California; Ihor John Basko, D.V.M., Hawaii; John Fudens, D.V.M., Florida; Robert Goldstein, V.M.D., Connecticut; Michael W. Lemmon, D.V.M., Washington; John B. Limehouse, D.V.M., California; Jack Long, V.M.D., California; S. Allen Price, D.V.M., Alabama; Phillip Racyln, D.V.M., New York; Norman C. Ralston, D.V.M., Texas; Robert J. Silver, D.V.M., Colorado; Carvel G. Tiekert, D.V.M., Maryland; and Neal K. Weiner, D.V.M., California.

I owe gratitude to my husband, Joe, also a medical writer, who helped me with many of the mechanical aspects of this compilation and who gave me strong psychological support, as he has throughout our marriage.

And I must thank Brendan Robinson, who stepped in and rescued the manuscript after a computer breakdown. Perhaps fittingly, it was Brendan's inspired work in devising a successful healing diet for his pet scheduled for euthanasia that started my interest in holistic veterinary medicine some two decades ago.

Contents

Keep Your Cat Healthy
the Natural Way

Introduction

How I Came to Write This Book

The first edition of this book (which was called *Keep Your Pet Healthy the Natural Way* because it covered both dogs and cats) was inspired by two small poodles who recovered from diagnosed "hopeless" cases of arthritis through dietary changes only. One of the dogs, Shiki, was my own.

Shiki also inspired this new edition, in even more dramatic fashion, many years later when holistic therapy allowed her to recover completely from diagnosed terminal cancer.

Even though the first edition was continuing to sell after more than sixteen years (a very long time in the publishing world), Shiki's return from paralysis and coma to sprightly health within a few weeks made me research the advances holistic veterinary medicine had made in those years. (I hadn't looked into them previously because I write basically on alternative medicine for humans.) Once I saw how gigantic those advances were, I knew it was part of my mission in life to tell other people about them.

While my *personal* inspirations for both editions happened to be dogs, I was also greatly inspired by the number of cats I learned of who were responding beautifully to holistic care: for instance, my tenant's Persian, Snowball, who had been pronounced hopeless with generalized red mange, an often fatal disease of the skin and hair. Before my eyes, within weeks of seeing a holistic veterinarian,

Snowball went from being a totally bald skeleton of a cat with terrible-looking, reddened bare skin back to his original fluffy, proud-looking self.

Also, Marty Goldstein, D.V. M., who was doing research on a new natural therapy for cancer (see chapter 11), treated me to a number of awesome before and after pictures of cats who had been diagnosed as terminal when brought to him.

There were also phone calls from elated readers of the first edition telling me of the wonderful results their cats had had with holistic therapy: Stevie from the Bronx (cancer), Sarah from Hawaii (kidney failure), Gorgeous from Arizona (recurrent cystitis), and many more.

Because holistic veterinary medicine had expanded so much over the years, I felt that I could not give cats the full advantage of all the new therapies for them if I once again lumped them in the same book as dogs. I asked the new publisher to let me separate this into two books, so that I could give cats their own book.

I would like to share with you right now the two case histories that inspired the first edition. If you don't mind, I'd like to hold off giving details about Shiki's return from the land of terminal cancer until later in this introduction. I realize that if you are new to the field of alternative medicine, Shiki's experience sounds preposterous. I would like to lead you gradually into an understanding of just *how* and *why* holistic medicine works to achieve what seem to be wonders to those who have not investigated the field.

The first edition began in the moment that my friends Brendan Robinson and Nick Cieri stood beside their totally crippled toy poodle, Little Boy, in their veterinarian's office and listened to the words: "This animal is far too advanced with arthritis to help in any way whatsoever. Put him to sleep. Please do it right now: Every moment he lives is torture for him."

Luckily for Little Boy—and for all the dogs and cats I believe will be helped by the little-known information in these pages—Bren and Nick chose to bundle up their little dog and take him home.

About a week later, I went over to visit. Little Boy was lying about six feet away from his bowl of food. He started a laborious attempt to crawl to his bowl. I say crawl, because walking—or even standing—had been impossible for the toy poodle for quite a while.

However, it was all too apparent that now crawling, too, was almost impossible. Each little leg crept out slowly, tentatively; and Little Boy squealed with pain at every movement as he tried to drag his small body along the floor.

While Bren and Nick fell over each other in a race to bring the food bowl to their pet, I found myself thinking something I never would have believed would cross my mind: He *should* be put to sleep.

A week later, Bren phoned. "Do you think the diet for arthritis in human patients might possibly work for dogs, too?" he asked. Bren had studied such therapies for human beings extensively; I am a writer in the same field.

I thought a moment. "It might," I said. Then I added, "If it doesn't, what have you and Little Boy got to lose?"

"Right," Bren agreed. "What have we got to lose?"

Bren set to work adapting human therapy to what he could only hope were the correct differing needs of a dog. He had no book to guide him because there was none. And we did not know then that a small but growing number of veterinarians across the country were already using natural therapies for their patients.

Several weeks later, Bren called again. "Come on over," he said; "we have a surprise for you."

I was led out to the yard, where a tiny poodle of seemingly limitless energy—obviously a puppy—was playing a game by himself of leaping constantly to and fro over a low bush. When he saw me, he bounded over, tail wagging, and greeted me as if he knew me.

"Oh," I said, charmed, "you have a new little puppy!" (At the same time, I was thinking sadly that this new puppy's presence in the house meant that the nine-year-old Little Boy had been "disposed of.")

"Everybody says that!" Nick said, delighted.

"That's Little Boy," Bren said.

"That's Little Boy?" I said. "That can't *possibly* be Little Boy."

"I know it can't possibly be," Bren said, "but it is."*

Several months after Little Boy's return from the land of the hopeless, I took my own little black miniature poodle, Shiki, who was only a year old, to one of the top orthodox veterinary centers in the country; I wanted the best for my moppet. Shiki had been holding her right hind leg up in the air in a little ball and hobbling around on three feet for progressively longer periods of time. Lately, she had not been able to put her leg down at all.

"It's arthritis," said the veterinarian. "You really can't do anything for it. Just give her half a Tylenol when the pain gets too bad."

As you will see later in this book, I deplore the fact that it often takes so long for new medical ideas to supplant old, embedded ones. Yet in Shiki's case, I myself almost fell prey to the thinking that keeps new ideas from being accepted in medicine.

Shamefully I must admit that it took me a full month to realize that there *was* something I could try for Shiki, despite the doctor's words. One night I was sitting at my typewriter unable to do much work as I sadly watched my courageous little black moppet playing happily by herself. She would throw her ball across the room, chase it, retrieve it, and then growl at it for having tried to get away. Obviously this was real fun, because she was repeating the game over and over. What bothered me, however, was seeing her hobble across the room on three feet; and maybe I was imagining it, but was she starting to have trouble with one of her other legs, too?

"Oh, what's the use?" I said to myself. "I'm a medical writer; I know what is probably going to happen. She's going to get worse and worse, until she's as crippled as Little Boy used to be. She's going to have to be put to sleep, just as Little Boy was supposed to have been."

I wheeled back and ran that thought through my mind again:

---

* Little Boy died five years later, at age fourteen, of a fast-acting virus. But he was still leaping effortlessly over that bush a few hours before the virus struck.

". . . as crippled as Little Boy *used to be*?" ". . . be put to sleep, just as Little Boy *was supposed to have been*?"

I leaped across the room to the phone, almost tripping over Shiki, who was crossing my path in pursuit of her errant ball.

Bren answered the phone. "What is the diet you made up for Little Boy?" I asked, without taking the time to introduce myself.

"Who is this?" Bren asked.

"Never *mind* who this is," I said impatiently, and inanely. *"Just tell me what the diet is.* It might possibly help Shiki, too."

"You know," Bren said, "I was thinking that just the other day."

"The other day?" I said. "What took you so long?"

There was a pause. "I don't know," Bren said. "What took *you* so long?"

That night I threw Shiki's "nutritionally complete" supermarket dog foods out with the trash and started Shiki on the more natural diet Bren had painstakingly devised (which, by the way, turned out to be extremely close to the diet used successfully by the nutritional veterinarians whose work is detailed in this book). One day later I reported happily to my husband: "Shiki was able to put her leg down today! For at least ten minutes!"

Two weeks later I was able to report: "Shiki held her leg up once today. For about two minutes."

Shiki remained free of arthritis until the day she died, of natural causes, almost two decades later.

How This Book Was Researched and Written

To start my research, I obtained a list of veterinarians who belong to the American Holistic Veterinary Medical Association. This list told me their addresses and the fields of alternative medicine they are trained in (nutrition, herbology, homeopathy, acupuncture, kinesiology, chiropractic, and so on). Almost all of the doctors I chose to contact practiced a broad range of therapies, some as many as nine or ten. Occasionally, for a specific reason, I opted for a doctor who specialized in one therapy. I also had a strong preference for the veterinarians who had worked with me on the first book. This preference came not only from loyalty, but from the fact that by now these doctors have more experience in holistic veterinary medicine than anyone in history.

The responses to the questionnaires I sent told me, among other things, the disorders the veterinarians have the most hands-on experience in treating. I chose several doctors to interview for each chapter. As I had suspected, they assured me that the therapies covered in the first book were still valid. As I also had suspected, the doctors now had numerous new therapies in their arsenal. (In the field of nutrition alone, there has been a virtual explosion of research in recent years. Many previously unknown nutrients have been discovered and studied, and new uses have been found for the ones that were known.)

I found that, for disorders in which the diagnosis of terminal sometimes didn't mean terminal to a holistic veterinarian years ago, now it *often* doesn't. I found these doctors using newly discovered nutrients for disorders they previously had to treat with drugs or surgery. (As mentioned later, all holistic veterinarians have first received a veterinary degree in orthodox medicine.)

In short, as I listened to these veterinarians talk about their work, I kept thinking that Columbus wasn't the only one who discovered a whole new world.

For the most part, I have not interrupted the practical thrust of this book to cite the medical studies on which these doctors have based their work; but you should know that the doctors *are* using solid scientific bases. (Actually, it is an undisputed basic medical fact that nutrients create every biochemical reaction in our bodies. For instance, if you have a hormonal imbalance, a holistic doctor will know how to give you the correct balance of nutrients to get your body producing the natural balance of hormones on its own—just as it always did before you got sick.) Also, you should know that when I give only one case history, it is only a representative case history chosen from many. I mention this because a number of the histories in this book will seem so astounding to you if you're new to alternative medicine that it would be easy to assume the doctors picked their one greatest success story to tell me about. And when I quote only one veterinarian, I do so only to personalize the information; it doesn't mean there is only one doctor who uses the therapy being discussed.

What This Book Is All About

Obviously, this book is all about saving the lives of cats. Dogs can also benefit equally from holistic therapy. (I will be publishing very shortly a book devoted exclusively to our canine companions, who get different diseases than cats do and who have different requirements for a basic preventive diet.) And, as "my" veterinarians repeatedly pointed out to me, natural therapies that can cure disorders such as glaucoma, arthritis, and cancer are known to cure them in humans, too.

In this book holistic veterinarians tell you simple ways to *prevent* the disorders generally considered inevitable: cancer, heart problems, diabetes, arthritis, and so on. As I detail in chapter 2, these steps basically involve feeding your cat the diet her body evolved to thrive on—which is most probably *not* the diet you're feeding her—and will save you money, too.

Of course, there will be those of you for whom this book's prevention program comes too late, those of you with a cat stricken with a serious disease. If you're too late for the prevention program, you can use the successful natural therapies that I detail for many disorders.

Has orthodox veterinary medicine despaired of your pet? Have you been told to put him to sleep? *PLEASE DO NOT PUT YOUR PET TO SLEEP BEFORE YOU READ THIS BOOK.* You will find that holistic veterinarians often have extraordinary success with the "rejects" of traditional veterinary medicine; indeed, the majority of the case histories in this book detail recoveries of cats who were given up on by orthodox veterinarians. As a matter of fact, time after time as I gathered material for this book, holistic veterinarians said to me sadly:

"So often we get to see only the pet who has been given up on by traditional medicine. That is because many people don't think of natural medicine until everything else has been tried and has failed. While it is true that we often get good results with 'hopeless' cases, we can do even so much more when we can treat a pet in the early or intermediate stages of a disease."

The natural therapies covered in this book differ in three basic respects from drug and surgery treatments:

- The natural therapies do not tend to have the negative side effects of drugs and do not carry the dangers of surgery.
- The natural therapies do not attack just the *symptoms* of the disorder. Instead, they rebuild the total health of the body—*and the body heals itself*. In this way, as you will see, pets being treated by holistic veterinarians for one disorder tend to recover from other, seemingly unrelated disorders, too.
- Often, the natural therapies are less expensive than drugs or surgery. When the natural therapy is more expensive, it is because you are keeping your pet alive to be *on* the therapy. (A fatal dose of anesthesia—that is, euthanasia—isn't all that expensive.)

You may wonder: If nutritional medicine is so successful, why doesn't my veterinarian use it? The answer to that can be given in two parts. First, the dissemination of new medical knowledge tends to be much, much slower than most of the public realizes; and it is quite possible that your own veterinarian simply does not yet have the information put forth in this book. Another possible reason lies in the natural conservatism and skepticism of the scientific mind. This skepticism may very well have saved us from a lot of dangerous quackery, but it has also labeled as "quacks" a number of scientists later proven to be geniuses. And, as I detail later in this book, it has sometimes slowed down the use of new therapies now recognized as being responsible for saving millions of lives. For instance, antibiotics—now relied on so heavily by orthodox medicine—weren't used until a decade after they were discovered.

It was obvious "quackery" for anyone to claim he had found a cure for not just one but a number of "hopeless" diseases in, of all things, the bark from a tree.

But times are definitely changing. The orthodox war against natural medicine—which at several points in recent history reached what might be called a fever pitch—has greatly died down in the last few years. It might be considered gratifying to note that the truce resulted in no small part from the will of the people. I think the tide turned when the prestigious journal for the union of orthodox M.D.s (the *Journal of the American Medical Association*) published a report that found that one in three Americans routinely visit alternative practitioners.

This surprising survey, and later results along this line that were even more surprising, led this union of orthodox doctors to urge their membership to consider learning alternative techniques.

By 1997, reportedly over one-third of this country's medical schools were offering courses in nutrition, acupuncture, homeopathy, massage, and—I might add—prayer. When I wrote the first book, virtually no medical school offered even an elementary course in nutrition—even though it was well established by then that nutrients create every biochemical reaction in the body.

Health insurance companies have started joining the bandwagon, having realized that holistic care prevents disease and that its therapies are generally shorter term and less expensive.

Before I end this section, I would like to add one other way in which holistic veterinary medicine differs from orthodox. Holistic doctors do not tend to consider healing a cat's physical disorders to be the be-all and end-all of their responsibility. The word *holistic* used to be more often spelled *wholistic*—because in this approach to healing, the whole entity that comprises the animal (or human) is treated.

Holistic veterinarian John Fudens, D.V.M., expressed that idea to me this way: "The holistic view is that life is an integration of the physical with the spiritual, mental, and emotional. The physical is only an expression of the last three worlds."

I have never come upon an orthodox veterinarian who actually ignored an animal's psyche. But holistic veterinarians do tend to make the cat's spirit a more important part of their treatment. For instance, Norman C. Ralston, D.V.M., treated a cat for severe emotional problems. "He had taken to attacking his owner something terrible," the veterinarian said. "He had started all this when she brought him home from another veterinarian after having him castrated and having him declawed, so you can sort of understand his point of view." When the woman brought the cat to Dr. Ralston, the animal was traumatized at finding himself in another doctor's office.

Dr. Ralston put the cat into a room with no surgical equipment and no examining table. "I spent four hours getting that poor guy untraumatized," the veterinarian said. "My crew were telling me, 'Well, you know, we can just grab this cat for you.' I told them, '*You are not grabbing this cat.*' "

The veterinarian treated the animal for his emotional problems. "We got him to the point where he forgave his owner and stopped attacking her," he states. "But he still didn't like her anymore. Now we're seeing signs of his old affection returning." A few weeks later, Dr. Ralston wrote me, "He now gets up in the owner's lap to be petted."

I hope and believe that the compilation nature of this book gives you broader information—and from doctors with more expertise in the problem being discussed—than if I'd taken the easy way out and reported the work basically of only one doctor, as many books do. For instance, I had read several references to a new virus in cats—AIDS. But there was no mention of a cure, or even a treatment. As questionnaire after questionnaire came back, I feared that holistic veterinary medicine didn't have an answer for this new cat virus. Finally, on one of those days that make the grueling work of a compilation so rewarding, I received a completed questionnaire from Jack Long, V.M.D., who had worked with me on the first book. Dr. Long had for years made the treatment of feline leukemia one of his specialties. "The AIDS virus in cats is very similar to the feline leukemia virus, and it has the same types of effects on the immune system," he wrote me. "I treat cats with AIDS using basically the therapy I use for leukemia, and I'm having good results." (See chapter 8 on infectious diseases.)

How to Use This Book

If you have a new kitten and apply the principles detailed in the prevention chapters, you very probably will never have any use for the chapters on therapy. However, you may want to look over those chapters now, anyway: Very possibly either now or someday you may be able to help a friend's pet by alerting your friend to the information in these chapters.

If you are reading this book because you already have a sick animal, please be sure you read the pertinent information carefully, especially if you do not already know a lot about nutritional medicine.

In some cases, treating your pet yourself is possible, and I have tried to indicate clearly when and exactly how you can administer treatment yourself. In treating your own pet, you *must* first have a clear-cut diagnosis from a veterinarian. Treating your pet for one disorder when he really has something quite different that just happens to have similar symptoms can be tantamount to killing him.

For the most part, however, I am against any medical treatment—either with drugs or natural therapies—that is not conducted by, or at least under the supervision of, a trained doctor.* The directory at the back of the book gives phone numbers of many holistic veterinarians from around the country. If you don't live near enough to one of these doctors to take your pet in directly, I can tell you that many of them mentioned to me that over half the work they do is over-the-phone consultation.

Before sickness strikes your pet, choose a holistic veterinarian who will work with you and your orthodox veterinarian by phone. (Most of the nutritional, herbal, and homeopathic remedies used by holistic practitioners have in recent years become available not only

---

* You will see later, for instance, that holistic veterinarians often use extremely high amounts of vitamins A and E. However, if you were to try giving the same high amounts of these two vitamins without consulting first with a veterinarian, you might cause your pet great harm. When veterinarians use large doses of vitamins A and E, they use the vitamins in a new, water-soluble form. The commonly available fat-soluble form can be highly toxic in large doses.

in health food stores but also in drugstores. Or holistic veterinarians will mail some therapies to you. So don't be afraid that your orthodox doctor won't have the medicines needed.) In making your choice of a holistic doctor to deal *in person* with your cat, keep in mind that while the vast majority of these veterinarians use orthodox techniques when necessary for the individual case, I found a few who absolutely refused to use drugs or surgery. When these were needed, they sent the animal to an orthodox veterinarian. Do you want your cat to lose valuable time in an emergency?

Speaking of emergencies, generally these are the times when orthodox techniques are most valuable. If you're not close to a holistic doctor, take your companion to a nearby orthodox veterinarian. Get the cat stabilized, and then have the orthodox doctor consult by phone with your chosen holistic veterinarian. It would be a shame if you lost valuable time waiting to talk to a holistic veterinarian only to find out he or she would start off with the same therapies an orthodox doctor would.

Cats are, unfortunately, quite prone to fast-acting diseases that give very little notice that the cat is ill until he is suffering an emergency. When you choose your friend's holistic veterinarian (consulting or personal), ask what homeopathics or other remedies you might keep on hand to help your cat until you can get veterinary help. A number of holistic veterinarians have told me they dispense lactated Ringer's kits to owners and teach them how to use them. These can often be the difference between life and death when the cat becomes dehydrated, which can happen very suddenly. (See chapter 8 on infectious diseases.)

One final note about choosing a holistic veterinarian: More and more orthodox veterinarians are incorporating holistic therapies into their practices, and I have found a few who think of themselves as holistic but who still rely most heavily on their earlier training. Ask the doctor you're talking to approximately how many times he uses orthodox as opposed to holistic therapy.

The index at the back of the book can be a valuable tool for you. Let's say you read something that interests you about probiotics, and you'd like to know more about how they work. Check the index under *probiotics*, and it will lead you to every mention in the book about them. Or if you're reading a section on a particular disorder, check the index to see if that problem is mentioned somewhere else, too.

You may be concerned about a disorder for which you can find no section in the text. It may, however, be mentioned in a section on another problem. Again, check the index.

A Note for Orthodox Veterinarians

First, I know that many of you have recently become interested in investigating holistic therapies for incorporation into your practice. Over the years I have received word from a number of orthodox veterinarians telling me that they were using the first edition as a basic starting point. That was certainly gratifying. But obviously the explosion of alternative medicine since 1981, when I researched that edition, has made the earlier book obsolete. Today's holistic veterinarians have assured me that nothing in the earlier book has proved invalid—but there is so much more that can be done today, just as there is so much more that can be done today in orthodox medicine.

I hope this new edition will serve as an update for you if you used the first book as a starting point in your investigation of holistic veterinary medicine, or as an introduction to holistic veterinary medicine if you're just learning the ropes.

The list of veterinarians at the back of the book has been expanded since the first edition, so I have been able to give you the addresses and phone numbers of more holistic doctors, should you wish to consult about something.

Now I would like to address myself to the more skeptical orthodox veterinarian.

I do not ask any orthodox veterinarian to abandon years of training, knowledge, experience, and success for an "opposite" field. I ask only that you consider adding to your success, experience, and knowledge with a successful adjunct therapy. You will see throughout this book that holistic veterinarians have not abandoned their years of training and experience in orthodox therapies. You will see surgery, antibiotics, and so on as a part of their treatment in a number of the specific case histories.

I think John S. Eden, D.V.M., expressed the above ideas very well. Dr. Eden once described his approach to veterinary medicine as "largely orthodox." He wrote me: "In my mind a combination of the two fields of knowledge seems the best of both worlds, and that is how I try to guide myself. . . . I deeply resent it when one side of this issue tries to debunk or discredit the other. It is a foolish waste of energy and only serves to prevent any exchange of information and to limit the capacity of both sides to solve problems." As Dr. Eden added, preventing this exchange of information "diminishes the ability to accomplish the common goal of seeking what is best for the animal."

The next time you have a pet in your office for which surgery or drugs offer no hope, won't you please consult this book to see if it contains an approach relevant to that pet, consult with one of the holistic veterinarians named in the directory, and try the suggested therapy before you put the pet to sleep? If the therapy doesn't work, you and your patient will have lost nothing. If it does, an animal will have been saved.

Shiki's Journey into—and out of— the Land of the Doomed

I know of countless cats who "miraculously" recovered from diagnosed terminal cancer and other problems deemed hopeless. I mentioned just a few of them at the beginning of this introduction, and you will read of many others throughout the book. All of them together—and each one individually—helped inspire me to write this new edition.

However, here I would like to share with you the true story of my miniature poodle, who was my strictly *personal* inspiration for writing this book.

Earlier, I said I'd like to delay telling you about my Shiki's "miracle" recovery from diagnosed terminal cancer. I wanted to wait until I had explained alternative medicine well enough for you to understand why I'd used quotation marks around the word *miracle*. They indicate that although many people might consider her recovery a miracle, holistic veterinarians would not because they know the scientific reasons behind such recoveries.

I hope Shiki's grim journey will serve as a further introduction to the success of holistic medical techniques—because her "miracle" is by no means unique. (See chapter 11 for the results of a study of many years on thousands of cats and dogs diagnosed with terminal cancer: About half went into remission—and remain cancer-free today or remained cancer-free until they died of other causes.) I also hope that Shiki's tale will serve as a very specific example of why I have urged in this introduction that you don't give up on your cat until you have tried holistic veterinary medicine. Finally, I believe Shiki's journey will give you a more specific overview of some of the ways holistic veterinarians work differently from orthodox veterinarians.

One morning, Shiki uttered a little cry and toppled over. My husband, Joe, and I ran to find out why her legs had suddenly failed her. She was lying there helplessly, screaming and flailing her legs in the air trying desperately to right herself so she could stand again. But soon all her terrified activity ceased.

Shiki was no longer only unable to stand. She was in a coma.

She was diagnosed by probably the most respected orthodox veterinary center in this country as having terminal cancer. (For skeptics who might ask why my "naturally raised" dog developed cancer, I'll repeat what I said earlier—that she didn't receive a natural diet early in life, because I didn't know then what a dog's natural diet was. Also, she was sixteen when diagnosed with cancer. That's an age—equivalent to age 90 in humans—at which most dogs have already passed on. Actually, her ancient age makes her recovery even more remarkable.)

The orthodox veterinarians told us that the cancer had invaded several internal organs and had metastasized to her brain. As if to confirm that she had cancer in her internal organs, Shiki came out of her coma just long enough to vomit up blood, then fell back into unconsciousness.

As you will see, she was saved by Marty Goldstein, D.V.M., who had worked with me on the first edition of this book and whom I had called to ask for advice on Shiki's condition.

After several days at the center, Shiki was out of the coma; but she still couldn't stand, let alone move, and she was still vomiting blood. All the center's veterinarians agreed that she would soon lapse back into a coma. They urged Joe and me to allow them to "put her out of her misery." With less optimism than Dr. Goldstein was expressing over the phone, Joe and I insisted on taking Shiki (alive) out of the center. When the attendant brought her out and put her down on the floor, Shiki fell over on her side and lay there helplessly, screaming; and the attendant glared at us for what we were doing to this poor little dog by not "letting her go."

Dr. Goldstein had, oddly (or so we thought at the time), urged us *not* to take Shiki immediately to him. "Keep her at home with you for two days," he'd said. "The first thing we need to do is to let her recover from the stress of separation and all the frightening things that are done to patients in a hospital. Give her a few days to feel all comfy and safe with you again."

But when we saw her crumpled there on the hospital floor, we felt that Dr. Goldstein was wrong. Shiki wouldn't last another two days without any medical care at all. But then again, the only medical care the center offered was to put her permanently to sleep. We carried her down to the street and propped her up on the ground while we waited for the car service to take us home. (She couldn't bend her legs to lie down face forward as animals do, you see. If you didn't hold her up, she toppled onto her side, and couldn't get up.) Joe and I took turns kneeling beside her and holding her upright. Then I decided to test Dr. Goldstein's idea: "Once Shiki feels she's going to be safely back home with you, you'll see improvement." Gingerly, I took one of my hands off her body. If she started to topple, as I was sure she would, my other hand could still keep her basically upright.

Eventually Joe said, "Let me know when you get tired holding her up. The last thing we need right now is for her to fall over and hurt herself."

"Joe," I said, "she's been standing on her own for ten minutes."

Shiki did indeed improve further in the two days of Dr. Goldstein's prescribed "cozy time" with us at home. In those two days, Dr. Goldstein had requested and received all the center's tests and records. As this book stresses, holistic veterinarians are all fully licensed as orthodox veterinarians, but their specialization gives them many additional tests and therapies from which to choose. So, for Dr. Goldstein, the orthodox center's tests and their results were only a starting point.

I had chosen Dr. Goldstein, of all the veterinarians who had worked with me on the first book, because I knew that he and his veterinarian brother, Robert, were conducting the research I referred to earlier and that it was showing much success. (His brother had at the time dropped out of clinical practice to devote himself fully to conducting that research.) When we walked into Dr. Goldstein's office—Shiki was slipping and sliding, but she was *walking*—the veterinarian said that, after looking at the center's information, Shiki couldn't be enrolled in the study he and his brother were running. "The center didn't prove the diagnosis of terminal cancer according to the stringent requirements of a solid scientific study."

For a brief moment, I felt that I might prefer to be dead rather than to be standing there listening to Dr. Goldstein. Shiki had fought so hard not to let this be her time to pass on, and now she wasn't eligible for a therapy that could help her because the center's veterinarians hadn't followed a particular protocol in their diagnosis. But then my mind went back to a basic tenet of alternative medicine: Bottom line, you don't treat the disease label, you treat the animal (or the human). "Well," I said hopefully to Dr. Goldstein, "even without an ironclad diagnosis . . ."

I didn't get to finish my sentence before the veterinarian said,

"Absolutely. We'll treat Shiki according to what's off base in her body."

Using his training as an animal chiropractor, Dr. Goldstein found a point on Shiki's spine that was "really out of whack," he said. "Even before all this happened to her, I bet she wasn't able to stand on her hind legs the way poodles can."

True. We had thought she'd just been getting too old for athletics. (As I report later in this book, "normal" aging is not considered normal by holistic veterinarians.) Dr. Goldstein slightly twisted Shiki's neck in a way that looked as if he'd just gently nudged her to look to her left. Then he lifted her off the examining table and put her down on the floor. "Who's her favorite parent?" he asked. Joe was, as much as I hated admitting it. "Okay, Joe. Hold your hand up high in the air, and let's see if she'll try to get to it."

Shiki stood up on her hind legs, reaching toward Joe's fingers. When she realized the fingers were too high, she made a straight-up leap in the air. (Remember that Shiki wasn't going toward food, because Joe had none. She wasn't even repeating a trick she had been taught. She just saw her person obviously wanting her to do something, for some strange reason, and—since she was now physically able to do it—she did it.)

I'm fond of saying, from my own experience, that actually seeing the results of an alternative veterinarian's or M.D.'s work is infinitely more powerful than spending years doing research and interviews. Joe's and my first thought was that we'd witnessed a miracle. But, as I have said, holistic doctors don't consider their results astounding, simply because they know the scientific bases behind them. Dr. Goldstein said only, "Okay. That's what was crippling her hind legs. Now we have to find out what's behind all her other symptoms."

Dr. Goldstein ran a sample of Shiki's blood through a number of tests that the orthodox center hadn't conducted, including tests for levels of all nutrients. He found two vitamin and three mineral levels that were "really out of whack."

Shiki's recovery wasn't quick or without cost. It was several weeks before she was back to her old spunky, bullheaded self. And the therapy was more complex than holistic therapy often is: It involved a rigidly controlled diet, several vitamin and mineral supplements, enzyme tablets, and two homeopathic remedies. But the cost of all this was about the same as it would have cost us to bury her.

Since everything in Shiki's therapy was natural and noninvasive, Shiki was spared the often gruesome side effects of surgery, radiation, and chemotherapy. Of course, she wouldn't have suffered these side effects anyway, because the major orthodox center refused to give these therapies, since she was "beyond help." She did, however, "suffer" from an intense hatred of the taste of one homeopathic. She found it so loathsome that Joe and I had to use most of our strength to keep her small flailing body pinned down on the couch, while one of us found some extra strength to pry open her mouth. But we didn't mind: We were vividly aware that this powerful, squirming dog only days before had so lost control of her brain and spinal cord that we'd been told she'd never be able to move again and would soon be dead. We found ourselves actually rooting for her to win over us.

By the way, as Shiki's body was restored to its natural balance, she recovered from cataracts, too.

PART 1

Preventing Disease and Premature Death in Your Cat: *This Is Almost Completely Within Your Power*

Chapter 1

How Commercial Pet Foods May Be Killing Your Cat—and Why

"Do you know what is in meat meal, the major constituent of dry dog food? . . . Urine, fecal matter, hair, pus, meat with cancer and T.B., etc."[1]

—*Wendell O. Belfield, D.V.M.*

"When the moist foods came out, we figured they must have a very strong preservative, because they need no refrigeration. Many of them do have a very strong preservative—formalin. Formalin is such a good preservative, in fact, that undertakers use quite a lot of it."

—*Thomas A. Newland, D.V.M. (in 1981)*

"When I started out as a veterinarian, I too told everybody. 'Yes, sure, the commercial foods are all fine. Go ahead and use them. Your cat will thrive.' But I was brain dead at the time."

—*John Fudens, D.V.M.*

25

If someone suggested you feed your cat rust every day, you would think the person was quite mad, wouldn't you? But maybe you do just that without knowing it. How about feeding her two substances that scientists use in laboratories to create brain defects in animals? How about taking a bottle marked POISON, with a skull and crossbones on its label, and sprinkling that over her food? If you feed your cat packaged or canned "nutritionally complete" pet foods—as so very many people in this country do—you may be giving her not only all of the above poisons but a number of others. This information may surprise you, because commercial food manufacturers—and even many veterinarians—tell us these foods are the "best" way to feed our pets. However, read on and see what researchers and nutritional veterinarians have to say.

What Is In Commercial Pet Food That Shouldn't Be?

To begin with, let us look at what commercial pet foods are composed of in general. In 1975 the Pet Food Institute said: "Forty percent of all pet food is meat by-products and offal [wastes]." One would think that the other 60 percent would have to be better than that, but the Pet Food Institute goes on to say that the other 60 percent is grain and soy meal not used for human consumption because of foreign odors, *debris*, *germs*, and so on.[2] You may remember the similar, even stronger statement by Wendell O. Belfield, D.V.M., on the first page of this chapter.

As we will discuss, today some nutritional veterinarians believe commercial foods are worse than ever.

By the way, you may have noted that Dr. Belfield wrote of tumors being put in our pets' foods. More recently I read a vivid example of that fact. A veterinarian visiting a meatpacking plant asked why the tumors being cut out from the dead animals were stored in bins, rather than thrown away. She was told there was nothing to worry about. The tumors would never reach human consumption; they would all be used in cat and dog foods.

Commercial pet foods contain a number of other "extra" substances, substances not present in natural foods and therefore foreign (toxic) to your pet's body. For instance:*

- **Sodium nitrite.** You have probably heard that sodium nitrite, which occurs in such processed foods as hot dogs and bologna, can cause cancer in human beings. But did you know that as long ago as 1972 the FDA stated that this chemical is also potentially hazardous to pet health?[3] That hasn't stopped commercial manufacturers from using it, however. You see, sodium nitrite is terribly important: It adds an artificial rosy color to some commercial pet foods. Manufacturers know that this makes a good impression on us; and we, after all, are the ones who shell out the money for these products. It is doubtful, however, that this pleasant red color makes much difference to your cat. Cats cannot see colors.

  Sodium nitrite isn't the only unnatural ingredient used in commercial foods to add pretty colors for the enjoyment of cats who can't see them. You may see mention on the

---

* Not all pet foods contain all the following harmful substances. Note also that this list does not comprise all the harmful substances that occur in various commercial pet foods.

label of red dye #2, blue dye #3, yellow dye some other number. A popular commercial cat food, which features on the box a picture of very colorful kibble, is honest enough to list several dyes as among the ingredients. But, as mentioned elsewhere in this chapter, if dyes aren't listed as ingredients, that is no assurance they aren't in your cat's commercial food.

• **BHA and BHT.** Scientists use these chemicals on animals in research laboratories—to produce serious brain defects. These additives also produce kidney and liver problems as well as behavior problems in laboratory animals.

• **Lead.** Researching this new book, I found indications that lead is not so prevalent in canned cat foods as it was in 1981. At that time, researchers at the Connecticut Agricultural Experiment Station had found that many canned foods contained so much lead that every time an animal ate six ounces of these foods he took into his body *four times* the level of lead potentially toxic to children. So, even if this terrible state of affairs has improved, we might ask why this amount of lead was ever allowed in the first place—and what else is presently being allowed that we don't know about.

John Fudens, D.V.M., comments that "you might still find lead in some of those canned cat foods you can buy for about a dime. But I wouldn't feed those to a cockroach."

• **Artificial flavorings.** These are used to make fake food taste the way it would if it were real food. About 25 years ago a California physician, Benjamin Feingold, of the Kaiser Permanente Hospital, came out with a radical theory that put his reputation on the line: Many children with autism, hyperactivity, and various other personality disorders could be controlled simply by removing artificial colorings and flavorings from their diets. His theory worked so well in practice that it has since been utilized even by some of the most orthodox physicians.

Veterinarians practicing the new field of nutritional veterinary medicine have been calling for the removal of such artificial flavorings from pet foods. R. Geoffrey Broderick, D.V.M., once said: "These same substances that are known to cause children to be unsociable, unable to learn—to choose to spend hours at a time sitting and banging their heads against a wall—these are the substances that cause your dog or cat to be nervous, hostile, and full of anxiety."

- **Salt.** This substance, while it does occur in nature, is added in unnatural proportions to many processed foods. Sometimes, Dr. Broderick said in 1981, such foods contain "one thousand times" as much salt as occurs in the natural food the processed food is imitating. You probably know the strong role excessive salt plays in causing human hypertension and heart disease. It does the same thing in cats and is considered one of the main reasons these two diseases, virtually unknown in our pets until fifty years ago, are now top killers.

- **Ethoxyquin.** The first questionnaire response I received for this new book came from a veterinarian who referred to himself as basically orthodox. He wrote that he had been using my first book to start to incorporate holistic medicine into his practice but doubted he knew enough yet to contribute to this edition. The one comment he did give, however, was that he felt I would find that commercial food manufacturers had "cleaned up their acts" since the first edition. Following a long tradition of veterinarians who don't specialize in nutrition, this doctor now believed that commercial foods would maintain animals' health. (Hoping, for the sake of all animals, that this doctor was right in his belief that some toxic substances had been removed, I skulked in my neighborhood reading labels, as I had done in 1981 for the first edition. No, everything I had mentioned before was still listed on labels. And it was only later that I found out, as I'll detail shortly, that a new law allows pet food manufacturers to put toxic substances into the foods without mentioning them on the label.)

To double-check myself, I asked Dr. Fudens if he thought commercial foods had got any better in the years since the first book. "You're kidding me," he said. "In my opinion and experience, commercial pet foods have recently got much worse than they've ever been, with the road kill and the diseased carcasses, and everything else they're putting in there."

I took the same question up with Carvel G. Tiekert, D.V.M., founder and president of the American Holistic Veterinary Medical Association. He pointed out that there had been a brand-*new* poison, ethoxyquin, introduced into many pet foods since the first edition, and he sent me an article by Gloria Dodd, D.V.M., from the *Journal of the American Holistic Veterinary Medical Association* (August–October 1992). You may remember I said at the beginning of this chapter that you might very well unknowingly be feeding your cat every day from a bottle with a label featuring, in all capital letters, POISON, with an additional skull and crossbones as a warning for those who don't read English. I was talking about ethoxyquin.

The article was actually a letter written by Dr. Dodd to a veterinary nutritionist responsible for pet food issues within the Food and Drug Administration. Previous to her letter, Dr. Dodd had run four years of research on ethoxyquin. She began this work when a breeder contacted her after suddenly losing four champion German shepherds in a row to liver cancer. The breeder had made only one change in rearing her dogs: She'd switched them to a new commercial food that had ethoxyquin as a preservative. Soon after, another breeder told Dr. Dodd that suddenly 82 percent of her puppies were dying. Many others came into the world dead to begin with, or were malformed. The only thing she'd done differently was to switch to the same pet food.

One of the first facts Dr. Dodd unearthed was that the FDA allows a maximum of 5 ppm of ethoxyquin in human foods—which would seemingly indicate that the FDA knows it can be toxic—but allows up to 150 ppm in pet food. So it's okay for our beloved companions to eat thirty times more of this chemical than it's considered safe for us to take in. That might make some sense if our cats weighed thirty times more than we do, but obviously . . .

Maybe by now you've run off to check the commercial foods you give your cat and have noticed with relief that ethoxyquin isn't listed on the labels. Although I have recently seen this chemical mentioned on labels, Dr. Dodd states that many manufacturers who use ethoxyquin in their foods don't mention it. You may say, "I thought there was an FDA regulation that all ingredients had to be mentioned on the label." So did I. So did Dr. Dodd.

Dr. Fudens addressed this issue in an interview with me. "This is what has happened in the last few years. Lobbyists for the pet food companies got a new pet food labeling act passed in Washington," he said. "There are only about five major producing companies, and they contract out their base meal to most of the other companies. These first companies put in their meat and whatever else—and then what goes on their label is only what they've *added* to the basic ingredients." Dr. Fudens sent me an article indicating that the "whatever else" he refers to as basic ingredients includes spoiled meat cuts, ground-up flea collars and "body bags" that come in with euthanized pets, and other ingredients I'd like to shield you from knowing about. "They're not required anymore to mention on the label any junk, garbage, or poisons that are in the basic ingredients unless they actually *added* it."

These major producing companies then contract out their base meal to other companies. If the latter companies do not add any more poisons, ground-up flea collars, or whatever, "they can call the food all-natural or anything else they want to call it," the veterinarian says.

"So if an enlightened cat owner tries to buy only commercial foods that say they're all natural, no preservatives, no artificial this or that," Dr. Fudens summarized, "the owner should realize that only God really knows what's in those foods."

In her long, impassioned letter, Dr. Dodd gives many more chilling facts. I'm giving only a few of them. "I further learned from the *Chemical Toxicology of Commercial Products*," she writes, "that ethoxyquin has a toxic rating of 3 on a scale of 1 to 6." She explains that a rating of 6 means that fewer than seven drops of a substance produces instant death. The rating of 3 given to ethoxyquin means, the veterinarian says, that it can produce slowly developing depression, skin irritation, liver damage, convulsions, coma, and eventual death.

Dr. Dodd states that the FDA approved ethoxyquin on the basis of a study conducted by its developer, Monsanto, over thirty years ago. She gives a number of specifics of what she calls the "slipshod" methods by which the study was conducted, concluding that "by today's standards of testing, [Monsanto's study] would be laughed out of the room."

But wait a minute. Let's look at one of the results Monsanto had. Of the sixty-seven puppies who were born during the study, thirty-two died, a mortality rate of almost 50 percent. You may remember that it was exactly an abnormally high rate of dead puppies that prompted Dr. Dodd's four years of research into ethoxyquin in the first place.

Dr. Dodd says, "The 'scientists' claimed the deaths were due to 'underdeveloped and weak puppies'!" I'm sure you don't need me to suggest to you that maybe those puppies were born that way not because of karma or a fluke of nature but because of ethoxyquin in their mother's diet.

Dr. Dodd, who studied with medical physicians in Europe and in South America, used a state-of-the-art electronic machine developed in Germany to scientifically analyze ethoxyquin's effects in the body. She found the chemical implicated in—and I'm giving only a partial list here—poor quality of skin and hair, weight loss, obesity, nausea, diarrhea, allergies, and numerous internal stress reactions. (Dr. Dodd notes, "There's nothing more stressing to the body than being poisoned!") She also found hypothyroidism, overall accelerated aging of the organs, tumors, and cancer of the liver with metastasis to the pancreas and spleen.

Some animals evinced strange behavior, such as incessant pacing or a "sudden development of a Dr. Jekyll–Mr. Hyde syndrome—quiet, loving pets changed to violently aggressive biting animals." Many of these were so violent that their owners euthanized them.

In those animals whose organs were not irreversibly damaged, Dr. Dodd was able to get a good recovery response in part by using a homeopathic remedy that negates the effects of ethoxyquin.

- **Euthanized cats and dogs.** Am I telling you here that the commercial foods your cat eats may contain ground-up parts of her own "people" who were put to death because they were unloved or were diagnosed as too sick to go on living? Unfortunately, yes, I am. I won't comment any further on this particular fact. I'm sure you can fill in your own thoughts.

What Isn't in Commercial Foods That Should Be?

Advertising for most commercial pet foods states that the products have all the nutrients your cat or dog needs. But do they?

If you were being paid to write ads for a cat food, would you stress that the food didn't contain any enzymes at all, even though enzymes are absolutely essential for every biochemical reaction in the body?

Yet enzymes occur, as Dr. Broderick and other holistic veterinarians tell us, in not one single commercial pet food. You see, enzymes occur in raw foods. (That fact is one of the major reasons that nutritionists urge people to eat raw fruits and raw vegetables.) Dr. Tiekert adds that a major reason nutritional veterinarians object to table scraps for cats is that people will then be feeding their cats basically *cooked* foods.

You probably won't find on your labels any mention of vitamin C. And yet, as we'll cover in following chapters, holistic veterinarians help prevent and cure a number of "unpreventable" and "incurable" pet problems with this vitamin. Cats—unlike people—manufacture vitamin C in their bodies, and this fact has traditionally led veterinary medicine to the conclusion that these animals don't need to get the vitamin from outside sources.

However, this conclusion overlooks the fact that cats always used to get additional vitamin C from outside sources: in the foods they ate before the commercial foods supplanted their natural diet. It also overlooks the fact that some pets produce much less C in their bodies than others. Further, it overlooks the fact that today's new environmental poisons (including those in commercial pet foods) actually rob the body of substantial amounts of vitamin C.

Animal behaviorists have pointed out that if your cat eats his own feces, he may not be a "bad boy"; he may simply be trying the only way he can think of to obtain some of the vitally important nutrients missing from his "nutritionally complete" commercial pet food.

Even when something that should be in commercial pet foods *is* in the foods, it may not be there in the proper biochemical form. For instance, that long list of minerals on some boxed or canned foods may look very impressive. However, those minerals are very likely to be *unchelated* minerals. These tend to pass right through the body without ever being used. Feeding your pet (or yourself) unchelated minerals can therefore be tantamount to not feeding her (or yourself) any minerals at all.

Chelated minerals, according to Richard J. Kearns, D.V.M., not only are absolutely essential in and of themselves, but also are necessary to help the body use vitamins. Therefore, unchelated minerals can sometimes seriously impair the function of the vitamins your pet gets. Moreover, unchelated minerals can sometimes store themselves in the body and help cause such modern-day problems as arthritis.

The reason for this lack of chelated minerals in pet foods is simple. As Dr. Broderick has pointed out, the unnatural forms of minerals "are a lot cheaper."

Now, what about the iron listed on your pet food's label? Well, as we have said, nutrients occur in different forms. Under the heading "iron," for instance, medical dictionaries list almost thirty different forms. One type of iron commonly used in pet foods is iron oxide. This form is more commonly known as rust. Then there is magnesium. This mineral is sometimes even announced on the label in the correct proportion to calcium, a subtlety not bothered with in some supplements for human consumption. (Too much calcium in relation to magnesium—and vice versa—can cause bone and joint deteriorations such as arthritis. The doctors Goldstein emphasize that the wrong calcium-magnesium ratio also can be a cause of neuromuscular problems.)

However, as Dr. Broderick has pointed out, the form of magnesium most commonly used in pet foods is the inexpensive magnesium oxide. "Since very little magnesium oxide can be utilized by the body," he said, "it is virtually impossible for the animal to *absorb* the correct magnesium-calcium ratio, even when the proportion in the box or can is correct."

In other words, even the best processed foods can be a direct cause of the new animal disease, arthritis.

What Exactly Is Meant by the Term *Natural Foods*?

Simply put, an animal's natural foods are the ones his body organs and structures are best equipped to utilize. Through evolution, the bodies of cats have superbly adapted to maintain health on the foods that were most easily available to them in the wild. These foods are called the cat's natural foods.

It goes without saying, of course, that the foods our pets' bodies have evolved to thrive on throughout millions of years are not the processed commercial pet foods that have been manufactured for only the past fifty years. Cats simply did not lug boxes of dry pellets around the wild with them, and they didn't take their prey home in a can. Nor was their prey stuffed with the dyes, preservatives, and other harmful additives we have shown are contained in today's pet foods.

As we have said, these commercial pet foods have been around for only about fifty years. This is not nearly enough time for a species to rebuild its body to utilize new foods for health. Three major diseases of today's pets are cancer, heart disease, and arthritis; yet in the millions of years cats ate their natural diet, cancer, heart disease, and arthritis were virtually unknown.* These three diseases are also, of course, the main killers of human beings; again, these diseases were virtually unknown in human beings until we started tampering with our own food one hundred years ago.

What were cats evolved to eat? There is no controversy here among scientists: Cats are basically carnivores, animals who naturally eat raw flesh.**

Those of you who are interested in nutrition may point out at this juncture that human beings are supposed to have evolved to be meat eaters, too, but that in the last thirty years medical science has discovered that animal fat—and animal protein—can be detrimental to human health.

The last part of that statement is quite correct: A growing number of authorities state that animal food is at least a contributing factor to a number of our serious disorders. However, while we human

---

* Scientists have ascertained this by studying well-preserved skeletons of wild cats, as well as veterinary records prior to fifty years ago.
** Please don't assume that you can't possibly feed your pet his natural diet because it contains meat. As we will show in chapter 2, it can cost you *less* to feed a healthful, natural diet than you are presently paying for even the less expensive harmful commercial pet foods.

animals may have been eating meat for a few million years, there has not yet been enough time for our systems to have evolved to accept animal protein as a natural substance.

Let's compare a cat's carnivorous body with ours to see how the cat is adapted to be a meat eater, while we are not. Open your cat's mouth and take a look at his teeth (provided, of course, you have a sweet-tempered cat who will let you do that). You will notice that all your cat's teeth are a lot sharper than ours. You will notice also those two extremely long teeth to each side, top and bottom. (Even in my six-pound tabby cat they looked ferocious.)

Now, why don't we have teeth like that? Because our teeth haven't evolved to be the teeth of natural meat eaters. They aren't sharp enough to kill another animal and tear it—raw—to pieces.

Take a look at your cat's nails. Unlike a dog, a cat tends to hide his nails so as not to harm friends. But if you've just angered him by poking around his feet too much to find those nails, you've seen that they are very long. Women who try to grow long nails for cosmetic purposes know that human nails will break, no matter how well they're nurtured, long before they get as long as a cat's.

You see, the nails of your cat have evolved to this length so that he, again, can kill and tear apart his natural food: animal flesh.

But the most important anatomical difference between our natural meat-eating pets and ourselves is the length of the intestines. Meat, in the presence of heat, tends to putrefy and send out poisons. Of course, intestines in any animal's body carry a lot of heat, so the shorter the intestines—that is, the quicker the meat can pass through the body—the less harm it's going to do to the body.

Our intestines are very long; therefore, it takes a lot of time for animal food to make its way through them. The length of time, then, that such food is exposed to the heat of our bodies is more than ample to allow it to putrefy and send toxins through our systems. A cat, again, does not have this problem. His intestines are quite short, even considering the fact that his body is smaller than ours.

Thus, cats—unlike us—have been carefully designed by nature to thrive healthily on meat. For this reason—and for all the other reasons we have detailed in this chapter—we are doing our pet's body a great disservice when we feed the animal the unnatural new commercial foods.

The story of the nutrient called taurine is an illustration of how natural food can maintain health, while unnatural food does not. Natural foods contain within them a number of helpful nutrients (such as taurine) that were unknown until a comparatively short time ago. Nutritional authorities believe that many others are still unknown. (Only by eating natural foods can you and your pet be certain to get the whole complement of nutrients, known and unknown, that have in the past protected our ancestors from such ailments as cancer and heart disease.)

The search that uncovered taurine began because scientists were puzzled by a new disease that was striking cats with increasing frequency: progressive retinal atrophy, a condition that leads to total blindness.

Dr. Broderick once gave a dramatic medical description of this disease. "You look in a healthy cat's eyes," he said, "and you see the optic disk with blood vessels radiating out from it." (These blood vessels carry blood and all necessary nutrients to the eye, and in this way keep it alive.) "But when you look in the eyes of a cat with this disease, the optic disk looks like a saucer set apart from the rest of the eye, with no blood vessels. In other words, you see this shiny globe looking back at you unseeingly; the cat is stone blind."

When researchers recently discovered taurine, they discovered also that a lack of this substance causes at least some cases of the "new" disease, progressive retinal atrophy.

Taurine occurs naturally in meat. Cats, of course, always ate an abundance of meat when they were left to their own devices in the wild. Now that taurine has been discovered, it has been added to most commercial cat foods. But for many pets the addition came too late.

The question remains: How many other presently unknown nutrients necessary to pet (and human) health are not included in unnatural foods?

*   *   *

The next chapter will tell you how you can prevent the grim diseases considered inevitable in today's processed-food–fed cat by feeding your cat his natural, healthy diet. As I have said, this diet should cost you less every week than the commercial foods you may presently be using. Be advised, however, that over the years the natural diet may end up costing you more—because your pet will probably live many more years to enjoy it.

One last word: You may at this point be vowing you will never, never, never feed raw meat to your cat because you have heard so much in recent years about the danger to us from parasites in undercooked meat. That danger is to *us*—not to natural carnivores. Again we're back to considering that our cats' bodies evolved to be quite different from ours. Trust that nutritional veterinarians will explain in more detail in the next chapter why raw meat is not harmful to our cats. For now, just let me give a basic clue as to why a cat is not affected by parasites while we are. Our bodies' basic pH balance is alkaline; our cats' bodies are basically acidic, the exact opposite of alkaline. Imagine what happens to a parasite if it's plopped into a body full of acid.

References

1. Wendell O. Belfield, D.V.M., *Let's Live*, April 1980.
2. Frances Sheridan Goulart, *Let's Live*, October 1975, p. 44.
3. *Ibid.*

Chapter 2

What Your Adult Cat Should Eat for a Long and Healthy Life— and Why

"We just seldom see the so-called inevitable diseases in our patients when we can get the owners to raise the pets on their natural foods."

—*Robert S. Goldstein, V.M.D.; Marty Goldstein, D.V.M.; Richard J. Kearns, D.V.M.; H. H. Robertson, D.V.M.*

"Everybody laughs at me; they say I'm a specialist in geriatrics, because all my animals get to be so old. That's simply because I try to have my clients feed their pets right in the first place."

—*Richard J. Kearns, D.V.M.*

"My greatest goal is to be known not for what I've cured and controlled, but for what I've prevented."

—*R. Geoffrey Broderick, D.V.M.*

"Even the so-called 'sickly' pet can get to live a long, healthy life with the proper diet."

—*Nino Aloro, D.V.M.*

As *the title* for this chapter indicates, this information has been given by holistic veterinarians for an *adult* cat. Kittens, elderly cats, pregnant or lactating cats, and half-starved strays all have special dietary needs that are detailed in chapter 4.

This chapter is also meant to *prevent* disease in a healthy cat. If your companion is already ill, he may need important adjustments to this chapter's recommended diet to compensate for existing biochemical imbalances in his body. The chapters on disorders indicate some of these special dietary requirements.

Cats in the wild usually did not—and still usually do not—become crippled or blind or deaf from the disorders that most veterinarians today consider inevitable. And cats today who are raised on the diets their ancestors ate in the wild seldom become crippled or blind or deaf from the disorders that have become "normal" since the commercial pet food industry took over our pets' diets.

It is not by some unexplainable "miracle" that a pet (or a person) can be kept healthy by feeding the body the foods it has evolved to thrive on. You probably know that everything you take into your body affects your cells in one way or another: Cigarette smoke adversely affects the cells of your lungs, for instance; Valium alters body chemistry so that anxiety may be alleviated temporarily; high-blood-pressure medication sets up another biochemical reaction in your body that lowers blood pressure for a while.

Now, what one general substance do you take into your body more often, every day of your life, than any other substance? Food.

And the various nutrients in food set up more biochemical reactions in your body, every minute of your life, than any one drug can do. Therefore, when you (and your pet) take in the right foods, these foods will set up healthy biochemical reactions; when you and your pet take in the wrong foods, they will set up destructive biochemical reactions in the body. It's that simple.

Frank L. Earl, D.V.M., once expressed the above idea this way: "I compare vitamins and minerals to the spark plugs in cars. These nutrients are the necessary energizers to move from one chemical reaction to another in each and every cell in the body."

So healthy, natural foods set up and maintain healthy, natural biochemical reactions in your body. These biochemical reactions set up a natural line of defense—a healthy immune system—that fights off bacteria, viruses, and parasites many times a day. Every veterinarian whose work is covered in this book has said to me in one way or another that without a healthy immune system we would all be sick every day.

For instance, let's say you're in a classroom or at a party with a person who has the flu. Ten of the twenty people in that room catch that virus; you're one of the unlucky ones. That virus didn't float mysteriously by the other ten in that room just to pick you out maliciously; it entered the body of the other ten persons, too. But the other ten had immune systems that were strong enough to say, "Get out of here; this is *my* territory," and to destroy the offending stranger.

In the same way, we all have cancer cells in our body every day. As long as our overall health is good, our immune system will keep knocking out these cancer cells.

Almost all holistic veterinarians I have interviewed over the years have asked me to please stress to readers that it is *not* bacteria or viruses that make pets sick; it is pets' weakened immune systems that allow the disease-causing organisms to take hold.

So by restoring your pet to his natural, health-giving diet, you can restore the myriad natural biochemical reactions that give strength to his immune system. This is the "magic" that keeps pets who are fed natural diets free of today's "inevitable" diseases—diseases that were, and are, virtually unknown among animals in the wild.

Later chapters are devoted to a compilation of the work of countless veterinarians working in the new field of holistic veterinary medicine. These chapters detail successful therapies for already existing diseases: therapies that use little or no dangerous drugs or surgery; therapies that often have amazing results with disorders currently thought basically "hopeless."

If you are lucky enough to be reading the chapter at hand on prevention because you're just starting to raise a new kitten, chances are this book will sit on your shelf for many years before you need the information in the later chapters, if you ever *do* need it.

Just as every one of these veterinarians expressed to me that his or her greatest satisfaction comes in preventing diseases rather than in curing them, so I hope that the months I have spent compiling information on the successful treatment of these diseases results in some of the least-needed chapters ever written in the field of veterinary medicine.

Your Pet's Natural, Healthy Diet Will Probably Cost You Less Than the Fake Foods You're Presently Feeding Him

Before I give information on how your cat can remain disease-free and live longer, let me get one stumbling block out of the way. The cat's natural diet is high in meat, a word that these days raises some trepidation in anyone on a budget.

First of all, holistic veterinarians do not ask you to feed your cat exclusively meat. (Actually, as we cover later, feeding your cat only meat can harm her.) Although the cat is more truly a carnivore than the dog, only 60 to 75 percent of the cat's diet should be in the form of what is commonly termed meat, and some of that can be other animal products, such as eggs and yogurt.

Secondly—and very importantly—you will most probably find that your cat eats less of his natural diet than he does fake foods. As a matter of fact, R. Geoffrey Broderick, D.V.M., has reported that almost without exception pets eat one-third less of natural foods than unnatural ones. Why should a pet be so obliging? He eats less of the natural foods because these foods contain all the nutrients his body needs for good health; therefore, his body tends to retain these foods, using them to build fresh new cells, healthy blood, and so on. On the other hand, the pet's body doesn't know *what* the heck to do with the newfangled fake foods, and most of these foods pass almost immediately through the body and out again. Therefore, instant hunger. As Dr. Broderick put it: "A pound of fake food equals almost a pound of waste," or feces.

As a matter of fact, many kennel owners who deal with numerous animals in close quarters express relief that the natural diet cuts down so drastically on the amount of waste they have to discard every day. Whereas their animals were previously discarding as foreign substances (which, indeed, they are) many of the chemicals and much of the diseased matter contained in processed foods, the same bodies are now retaining the nutrient-rich natural foods for the purposes of building healthy new cells, strong immune systems, and healthy blood.

Robert Goldstein, V.M.D., and Marty Goldstein, D.V.M., have added that excessive—and costly—eating may be caused also by addiction to the chemical appetite stimulants and preservatives in fake foods. When you feed your pet natural foods, he will eat only enough to satisfy natural hunger—not to satisfy an addiction.

Another thing: Nowhere will I be asking you to feed your pet expensive steak as the basis of an optimal diet. As a matter of fact, please do *not* feed steak as the basis of your pet's diet, even if you can afford to. As we'll see a bit later when we follow your pet's ancestor through the wild, he first ate the organ meats of his prey (the heart, gizzard, liver, tripe, spleen). Steak is actually less nutritious overall than these innards. Indeed, your pet's great-great-etc.-granddaddy didn't deign to eat this inferior type of meat—steak—unless his prey happened not to have been spirited away when he returned to the scene hours after dinner for a midnight snack.

Now let's compare some specific costs using present (1998) prices in my neighborhood. I'm asking you to pass up a box of embalmed kibble ($1.75 a pound) or a can of cat food ($1.80 to $2.50 a pound). I'm asking you instead to buy a pound of chicken hearts, gizzards, or livers at 99 cents to $1.19 a pound. Or a few eggs ($1.00 a dozen) or carrots (three pounds for $1.00) or a few apples (49 cents a pound). Then I'm reminding you that since your cat's body can actually *use* all the natural food it gets, your pet will probably eat only two-thirds of a pound of her natural diet for every pound of fake food.

You can probably even get your butcher to give you free some of the animal parts he normally discards that would be highly nutritious for your pet.

All this is not even considering the money you probably will not have to spend in veterinary bills trying to save your beloved pet's life from an illness caused by unnatural foods. In my own case, I spent a small fortune raising (and almost managing to kill) my little black poodle Shiki on the "nutritionally complete" kibble and canned foods my veterinarian—and all the ads—assured me were all she needed. She had the "inevitable" worms three times in her first year; she had gastroenteritis twice; then, at the end of that first year of her life, she developed the "hopeless" arthritis that caused her to be half crippled.

Luckily, it was at that time that I discovered what a dog's natural diet was. Changing Shiki to the diet her body had been built for kept her free of the "hopeless" arthritis for sixteen years, until she died a natural death.

Since then I have raised three other dogs on a diet of real foods. They are all extremely healthy, extremely energetic, and extremely old. My cat, Puddy, was 20 when she died in an accident.

I would say that Shiki's one year on fake foods cost me about $800 in paying for her orthodox therapies. (This was in the 1970s, so you can imagine how much more it would have cost me now.) Total cost of therapy—throughout their lives—for Puddy and my three ancient dogs raised on their natural diets: $000.

One more word about how a natural diet can save you money. As you probably know, a number of dog and cat diseases can be passed to their owners. If you have a healthy pet, you may never know how much this may have saved you in medical bills—or even in the possible loss of a loved one.*

What Your Cat's Ancestor Ate

Let's start with the average day in the life of your pet's ancestor in the wild, a day in which he had no loving owner around to provide him with things his body had not been built to deal with. I want to go through this day with your pet's great-many-times-over-grandfather so you can more readily visualize the reasons for the specific suggestions we will cover later.

Ruff wakes early in the forest. There is no bowl of kibble in front of his nose for breakfast, but that doesn't surprise him. There never has been a bowl of kibble there. What does surprise him is that the half-eaten prey he had been guarding overnight has disappeared from between his front paws, spirited away in the middle of the night by some darned animal. Well, that happens. Up and at 'em. Walk, search, climb, stalk, run—in other words, exercise.

Now, when great-great-etc.-granddaddy killed his prey, he ate the intestines, liver, heart, stomach, and spleen first. He didn't know it, of course, but these are what we call organ meats, and they store up certain nutrients that are not stored in the bones and muscles. The organs of the prey also contained partially digested vegetables, fruits, and grains. These nonmeat foods provide certain other nutrients, such as unsaturated fats and carbohydrates, which

* Wendell O. Belfield, D.V.M., for instance, reported that human beings may contract cats' upper respiratory diseases. The veterinarian also pointed to the fact that heartworms—previously thought confined to dogs—were starting to be reported in human patients. Also, Dr. Belfield pointed out that a pregnant woman can contract a serious disease—if her cat *has* the disease, of course—while cleaning feces from the litter box. The disease, caused by *Toxoplasma gondii*, can destroy the brain of a fetus. (To be safe, if you become pregnant, you might want to prevail upon another family member to clean up after the cat until the baby is born.)

are necessary for the cat, who is not totally carnivorous. Many holistic veterinarians have told me horror stories of desperately sick cats raised by well-meaning owners who were determined to raise their pets on "natural," nonsupermarket foods. However, these owners mistakenly thought their pets were total carnivores and thus needed only meat for their natural diets.

Next the cat went on to eat his prey's bones, fat, and muscles, to round out a full complement of vitamins, minerals, enzymes, carbohydrates, proteins, and fats.

As he later lazed in the sun, digesting his feast, he might occasionally catch himself an insect for a bit of dessert. An insect? Yes, insects contain protein and B_{12}, both of which are necessary parts of a cat's diet. I hope this paragraph cuts down the number of letters I see in veterinarians' magazine columns from distraught owners who are sure their pets are going to die because they catch and eat flies.

After his feast, our great-etc.-granddaddy cat rested awhile or otherwise amused himself before he decided he would go to the nearest watering hole for a drink. He didn't know, you see, that centuries hence, many fake food labels would be saying it was best to set out a bowl of water with each feeding, or even to mix water directly with the "food" to make a nice fake gravy. Of course, neither did he have nutritionally oriented veterinarians such as Dr. Broderick around to tell him, "Drinking water at the same time as eating will make minerals pass through the body without being used and will upset the acid-alkaline balance of the system." He didn't need such specialists; it's only modern pet owners who do.

As H. H. Robertson, D.V.M., once told me, "All you have to do is watch a pet today who is not confined in a small apartment with his food bowl and his water bowl filled up under his nose at the same time. A free pet today will still eat first, and then later he'll go looking for a drink of water. But he'll never eat and drink at the same time."

Actually, though, your cat's ancestor didn't make many trips to watering holes. Since he was eating the diet his body had been designed to thrive on, he got most of the moisture he needed from the body of his prey. The chapter covering disorders of internal organs discusses in particular the damage dry commercial food (kibble) can do to a cat's body.

The Optimal Preventive Diet for Your Adult Cat

The Optimal Diet

The following is meant merely to sum up what we say elsewhere in this chapter. Please read the text for important details. *Also, see page 50 for tips on how to feed this diet to your pet quickly and easily. Remember always that variety is important.*

- **Animal foods:** About 60 to 75% of the daily food ration should be animal products, especially meat, raw preferably. Approximately one-sixth of the weekly meat ration should be organ meats—heart, kidney, gizzard, spleen, tripe. Provide fish perhaps twice a week and chicken and turkey often. Do not give any type of bones.
  Milk products: Yogurt or raw (unpasteurized) milk should be given several times weekly.
  Eggs: Give your cat one or two soft-cooked eggs a week. (Cats in the wild are not above swiping an egg from a bird's nest.)
- **Vegetables, fruits, grains:** Most of the rest of the daily ration should be cooked brown rice or cereal, cut-up raw fruits and vegetables, and occasionally chopped nuts.
- **Fats:** Polyunsaturated fat (in the form of safflower oil, sesame oil, and so on) should be given daily.
- **Prepared cat food:** Occasionally supplement with one of the purer foods for cats from the health food store.*

* Please see text for the relatively rare occasions this book recommends these foods.

- **Pure water**
- **Vitamin and mineral supplements** (some nutritional veterinarians consider these optional for the healthy pet):
  Vitamin C (in the form of sodium ascorbate)
  Vitamin E
  Cat multivitamin and mineral pill

Quick and Easy Tips for Feeding Your Cat His New, Natural Diet

- You might want to start simply by using, for a few weeks, a high-quality noncommercial cat food in place of the supermarket cat food you and your pet have been using. This will give your cat's body a chance to become free of addiction to the impurities in the commercial cat foods. Meanwhile, you can continue your habit of simply filling your cat's bowl with prepared food a few times a day.
- Then start adding a bit of chicken, turkey, or meat from your family's own dinner—perhaps a bit of leftover that might otherwise be thrown away—to your cat's bowl.
- Next, as you chop up raw vegetables for your family's salad, chop up a few extra pieces for your pet and put them into his bowl.
- Gradually start adding grains.
- Build a routine for your cat's diet, based closely around the one you follow for your own meals. This routine will mean you do not have to make new choices every day for your cat's menus, and it will also mean you don't have to make a separate work process out of feeding your pet.

  Chances are, for instance, that you tend to eat grains for breakfast. Make breakfast the meal you give your cat his grains. Chances are also that you eat salad and meat, fish or fowl at dinner; give your cat his meat and raw vegetables at dinner.
- The gradual change of your cat's diet, as recommended above, will give you a chance to reread this chapter leisurely so that the information can become "second nature" to you. After all, you don't want to have to go skimming

through the chapter every day for weeks just before your pet's meal to check out something you don't remember clearly.

- When for any reason you cannot fulfill the recommendations for your cat's natural diet, it's important that you don't feel guilty. Your cat's health will not deteriorate because of an occasional deviation from the recommended diet; remember, we have termed this diet the optimal diet. Keep on hand a non-commercial preformulated cat food and dump that into your cat's bowl when you will be away for an extended period of time. If you oversleep and don't have even a split second to pour this food out for your cat before rushing off to work, consider his day without food a partial fast; fasts are recommended by many holistic veterinarians, as we state later in this chapter, if your pet is not chronically ill.

- The bottom line is that you should read this chapter carefully and adhere to every suggestion as closely as possible, as often as possible. If, for any valid reason, one or two recommendations are impossible for you to fulfill, then they are just that: impossible for you to fulfill. Realize that every step you take to remove your cat from a total diet of supermarket foods is bringing him that much closer to a long, disease-free life.

Meat

Wild cats ate basically rodents, small rabbits, and birds. I doubt that many of you will choose to spend your days catching mice or rats to offer to your cat. However, if you do have a mouse running around, chances are your kitty won't need a mousetrap to help him catch it. If you do choose to feed rabbit to your cat occasionally, see our later admonitions against feeding rabbit raw.

In the first edition, many nutritional veterinarians recommended chicken and turkey wholeheartedly, not only because the cat evolved to thrive on birds, but because fowl tended to be—along with veal and lamb—one of the least polluted sources of animal protein available outside of health food stores. But Dr. Fudens alerts me to the fact that today the fowl bought in supermarkets has often been given hormones and antibiotics.

As we've discussed, one-sixth of your cat's meat allotment should be in the form of organ meats—thymus, spleen, kidney, heart, liver—not only because cats ate that proportion of organ meats in the wild, but because these meats contain many nutrients that are less abundant in other parts of the animal.

Cut up your cat's meat into approximately bite-sized pieces.

DON'T MAKE THE MISTAKE OF FEEDING ONLY MEAT TO YOUR CAT. When the cat is referred to as a carnivore, some members of the public can be misled. For that reason, many nutritional veterinarians are careful to refer to the cat as "almost a true carnivore," or "more truly a carnivore than the dog." Also, as I've pointed out, medical dictionaries define the family Carnivora as eating basically— but not exclusively—flesh.

Dr. Aloro once told me a chilling story of a lady who breeds cats. She latched onto a "carnivore" label years ago and tenaciously refused to believe that a carnivore should eat anything except meat. Not only that, but she decided that beef is *the* food, and fed her cats nothing but beef. As I keep pointing out, variety is important, since no one food contains all necessary nutrients for any one body. Also, an allergy to any food is always possible, and to keep bombarding a body with an allergen may be tantamount to murder.

But, as Dr. Aloro told me, "I have never been able to convince that breeder that there is no such thing as a good all-meat diet for dogs or cats. She has one cat that was bred to be a champion. And that poor cat has bad kidneys; he has chronic conjunctivitis; his coat is terrible looking because his body is so sick. She keeps looking for drugs to take care of these health problems and to make his skin look good, because, after all, he was supposed to be a champion for her. And I tell her, 'You can look from here to eternity, but unless you change the diet, that cat will not look good.' "

Another client purchased a young cat from this same breeder and brought it to Dr. Aloro only a month after buying it. Dr. Aloro told me sadly, "That poor thing was so weak, I couldn't do anything at all. He died."

Just one of the things wrong with an all-meat diet is that it's low in minerals. Your pet needs minerals (although as a result of the cat's having evolved as basically a meat eater, he does need less in the way of minerals than we do, or even than dogs do). Not only does your cat need minerals for all the good they can do for the body, but minerals are necessary before vitamins can be put to use by the body. Depriving your cat of minerals is tantamount to depriving him of vitamins, too.

Another problem with an all-meat diet is that carbohydrates, which are present in grains, fruits, and vegetables but not in meats, are needed to help your cat's body use proteins. Without carbohydrates, your cat can't efficiently use the proteins in meat that his body needs so much.

For these reasons, our nutritional veterinarians emphasize that besides feeding your cat the recommended variety of meats, you should add a small amount of grains and mashed raw vegetables and fruits. Remember, if you were to set your cat loose today without his food bowl, he would eat not only his natural prey (meat) but also the nonmeat contents of his prey's stomach.

Many nutritional veterinarians recommend cooked brown rice as a common supplement to your cat's meat diet. Why *brown* rice? Because it has more nutrients in it than white rice, including more B-vitamins that are necessary for the health of the brain and the spine.*

While we're on the subject of brown grains versus white grains, let me digress to the subject of bread. Even if you've never previously made it a point to read about nutrition, you've probably heard that white bread has many of the vitamins processed out of it. True, the labels on white breads state proudly that certain vitamins have

---

* Our veterinarians have asked me to stress that rice must be cooked very, very well or your pet may not be able to digest it. On the face of it, this may seem inconsistent with our previous warnings that cooking destroys many nutrients. However, rice and other grains grow naturally in very hot, sunny climates. As a result, the nutrients in these foods are unusually stable when exposed to heat.

been added to the bread. What you're not supposed to know is that these added vitamins are a partial replacement for the vitamins the manufacturers have robbed from the natural grain in the manufacturing process.

RAW MEAT VERSUS COOKED MEAT. In the first edition, all nutritional veterinarians agreed that raw meat (accompanied by raw vegetables and fruits and cooked grains) was the optimal diet for cats—for the simple reason that cats' bodies were designed by evolution, God, or Mother Nature (your choice) to thrive on these foods, and cats fed otherwise do not thrive.

In the intervening years, the public has heard a lot more about the dangers of parasites in raw meat. But those are dangers to humans, not to cats or dogs. You see, cats' bodies are acidic in their pH balance, while ours are alkaline—the opposite. If cats were sickened by parasites in raw meat, the wild would never have had an adult cat.

For this new edition, Dr. Tiekert told me, "I think the risk of giving raw meat is far outweighed by the risk of *not* giving it. The potential for parasitoxicity with raw meat is pretty small."

Dr. Fudens says that he has good success in getting his clients to give their cats raw meat once he gets them "over their fear of salmonella and *E. coli* and all the other garbage misinformation that's out there about parasites and cats and dogs."

Veterinarians do warn, however, that you should never feed your cat raw pork or raw rabbit. These meats do carry parasites to which cats are susceptible.

Raw versus Cooked Foods for Cats

One of medical history's most dramatic scientific studies of the effect of raw versus cooked foods for cats was begun, oddly, because an M.D. was trying to do research on something quite different. The doctor, Francis M. Pottenger Jr., was trying to standardize adrenal cortical material, and he was using cats for this research. However, he was in a quandary. So many cats were dying that he was having difficulty carrying on his study, and he did not know why the cats were dying.

It occurred to Dr. Pottenger that animals in zoos contracted the same diseases as man and died earlier than animals in the wild. It also occurred to him that animals in the wild ate raw foods, and animals in zoos often did not. And it did not escape him that he had been feeding his laboratory cats cooked meats.

Thus, Dr. Pottenger embarked on a ten-year study of three generations of cats. He fed half the cats the customary cooked meats and pasteurized (or cooked) milk; the other half he fed raw meats and unpasteurized (raw) milk. It didn't take even the first generation of cats fed cooked foods long to develop some of the new "inevitable" disorders of both animals and man: tooth loss, paralysis, irritable behavior. As time went on, heart lesions became common; so did arthritis, nephritis, hepatitis, cystitis, and so on.

Miscarriages in the first generation were about 25 percent—that is, one in four should-have-been-born kittens never made it into the world. By the second generation, 70 percent didn't make it. Of those kittens who did see the light of day, many died soon after. Many mother cats died in labor.

Lice and internal parasites were common among the "cooked-food cats"—that is, among those who lived long enough to suffer these things in the first place; so were skin lesions and allergies.

Meanwhile, the cats being "pampered" with raw foods rarely suffered abortions, lice, parasites, or infections. They also had calmer, more even-tempered personalities.

If you remember, Dr. Pottenger began those experiments because not enough cats were surviving the operations he was performing in his research on adrenal cortical material. Once he started giving raw foods to some of his cats, he found he could perform these operations on them with little or no problem.

By the way, my summation of these experiments is not meant to give you a sense of hopelessness if you happen to have raised a cat on an unnatural diet and he now shows some of the signs of Dr. Pottenger's "cooked-food cats." You should know that in the fourth generation, Dr. Pottenger fed his "cooked-food cats" raw foods. In many cases, he was able to restore them to health.

Fish

Some books written by veterinarians without a special interest in nutrition have stated that fish is not a natural food for the cat. However, as Dr. Newland once pointed out, "Cats in the wild are natural fishermen."

Fish can be a good addition to your cat's diet. Fish contains polyunsaturated fats, for instance, which meat does not. We will cover how crucial polyunsaturated fats are in a following section.

Here again, however, I must emphasize that you should not concentrate on fish for the mainstay of your cat's diet. Like any other single class of food, fish does not contain all the nutrients necessary for health. For instance, fish is low in vitamin E, and cats happen to require very high amounts of E. One of the terrible things that can happen to your cat if he eats too much fish (particularly tuna) is a disorder known as steatitis, caused by a deficiency of vitamin E. First your cat will become extremely nervous; then every time something or someone touches his skin, he will meow and cringe in extreme pain, because the disorder will have caused his nerve endings to become excruciatingly sensitive. Veterinarians can often cure this disorder with massive amounts of the missing vitamin E; but why cause it in the first place? By the way, many commercial cat foods are high in tuna because tuna has such a strong taste that cats often will become addicted to it. The idea is that you're supposed to notice that your cat will "only eat" X brand, so you buy it for him all the time. You're not supposed to know about vitamin E deficiency and steatitis. Fish is also low in vitamin B_1 and, as Dr. Kreisberg has pointed out, "a B_1 deficiency can cause vomiting, weight loss—and brain damage."

Vegetables, Grains, Fruits

As we've mentioned, 60 to 75 percent of the cat's daily food should be meat. The rest should be fruits, vegetables, and grains. The latter foods give your cat a number of nutrients that don't occur at all in meat but are still necessary for her health, including carbohydrates and essential fatty acids (or polyunsaturated fats).

Now, while the cat's body has evolved to thrive best on raw, cut-up meat, it has also evolved to thrive best on partially ground-up vegetables, fruits, and grains. Remember that the bulk of these latter foods are obtained in nature partially digested from the intestines of the cat's animal prey.

An animal who has evolved to thrive mainly on raw fruits, vegetables, and grains has a set of intestines long for its body. Such animals are called herbivores, not carnivores. As I've mentioned, the cat's intestines are quite short. If you feed your cat uncut-up fruits, vegetables, and grains, the high amount of fiber and bulk in these foods will make it difficult for her short intestinal tract to digest them. In other words, your pet's body won't be able to utilize the necessary nutrients from these foods. Therefore, you should feed your pet her daily ration of fruits and vegetables raw; because, again, cooking destroys enzymes, vitamins, and minerals. However, cut up these foods for your pet.

Polyunsaturated Fats (or Essential Fatty Acids)

All holistic veterinarians agree on the importance of polyunsaturated fats in the diet of your cat. Dr. Robertson once told me: "These are the most critical nutrients that we have to deal with today; it is absolutely essential that cats get adequate amounts of these nutrients."

As we'll see in later chapters, nutritional veterinarians use these unsaturated fats to help in the treatment of a number of disorders, from skin problems to cancer. As always, it's easier, cheaper, kinder, and safer to prevent than to cure.

"If the animal is getting the proper proportion of fresh whole grains," said Dr. Robertson, "he's probably getting adequate essential fatty acids. If he's not getting enough whole grains, then the owner had better supplement. The lack of unsaturated fats is the major cause of skin problems and the major reason that cats don't absorb calcium." (The malabsorption of calcium can lead to a number of bone and joint problems.)

Research in essential fatty acid deficiency has shown that such a deficiency can also lead to stunted growth, reproductive problems, and degeneration of lungs, liver, and kidneys. Too little essential fatty acid intake is also implicated in rheumatoid arthritis and multiple sclerosis.

If you want to offer your pet an optimal preventive diet, you might add one teaspoon to one tablespoon (depending on your pet's size) of essential fatty acids a day to his diet—even if you're fairly sure he's getting enough whole grains. A bit more than necessary won't be harmful. A supplement of essential fatty acids is quite easy to obtain. Just buy a bottle of soybean oil, corn oil, sunflower seed oil, or safflower oil—the cooking and salad oils you can buy in the supermarket. The highest-quality oils you can buy are cold pressed. These are available in health food stores and some supermarkets. If the oil is cold pressed, it will say so in bold letters on the label.

Dr. Robertson stated that the best source of the most potent fatty acid (gamma-linolenic) is oil of evening primrose. You may have trouble getting this particular oil outside of health food stores. Dr. Kearns had a preference for cold-pressed sesame oil. "This oil does everything other unsaturated fats do," he told me, "but it also stimulates the thymus to produce T-cells, which help fight infection and cancer." Dr. Robertson and Drs. Marty and Robert Goldstein also agreed that cold-pressed sesame oil is a top choice.

As for other oils, wheat germ oil is high in vitamin E and octacosanol, and safflower oil is very high in vitamin F. Joseph Stuart, D.V.M., believed safflower oil is the best oil for cats.

Vitamin and Mineral Supplements

For those of you whose budgets are very, very tight, I can say that a few of the veterinarians surveyed believe you'll be able to have a healthy, long-lived pet without supplements, as long as you feed him the natural diet as detailed in this chapter and give him the supplements mentioned in chapter 4 for special times in his life. For those of you who can afford a few more pennies a day (and that's all it will cost), you're on much safer ground if you give your pet supplements in the manner explained a bit later.

Readers who have been following this book closely may now be thinking they have discovered an inconsistency: "Cats," you may say, "never had vitamin and mineral supplements in the wild." You're quite right, of course; they didn't. However, they also did not eat foods grown in nutrient-depleted earth (which both you and your pet are doing, unless you buy all your foods from well-chosen health food stores or grow all your own foods organically). And they didn't have to use much of the nutrients in their bodies for the extra job of fighting off stress from all the new poisons in the environment.

When choosing supplements, I hope you will not "build your own" vitamin and mineral supplement, for either yourself or your pet. I hope you will buy a good multivitamin/multimineral supplement, preferably from the health food store, where the nutrients are likely to be from natural sources. (Health food stores carry vitamins especially formulated for cats.) Often, the vitamins and minerals available in drugstores are chemical copies of the real thing.

First of all, if you build your own from different sources, it will probably cost you several times more than getting all the same nutrients in one pill. But my main concern is that by prescribing your own balance of vitamins and minerals, you may very well do your pet—or yourself—more harm than good.

For instance, you may read something somewhere that convinces you that your pet needs vitamin B_6. If you give him isolated B_6 without the direction of a veterinarian, you can increase his need for the other B-vitamins. In other words, you can, by giving him B_6, make him *deficient* in the other B-vitamins. This can cause severe central nervous system damage, as well as other problems.

In another instance you may read rather simplistic statements that pregnant and lactating cats, as well as growing kittens, need extra calcium. This is true; but what these other sources may not tell you is that you can't give a pill containing only calcium. Calcium has to be combined in a delicate balance with phosphorus, as nutritional veterinarian Dr. Kreisberg has stressed. It also has to be given in a certain ratio to magnesium or you stand the chance of causing the very health problems you're trying to prevent. In addition, vitamin D is needed or the calcium can't even be used by the body.

I have deliberately tried to make the balancing of vitamins and minerals sound complicated—because it is. I hope you will not attempt to do it on your own. For preventive purposes I hope you will follow the recommendation given here by veterinarians who have devoted their careers to the specific problem of nutrition for pets: Select an already balanced multivitamin and mineral supplement, and add vitamins C and E.

Holistic veterinarians have recommended to me that you add to the multivitamin/multimineral supplement 500 mg of vitamin C for your adult cat unless there is already part of that amount in the pill. The total vitamin E you should give him daily is 100 IU. If you can't get exactly those amounts by combining the multivitamin/multimineral with separate supplements, it is better to go a bit above these recommendations than below them. (Dr. Tiekert, however, in reviewing this chapter in manuscript form, wrote me that the original recommendations of 500 mg and 100 IU are "probably more than needed." Saturated fat is necessary for a number of nutrients to be absorbed by the body, so feed the supplements to your guy or gal along with meat.

Ideally, you should buy a powdered supplement. If that's not possible, mash up the multivitamin/multimineral tablet into your cat's food. Why? If your cat's digestive processes are not tip-top (and if he has been on processed foods, chances are his digestive juices are *not* tip-top), the pill may pass through his system and out again without being used at all. As S. Allen Price, D.V.M., once put it: "Sometimes we give a vitamin/mineral tablet to a cat, and it comes out again later, still a whole tablet." You can see that those vitamins and minerals have not been used by the body.

One more important point: There is always the possibility that a tablet might get stuck in the throat of a small animal.

How Not to Poison Your Pet with Water

Every time you fill your pet's bowl with cool, fresh water from your faucet, you may very well be bringing him that much closer to cadmium poisoning, copper poisoning, and/or lead poisoning. Yes, the same lead poisoning that the public is generally led to believe is caused only by eating paint peelings.

These dangerous heavy metals, of course, find it just as easy to get from your water pipes into your glass as they do to get into your pet's bowl. Many plumbing pipes are made partially from cadmium, copper, or lead; and as these metals start to erode, the water carries particles of the metal out with it.

An overload of heavy metals in your pet's body, and/or your own, can cause kidney damage, emphysema (there's a lot of the heavy metal cadmium in cigarette smoke, by the way), high blood pressure, heart disease, mental retardation, anemia, miscarriages, epilepsy, depression, and arthritis. That's only a partial list.

There is another substance that is being added *on purpose* to our drinking water. In many cities fluoride is added as a form of mass medication to help us prevent tooth decay—which might be more safely prevented by cutting out sugar, of course. Medical studies on everything from the fruit fly to mice to human beings have shown increased incidences of cancer caused by fluoride.

Dean Burk, Ph.D., once made a strong statement: "Our data in the United States indicate in my view that one-tenth of all cancer deaths in this country can be shown to be linked to fluoridation of public drinking water. That comes to about forty thousand extra cancer deaths a year. . . . [That] exceeds deaths from breast cancer."

Dr. Burk was for thirty-five years a high-level researcher at the U.S. Public Health Service's National Cancer Institute in the Washington, D.C., area.[1]

That's a brief overview of the dangerous substances we drink in our tap water every day. Of course, there are other contaminants, too. As I wrote the first edition, a TV reporter was announcing with some amazement that "thousands of towns" across the country had recently suffered increased incidences of various diseases and that "these diseases have been traced to human waste in the water." You have probably read similar statements quite recently.

Of course, you can't cut out water, either for yourself or for your pet. Water is needed to carry wastes out of the system, not only digestive wastes but also dead body cells. However, as Dr. Robertson has pointed out, impure water does not have the "carrying power" of pure water, and many toxins and dead cells are left to float around in our circulatory system a lot longer than they should.

By now you're wishing I would stop telling you horror stories about tap water and give you a clue as to what you can do to get all those poisons out of your pet's bowl and out of your drinking glass. One simple and inexpensive thing you can do is to let your water run for five minutes before you use it. This will allow time for particles of eroded heavy metals from your pipes to be carried off harmlessly down the drain, although it won't do anything for the more than three hundred contaminants that can be found actually in the water itself.

You can help your and your pet's health even more by investing a small sum in a water filter that you can put permanently over your faucet. Investigate before you buy, however; some filters screen out more contaminants than others. You might call the offices of one or two holistic veterinarians and ask an assistant what filter the doctor presently uses.

Probably you have heard of both springwater and distilled water as alternatives for the chemical-laden water that comes from our faucets. Nutritional M.D.s and D.V.M.s alike argue among themselves as to whether spring or distilled water is the better alternative. I

asked a number of nutritional veterinarians to tell me their preference and their reasons for it.

From their responses it seems that your safest bet may be distilled
water. Even those veterinarians who prefer springwater have warned
that often such water is contaminated. If you elect to use springwater, do a bit of research to make sure it comes from pure sources.
Just reading the label won't do. After all, no distributor is going to
state on the label: "Bottled exclusively from contaminated springs."

Still, some nutritional writers have maintained that distilled water
can be dangerous because it not only lacks desirable minerals but
can also leach minerals out of the body. As for the argument that distilled water contains no desirable minerals, Dr. Robertson has
stated, "The inorganic minerals that are in water are practically useless to the body." Addressing themselves to the argument that distilled water robs the body of minerals, Drs. Robert and Marty
Goldstein have told me that the minerals leached out by distilled
water are undesirable, inorganic minerals. "Distilled water also
leaches out other morbid wastes," the latter two doctors stated. Indeed, as we will see later, nutritional veterinarians use distilled water as therapy for conditions such as arthritis, just because it *does*
leach out undesirable minerals from the body.

Bones for Your Cat?

I know that many people have heard that bones are indispensable
for their cat. When I researched the first edition, I personally had
doubts about bones because of the possibility of choking, so I asked
ten veterinarians to give their recommendations about letting pets
gnaw bones. Seven of the ten veterinarians voted no, two voted yes
but only for a specific type of bone, and only one doctor voted
wholeheartedly for bones. He cited the fact that carnivores in the
wild always chewed on bones—and still do—as a way of cleaning
their teeth. This doctor stated that in thirty years of practice, he had
never found a pet who choked or otherwise had problems caused
by a splintered bone.

Unfortunately, other veterinarians *have* seen pets who have had problems, and they voted against bones because of the possibility of choking or of the cat's getting splinters into the intestines. Dr. Craige, for instance, said, "I remember a pitiable little Boston terrier who died with a string of lamb bones blocking his intestines. I have also seen countless animals who couldn't pass their feces without pain from bone splinters." Since cats are usually smaller than dogs—with proportionately smaller throats and intestines—we might expect them to be at a particularly high risk.

I once suggested to a neighbor that she stop giving bones to her dog, Lucky. "Don't fret your head, sweetheart," she told me. "Lucky's been gnawing on bones all his life without a problem. It keeps him happy." A few months later, the dog was dead. He'd choked on a chicken bone. The neighbor was stunned. "That never happened before," she said.

It seems to me that, while problems with bones may be rare, bones can kill. In this regard, I remember one of my earliest interviews with an M.D. when I was starting out as a medical journalist. "My editor wants you to comment on the fact that this form of cancer affects only 10 percent of men," I said.

The researcher answered: "The comment I have is that when a disease affects 10 percent, or 5 percent, or even 1 percent of the population, if it happens to *you*, the statistic is 100 percent."

Dr. Aloro was most strongly against giving bones to pets. He stated that bones, far from keeping the teeth healthy, can harm them quite drastically. "When my clients don't listen to me and give their pets bones, I find the teeth get chipped; they break; they get otherwise ruined because the roots get weakened." As if that weren't enough, sometimes the teeth even get "filed down to the gum line." Dr. Aloro did, however, recommend soup bones—which don't tend to splinter—*for teething pets,* whose baby teeth are meant by nature to come out soon, anyway. These bones help loosen the baby teeth.

Dr. Tiekert, who entered "the bone question" for this new edition, says, "I'll throw this in for whatever it's worth. I like to give animals oxtails if the owners can get them. Animals are not likely to break teeth on these bones. I do a lot of veterinary dentistry, so I see many animals who break their teeth off chewing on *hard* bones. But with the oxtails, animals get quite a bit of gristle, so they get a lot of precursors for ligaments and cartilage." (That means that gristle sets in motion in the body the biochemical reactions that produce two substances vital for healthy joints and bones. Thus, gristle can help prevent disorders that cripple.)

Does Dr. Tiekert know of any animals who have choked on oxtail bones? "I've never seen that happen. But of course there's always a potential for choking whenever an animal chews on anything."

Drs. Robert Goldstein and Marty Goldstein have told me that most of today's cats who are raised on processed cat food "do not have strong enough teeth or digestive juices to handle bones as safely as their ancestors did"—and still do—in the wild. In contrast, cats who have been on natural diets for long periods of time tend to have strong digestive juices that can dissolve bits of bone, preventing these bone fragments from getting embedded in the intestines.

The doctors Goldstein recommended that you give your cat a firm biscuit made of whole grains. This can give him almost as much a challenge to chew up as a bone would.

If you have always heard that cats absolutely must have bones, maybe this discussion has not convinced you otherwise. Please at least don't let your cat have bones small enough to swallow or fragile enough to splinter as he gnaws on them. And please take the advice of many holistic veterinarians *not* to cook any bones you give your pet. Dr. Craige explains that cooking denatures the collagen (a protein) of the bone, making it harder to digest.

For this new edition, Dr. Fudens has recommended raw (*again, not cooked*) chicken neck for cats. He says this is "great for teeth, nutrition, and psycho/emotional enjoyment. The bones of chicken necks are soft, so they are readily chewed, swallowed, and digested." He adds that "cats love them—at least once they get used to eating like their wild brothers and sisters."

Dr. Tiekert comments that he, too, recommends chicken necks for cats.

I have been talking until now about real animal, fish, or bird bones. What about plastic bones, rawhide bones, and milk bones?

When you buy these you are using the fake products holistic veterinarians spoke against so strongly in chapter 1. One veterinarian warned, "These artificial products must be excluded from the diet of *all* pets." And this was the veterinarian most strongly in favor of *real* bones for pets.

Additional Tips

A Chocolate Treat for Your Cat? No!

I'd often read that chocolate was dangerous, even sometimes fatal, for dogs. I hadn't seen any mention of it being a problem at all for cats. So all my reading indicated—as all your reading may have indicated—that you don't have to worry about giving an occasional chocolate treat to your cat.

But, as you may have noticed by now, I try never to *assume* anything. I took my question to Dr. Tiekert: Is chocolate just as harmful for cats as it is for dogs? "It probably is," he said, "and I suspect that cats are even more susceptible. But I've never heard of chocolate poisoning in a cat, probably for two reasons: Cats don't usually like sweets, and what owners would consider giving chocolate to their cats?"

That said, we both realized we had no way of knowing what every single reader might or might not do, so Dr. Tiekert checked a top reference book from his library. We found that "many dogs and some cats love chocolates.... Chocolate contains theobromine, which is quite toxic to dogs and cats and may cause urinary incontinence, seizures, and death."

Dr. Tiekert, who has never had a case of chocolate poisoning in his practice, told me he knew of no effective treatment. Dr. Fudens, however, tells me that if you catch chocolate poisoning early, you can help the cat by inducing vomiting. "Otherwise, there are several homeopathic remedies that can help."

Food Combining

How you combine food groups can be crucial to your cat's health. Why? The digestive organs secrete enzymes to break down food so it can be properly used by the body. When carbohydrates and proteins are eaten at the same time, the protein enzymes go to work first, and the digestion of carbohydrates must wait. While the carbohydrates are waiting around to be digested, they ferment and release toxins in the body.

Proper food combining might more aptly be called *not* combining foods: Give only meat (or other heavy proteins such as eggs or milk) at one meal; give carbohydrates (fruits and grains) for the other meal. Vegetables, though, may be given with either grains or heavy proteins.

This easy step can not only be helpful in preventing the release of toxins in your cat's body, it can also help prevent pancreatitis (inflammation of the pancreas). Holistic veterinarians discuss just how serious this disease is—and how many other conditions it can lead to—in chapter 9, which deals with problems of internal organs. You see, the pancreas spends much of its work time producing enzymes to aid in digestion. Asking it to try to produce two sets of enzymes at one time—to help digest both proteins and carbohydrates—can cause this hard worker much distress.

Is all this true for people, too? Yes. Rather than eating cereal and toast with ham and eggs for breakfast, you might consider eating cereal, fruit, and toast—all carbohydrates. If you are troubled by puzzling bouts of gas, you might see if proper food combining puts an end to them.

Don't Spring This New Diet on Your Cat All at Once

Don't spring *any* new diet on your cat suddenly. For one thing, any quick major change in a diet can prove upsetting to the body and cause digestive disturbances. For another, a cat addicted to sugar or other unnatural additives in commercial foods is not unlike a person addicted to alcohol. If you take away all his additives abruptly, he may "lose it." That is, he may go into withdrawal symptoms.

Start slowly. Add just a bit of his new diet at a time for about a week, then gradually add a bit more. In this way, not only his digestive system but his taste buds can get a chance to become adjusted to the new (though ancient) diet.

How Much to Feed Your Pet and How Often

First I am going to repeat the information on calories from the first edition. I'm doing this because I think calories are still the general approach to the idea of how much food you should feed your cat. But dealing with calories can become complicated for someone who isn't a nutritionist. After the information on calories, I will tell you about a newer, easier approach given me by two holistic veterinarians I talked to for this new edition.

You may be surprised to know that most nutritional veterinarians are loath to recommend how many calories you should feed a cat. And rightly so. As Dr. Aloro has said, "Of course I have in my office all those nice charts about calories and fat, et cetera, per pound of the animal's weight. But for practical purposes, they are fairly useless. The charts deal with the average animal. In reality, most animals are not average; each pet is an individual."

What Dr. Aloro said is true. Feeding the same number of calories to a twelve-pound cat who spends his days climbing trees and to a twelve-pounder who spends half his time cuddled in your lap and the other half snoozing on top of a cabinet could result in one half-starved cat and one bloated butterball.

Even feeding an equal number of calories to two cats of the same weight, age, and exercise habits won't work for certain to maintain perfect weight. These two animals might have quite dissimilar metabolic rates: One cat might burn up only half as many calories a day as the other. As Dr. Newland once pointed out, the same disparity is true of people. "We all know people who eat everything and stay thin, and we all know people who eat little and get fat."

Nutritional veterinarians recommend this sublimely common-sense rule of thumb: If your cat starts gaining weight, cut down a bit on his food and encourage him to exercise more. If he starts losing weight, indulge him in a bit more food. Another easy-to-follow rule of thumb about your cat's weight: You should be able to *feel* her ribs—that means she doesn't have a lot of extra fat around them. But you should not be able to *see* her ribs—that means she doesn't have enough fat around them.

However, I'll give you a base to start from, because I know your cat's new natural diet won't be coming out of a box or can that provides you with simplistic instructions for your "average" cat. Try starting him with about 75 calories a day for each pound he weighs. But no matter how many calories you include in your cat's new diet, watch his weight carefully for a while.

The following is an example of why Dr. Aloro and other nutritional veterinarians are reluctant to deal with *average* calories for *individual* animals: The average recommendation of 75 calories per pound of body weight added up to 750 calories a day for my tabby cat, Puddy. But she started to turn into a butterball when I offered her that much food. When I cut back about 100 calories, she once again became a fine figure of a cat and stayed that way.

You can easily get inexpensive books and pamphlets that give calorie counts of most foods. Maybe over breakfast one day, circle those foods you'll be feeding your cat. Then you'll be able to find the calorie counts quickly. You'll probably be surprised how fast you memorize them and don't need to look them up anymore.

Now that was, as I said, the traditional advice about doling out your pet's food. But for this new edition, several veterinarians have told me that they now go by *volume*, not calories. In other words, if your cat maintains her weight on a cup of food a day, 60 percent of that cup should be meat. At her other meal, give her 40 percent of a cup of grains or vegetables.

How often should you feed your cat? As cat breeder Celeste Yarnall points out, for many years veterinarians have advised owners to open a can twice a day, and to leave dry food out for the cat to eat at will all day—"rather like raising a child on Spam and Cocoa Puffs," she comments.[2] I checked out whether this advice is still on cat food labels. I found out that yes, we are often advised to dump some kibble into our cat's bowl every morning and to let him "nibble" throughout the day.

This advice is a far cry from that of veterinarians who specialize in nutrition. First, of course, these doctors don't recommend foods in cans or boxes. Second, "we don't like to feed them what is called free choice, leaving any food down all the time," Dr. Limehouse tells me. "We like to feed them twice a day, and what they haven't chosen to eat after maybe thirty minutes, we advise you just to go ahead and pick it up." Dr. Limehouse explains that the reason for this seeming cruelty to kitty is, as always, the goal of keeping your cat's carnivorous body as close to nature as possible. "In the wild, cats stalk their food, they chase it, they struggle with it, and after the kill, they play with it. So by the time they get ready to eat it, their bodies have worked up to producing what you might call a crescendo of enzymes. I feel that when we let a cat nibble throughout the day, they're not developing a sufficient amount of enzymes to always do a good job of digesting their food and actually *using* the nutrients." The veterinarian adds that often with cats who have been allowed to nibble at will, "we wind up having to supplement them with extra enzymes" to get them back to full health.

To express this from a somewhat different angle, remember that cats' bodies weren't formed to be those of grazers (such as cows, who *can* stay healthy by nibbling all day). Yarnall points out[3] that cats need "fasting" time between meals so their bodies can become acidic, their normal healthy state. "Smelling food and nibbling all day keeps cats' systems alkaline," she states. Alkaline is the *opposite* of acidic. She points out that feline urological syndrome is directly related to nibbling. (In a later chapter, we discuss that this syndrome can be fatal, and that it is among the most common health problems in cats. Indeed, some veterinarians believe it is *the* most common problem that strikes cats.) Yarnall cites studies showing that free feeding of dry food causes the urine to be more alkaline for longer periods of time, and that this forms an environment conducive to the creation of urinary crystals and calculi.

Norman C. Ralston, D.V.M., summed up these facts in another

way while talking to me about heart problems for a later chapter. Expressing himself passionately, as he usually does because he cares so deeply about animals, he interrupted himself to say, "You can talk about heart problems, you can talk about urinary problems, you can talk about other problems. But the biggest mistake people make with cats is to overlook their basic nature. Cats were designed by God—or nature if you don't want to talk about God—to go from feast to famine." After discussing some of the facts given above about necessary changes in a cat's body, Dr. Ralston said, "Cats need to get hungry so that they can stay healthy."

He added that "I once had the same problem in my house: My wife was wanting to leave food out all the time for our cat. 'Well,' she said, 'I'm afraid he might get hungry.' " Dr. Ralston managed to convince her that "He's *supposed* to get hungry." Before going back to the subject we had been talking about, the veterinarian commented, "Now our cat is seventeen years old, and he's a healthy son of a goon."

Fasting

Here, we're talking about longer-term fasting than we were in the previous paragraphs. If you already believe in occasional fasting for yourself because you feel that the digestive system should have a rest now and then to let the body rid itself of toxins, you'll be glad to know that there's a rationale for fasting your cat occasionally, too. Do you remember Ruff, our composite great-great-etc.-granddaddy of today's cats, whose evolving body shaped the carnivorous body and needs of your cat? Well, Ruff didn't get lucky enough to snare a catch every day. So Ruff and all his billions of descendants have bodies designed to be healthy if they have to fast occasionally for a day.

All the recommendations I know of suggest you fast your adult cat over two years of age for twenty-four hours once a week—if you want to "get into" fasting at all. *Of course, you must give him water during the fast.* If your cat is between four months and two years of age, fast him for only half a day every week, and a full day once a month.

Warning: Do not fast your chronically sick pet without the *personal* guidance of a veterinarian who thoroughly understands fasting. (Close guidance by phone is okay, if you feel assured the veterinarian will be quickly available by phone in case of an emergency.) The poisons that concentrate in the body before they are expelled can kill a degenerated pet. You may have read elsewhere that fasting can help many sick cats recover—and it can. But don't use this technique on your own, even if the book or article seems to have given you precise instructions. Sometimes writers give detailed instructions for something they know should be done only under close professional guidance because they fear readers won't consult doctors for one reason or another. The writers feel they should at least give some structure to what readers might otherwise "make up on their own."

Yarnall[4] gives a few tips about nurturing your cat if you opt for occasional fasting: "I only fast my cats when I have time to give them special care. . . . If you choose to fast your cat, the fasting day is a wonderful time for grooming and cuddling. Do not fast your cat when you are not home. She needs the extra attention when deprived of her food!"

Here I feel I should address myself to readers who may think that cats don't have the same "feelings" as humans. (I doubt that many of you reading this book believe that, but I try to cover all bases; and I've known compassionate "animal people" who have told me in no uncertain terms that cats aren't affected by the death of loved ones. Also, I have read articles saying that if you lock a cat away all alone in a strange room while someone renovates your house, the cat cries piteously only to get your attention—not because she is suffering emotionally.) It's true that Ruff, your cat's great-great-ancestor, didn't have a human around to console him whenever he had to go without food for a while. But Ruff *never* had a human. Your cat *always* has, and so he has learned to depend on you for many things that Ruff never dreamed of asking a two-legged animal for. Faced with no food for a day, Ruff would probably have said to himself: "Heck, no food today. Okay, I've survived this before. Let me take a nap and I'll go hunting again tomorrow." Your domesticated cat may think, "Oh, no. No food in my bowl! This has never happened to me before. I can't get out of this domicile to hunt, because I'm all locked in. I'm doomed!"

Some nutritional veterinarians suggest that you take a more hands-off approach toward regular fasting. "Your pet is the one who knows when he should fast," Dr. Robertson once told me. "Whenever a cat doesn't feel in top form, the first thing he'll do is stop eating. Leave it to him. He has a better idea of when he should fast than we do." (In this regard, you should have some concern if your pet goes off his food. But if he does, perhaps the worst thing you can do without professional guidance is to force-feed him. Think back, for instance, to the times you've felt nauseous: Would you have thanked *your* loved one for forcing you to take food into your stomach?)

Milk Products

I know that many people consider cats and milk practically synonymous with each other. This *is* true of kittens: After all, all mammals start life living exclusively off the milk their mothers so graciously provide. However, let's investigate this for a moment. If you're feeding your grown cat milk, you're feeding him cow's milk, aren't you? (That's pretty much the only kind you can buy in most stores.) As a kitten your companion got milk, naturally, from his mama—*cat's* milk. Just as puppies naturally get dog's milk from their mamas, and human babies naturally get human milk from their mamas.

Let's go back again to our average day in the life of our cat's long-ago ancestor, Ruff, to check out if milk is a natural food for your grown cat. Ruff is now weaned; he wakes up and starts his day looking for prey. He strikes it rich with a bird. No milk there. (If Ruff were a dog, he would wait awhile and then go to the spring for a drink, where he wouldn't find any milk either. But Ruff got most of the moisture he needed from his natural prey.) Assuming he would still have a longing from his babyhood for the milk his mother can no longer give him, where would he find milk in the wild? There is no dairy he can loot, and we can assume he doesn't know how to milk cows. The answer, then, is inescapable: Contrary to a popular myth, milk is not a natural food for our grown cat.

Dr. Kearns stated the idea this way: "I feel that milk is an unnatural food unless it goes from nipple to host by suction." The doctors Goldstein pointed out to me that cow's milk contains growth hormones that serve to take a forty-pound calf and build him to a seven-hundred- to thousand-pound cow. "This is great for the cow," the doctors said, "but not for the cat."

Having said all these negatives against milk, let me add that nutritional veterinarians believe that raw, unpasteurized milk (especially raw goat's milk) can be a good addition to your cat's weekly diet—*if your cat shows no signs of being allergic to milk*. On the plus side, milk contains calcium. In the wild, cats got calcium from chomping on the bones of their prey; this book asks you to consider very carefully before giving bones to your pet. Therefore, you must find other means to give him the calcium his body evolved to thrive on. Raw goat's milk is a good way.

Yogurt may be an even better way to provide your pet with calcium. Yogurt tends to cause fewer animals (and fewer persons) allergy problems. It also contains a type of "friendly" bacteria that is extremely important to the digestive health—and therefore the total health—of your pet (and yourself).

The common belief is that allergies cause basically only stomach and skin problems. However, Alfred Jay Plechner, D.V.M., who has studied allergies extensively, once told me, "Nearly any disease in the body may be primarily or secondarily related to a food allergy." Nutritional M.D.s make similar statements about human diseases.

If your cat has bouts of diarrhea, simply cutting out milk might "miraculously" cure the diarrhea. However, as we've said, allergies can cause almost any symptom. So if your pet has *any* problem that your veterinarian has not been able to explain or treat successfully, ask the doctor to consider the possibility of allergies to milk and other foods.

Temperature of Your Cat's Food

Your cat will have a better appetite and better digestion if you serve his food at a tepid temperature—neither cold right out of the refrigerator, nor hot right off the stove. Many people who are owned by cats have noticed this revulsion to hot and cold foods and have passed it off as a profound finickiness on the part of their pampered prince or princess. It's not finickiness; it's a desire on your cat's part that his food be served at its "proper" (natural) temperature. The temperature of the body of Ruff's newly killed prey was always tepid. Other writers have noted that our cats' reputation for finickiness when they pick at their fake food is a bum rap: Cats just want their food the way it *should* be, the way Ruff always had it.

Your Cat's Food and Water Bowls

Dr. Stuart once pointed out to me that your pet's bowl should not be the common plastic ones that so many owners use. Dr. Kearns agreed, adding that there is a chemical reaction that can cause many pets to lose pigment from their noses. Dr. Kearns also advised that aluminum dishes can cause aluminum toxicity and ceramic dishes can cause lead toxicity. He recommended stainless steel or glass dishes as the safest. Nutritional M.D.s make the same recommendations for us.

If your cat's water bowl starts to show discoloration, look to your tap water. In a recent book on psychiatrists who treat mental problems using natural therapies, I included the case history of a woman who for years had been diagnosed as having a serious psychosomatic disorder that refused to yield to psychological therapies. It was "psychosomatic," you see, because no physical reason for her array of symptoms could be found on the usual orthodox diagnostic tests. When her puppy also developed some of her "imagined" symptoms, the woman found it hard to believe that a pet could catch "mental" disorders from his owner. A discoloration in his water bowl led her to have her water pipes tested. They had many times the level of copper considered safe. She and her puppy had copper poisoning, and both were easily cured of their symptoms by nutritional doctors.

How to Supplement Your Cat's Diet with Inexpensive Packaged Foods

Your pet's healthy diet might include occasional servings of pre-pared cat foods bought at a store. Right now you're getting ready to throw back at me all the grisly facts we covered in chapter 1 about packaged pet foods from supermarket shelves. What I am recom-mending here are packaged pet foods available primarily at health food stores and some enlightened pet shops and grooming shops. The prepared foods I'm referring to are more closely tailored to your pet's needs, tend to come from more natural sources, and do not contain the poisons that plump out the commercial pet foods.

These purer prepared foods can serve as a nice source of bal-anced nutrition now and then: for instance, when you're not going to be home overnight. And they can be just about invaluable when you have to leave your cat in the care of someone else. You can more easily expect a friend or kennel owner to shake out some kib-ble from a bag than to deal with raw meat balanced with grains and raw fruits and vegetables.

Surprisingly, these more natural prepared foods are often no more expensive than the lethal packaged foods in supermarkets. Are these distributors, then, philanthropists? No. But for one thing, as we covered previously, the more nutritious a food is, the less a pet will eat of it, because he will need less to fulfill his body require-ments. For another thing, you don't have to pay these distributors for nationwide TV ads. As Dr. Newland pointed out to me in 1981, "A few seconds' TV commercial costs $60,000 to $150,000. I ask you, is there any nutritional value in this hot air? If you buy the product, you are paying for this advertising, right through the nose." Obviously, today you are helping the distributors to pay much heftier fees for their ads.

Now, if there are fairly good prepared foods available, why have I bothered you with everything I've told you in the earlier part of this chapter? Because your cat cannot thrive on these foods as a *mainstay* of her diet. They should be used only as an occasional supplement. And if they are used often, they themselves should be supplemented with the nutrients they're lacking. These more nutritional canned or packaged foods are still not raw, and they're missing the enzymes that can be found only in raw foods—more accurately, your pet is missing out on them. I think you'll find that adding the enzymes already makes the packaged food more expensive than a completely natural diet. And some of these less poisoned foods consist mostly of lamb and rice, or another combination of basically two ingredients. If you use these as a basis of your cat's diet, in addition to enzymes, you'll have to supplement with omega-3 and omega-6 fatty acids to make up for the fact that she doesn't have any fish in her diet. These "two-ingredient" prepared foods also leave your pet vulnerable to developing allergies because of eating the same foods every day.

Another argument against serving even the purest packaged foods as a mainstay of your cat's diet is that the longer foods sit around in packages or cans, the more nutrients they lose. And once you open the package or can, exposing the food to air, the nutrients start disappearing even faster, through the oxidation process.

Here you might have every reason to expect me to make things easy for you by simply giving you the brand names that holistic veterinarians recommend for occasional supplementation of a natural raw-food diet. I did do that in the first edition, although some veterinarians warned me not to, saying that many producers of the purer prepared foods become greedy over time and start substituting artificial ingredients for the more natural ones in order to make a bigger profit. When I tried again to list brand names for this new edition, I found that holistic veterinarians were telling me that until recently they were recommending, say, three brands, but that that was now down to one because the other two had started tampering with the quality of their products.

But do you know what? I *can* simplify the choice for you. Call the offices of a few holistic veterinarians (see the list at the back of the book) and ask what they're recommending at the precise time you're reading this. I suggest calling more than one holistic veterinarian because you might find brand X, say, to be one of four choices of the first doctor, but brand Y is a choice of that doctor as well as two others. I'd assume, then, that brand Y would be the more educated choice. Since busy veterinarians can sometimes be hard to get on the phone for a simple question like this, try just asking the secretary what the doctor recommends.

If, for some reason, you'd rather "go it alone" on choosing a prepackaged food for an occasional supplement—or if you want to double-check the veterinarian's recommendation—here's a very quick rundown on what you should look for on labels once you think you have found a noncontaminated food in a health food store, pet shop, or grooming shop. First of all, the label should state that there are no artificial preservatives, colors, or flavorings. Recently, even some supermarket foods state "no artificial preservatives or colors." If you read the label carefully, you'll probably see that there are artificial flavorings. That's not good enough for your cat. Some labels state "no added" preservatives or whatnot. The word *added* is a clue that the sources of the product might have *started off* with preservatives or whatnot. In addition, the label should not contain the words *meal* or *by-products* after any of its ingredients, for the reasons given in chapter 1. And the label shouldn't list any of the other "no-no's" covered in that chapter.

Somewhere along the line, the label should read that the product has one or more preservatives. But haven't I said that preservatives are practically going to make your pet keel over on the spot? I've warned against *artificial* preservatives. If you don't have any preservatives at all in prepackaged food, there's nothing to prevent it from spoiling while it sits on the shelf—before you even buy it. The label you're investigating should specify *natural* preservatives, such as vitamins C and E.

Avoid using too often a product that lists fish early on the label, which indicates it's a major ingredient. Although cats need fish in their diet, remember that *too much* fish can keep your cat from getting sufficient vitamin E and cause that gruesome disorder steatitis covered earlier in this chapter.

And if you come across a product that claims you can use it for both dogs and cats—as I have—ask yourself: How can a product fulfill at the same time the needs of dogs, who thrive on a diet of 33 to 50 percent meat, and the needs of cats, who thrive on a diet of 60 to 75 percent meat?

Let me add a final word to discourage you from using prepared foods often: As covered in chapter 1, a new labeling act allows labels to claim products are "all natural" even if they contain many poisons.

A Vegetarian Diet for Your Cat?

In the first edition, I reluctantly gave specifics of a vegetarian diet that came as close as an unnatural diet *could* to having the potential to keep a cat healthy. I pointed out that people who were vegetarians themselves because they believed meat wasn't healthy for humans were on the right track because our bodies aren't those of carnivores. But they were definitely on the wrong track if they tried to "make" their carnivorous pet into a vegetarian. However, I felt I couldn't offer an argument for readers who refused to feed meat to their pets because they couldn't bear to contribute to the slaughter of other animals. I was afraid that these readers might feel they should switch to poisonous fake supermarket foods, and I hoped to help them do less harm by suggesting the best possible vegetarian diet.

Remember that one reason animals are killed is to provide animal parts to manufacturers of your cat's supermarket foods. So, by paying for these foods, you are still helping to contribute to the death of these animals. But instead of giving your companion the parts of the animals that can bless her with a long and healthy life, you're giving her tumors and the like. Perhaps the fact I discovered for this new edition—that the commercial foods contain parts of bodies of euthanized dogs and cats—will solidify your decision not to switch your cat to these foods.

For this edition, I questioned a new batch of holistic veterinarians about whether it is ever okay for owners to feed a vegetarian diet to their cats. The responses I got were even more vehement than they were in 1981. For instance, Dr. Fudens answered me—and I quote him directly—"Never, never, never, never. Absolutely no. Never."

The veterinarian continued: "I don't care what your own religious or philosophical viewpoint is. You don't love your animals if you try to make them vegetarians." Referring to the vegetarian cats and dogs who have been brought to him in ill health in his thirty-four years as a veterinarian, Dr. Fudens said that the pets had become vegetarians because of their owners' perspectives, "not from the animal's point of view." He added that "once you balance out these sick animals' diet with some meat, you should see how happy and healthy they become: like fleas on a sick dog.

"Dogs and cats are not herbivores," Dr. Fudens summarized. "God made them as carnivores—whether we like it or not—and they need animal protein."

Dr. Tiekert said: "These are cats and dogs we're talking about; they're not little people. And I think we should use diets that are appropriate for their digestive systems—not ours. If we force on dogs and cats our philosophical desires about vegetarianism, I don't believe we're thinking about what we *have*. If you've chosen an animal who's by nature a carnivore, and now you want to make him into a vegetarian, why did you get that animal in the first place?"

Dr. Tiekert suggested that people considering buying or adopting a cat and feeding him a vegetarian diet should first look at a lot of pictures showing wild cats carrying dead animals in their mouths as they go about their daily lives.

I still have a nagging fear that some of you will continue your cat on a vegetarian diet. If you absolutely must do that, at least have a diet drawn up by an animal nutritionist who knows how to balance amino acids.

But you can see why I'm not including a vegetarian diet in this edition. It would go against my conscience. Also, I'm afraid the veterinarians who worked with me on this book would shoot me.

Summary

The holistic veterinarians who worked with me on this chapter have given you detailed information on nutrition, which is the source of every biochemical reaction in our bodies. You now are armed with the most important information presently known to give your adult cat a supremely healthy and long life. Specific nutritional information for kittenhood and other special stages in your cat's life will follow in chapter 4.

But first, in the next chapter, I'll give you information on the misuse of vaccinations—yes, orthodox veterinary medicine's major way of attempting to prevent disease. Holistic veterinarians consider standard vaccinations to be almost as important—some consider them of equal importance—in destroying our pets' health as a steady diet of unnatural and poisonous food. These veterinarians will tell you how you can vaccinate your cat safely—and with less expense—than you can with the regimen presently recommended by most orthodox veterinarians. We'll also see that the present regimen is falling out of favor even with conventional doctors.

As usual, this information will also be relevant to the health of you and your human family.

References

1. Jonathan Rothschild, *Let's Live*, January 1982.
2. Celeste Yarnall, *Cat Care, Naturally* (Charles E. Tuttle Co., Inc., Boston, 1995), p. 82.
3. *Ibid.*, p. 83.
4. *Ibid.*, p. 87.

Chapter 3

Vaccinations Can Be Your Cat's Worst Enemy or His Best Friend: How You Can Make the Right Choice

"Standard vaccines are the single biggest cause of immune system damage in humans and animals. All chronic disease in animals is traced to genetics and standard vaccinations before anything else."
—*John Fudens, D.V.M.*

"Overvaccination is the *main* problem (along with malnutrition) that affects our pets today."
—*Michele Yasson, D.V.M., C.V.A.*

"A practice that . . . lacks scientific validity or verification is annual revaccinations. Almost without exception there is no immunologic requirement for annual revaccination. Immunity to viruses persists for years or for the life of the animal. Successful vaccination to most bacterial pathogens produces an immunologic memory that remains for years . . ."
—*Tom R. Phillips, D.V.M., and Ronald D. Shultz, D.V.M., in* Current Veterinary Therapy XI, *p. 205*

"Since I have been using homeopathic vaccinations—for the last ten or twelve years—I have never had, to my knowledge, a single animal come down with any disease that was vaccinatable."
—*John Fudens, D.V.M.*

When I worked in 1981 with numerous holistic veterinarians for the first edition of this book, I didn't find any who really liked the idea of giving vaccinations, because of the potential dangers to the animal. But there were basically only two choices in that era: either give standard, orthodox vaccinations or give none. So I included in the book the details holistic veterinarians provided for making standard vaccinations as nontoxic and as effective as possible. (I repeat these details at the end of this chapter for those of you who might still feel, after reading the following new information, that your cat's health can benefit most from a specific standard vaccination. You can also use these details if you still feel you want to give your cat the full regimen of standard vaccinations throughout his life. But I'm betting that you won't want to do that by the time you get to the end of this chapter.)

One major reason I wanted to update the first edition was that I knew that holistic veterinarians, in the last decade and a half, had been trained in homeopathy, a natural field of medicine that they were only beginning to use in 1981. (Homeopathy is not, however, a new, untried field; it was developed in the late 1700s.) Just before starting to work with doctors for this present edition, I found that holistic veterinarians were now using homeopathic vaccinations. I wondered where that would lead.

The first veterinarian to answer my 1997 questionnaire, Dr. Fudens, wrote me a heavily underlined note stating that genetics and vaccinations were the major causes of disease in our cats. One of the skills I draw on in compiling the work of many doctors is that of balancing extreme views against conservative—and giving readers all views—when there is a medical debate. (That way, I believe, readers will know all sides of the issue and can make an educated decision on their own, or at least can initiate a knowledgeable conversation with a veterinarian.)

My first thought was that this veterinarian was probably on the extreme edge of the vaccination issue. But within days I'd received several more filled-out questionnaires from holistic veterinarians, all of them saying that standard vaccinations were one of the two major causes of disease in animals, and all heavily underlined for emphasis. I should stress that in the questionnaire I never asked for any doctor's thoughts on vaccinations. These were all veterinarians who—in part because they now have homeopathic vaccinations as a safer, surer way to prevent diseases than the standard vaccinations— at last feel free to warn strongly against the conventional vaccinations that they had never believed in seventeen years ago.

After talking to other veterinarians, and doing some reading in technical publications, it was clear that I couldn't just easily update the first edition's several paragraphs on vaccinations, as I'd planned. This subject was of the utmost importance and warranted its own full chapter. I knew that most of you have been taught to believe— and I believed this, too, until I researched the first edition—that standard vaccinations are the most important step we can take to prevent disease in our animals. I know my readers to be intelligent, seeking people; and I wasn't going to convince many of you to give up the usual vaccinations by saying, in a few paragraphs, "They're bad because I've looked into the matter and have deemed them to be bad."

As I said earlier, my goal in the first edition was to tell you what holistic veterinarians advised you to do to avail your cat of the *best* that standard vaccinations offered, while advising you how to save your cat from the *worst* they offered. My goal now is to give you suggestions as to when you can safely do away with harmful standard vaccinations altogether; when you can safely use only homeopathic vaccinations; when your best bet might be to mix and match; and when your cat may be better off with no vaccinations, either standard or homeopathic.

The bottom line as always, though, is that you should consult, at least by phone, with a holistic veterinarian for advice about your own, unique cat. (See the list of veterinarians at the back of the book.) You may wonder why these doctors can't just draw up a simple regimen, as orthodox doctors do: vaccination X for all cats at such and so an age, vaccination Y every so many years throughout the cat's life. Orthodox veterinarians sometimes think in terms of "a cat is a cat is a cat," while holistic veterinarians tend to think in terms of: "Okay, this animal is a cat. Now what are his or her specific needs?" A lot will depend on your cat's age, general health, lifestyle, and—as we will see later—even the part of the country in which he makes his home.

If you don't live anywhere near a holistic veterinarian, don't worry that you won't be able to avail your cat of homeopathic vaccines. As I detail later, this is as easy as waiting a few days after talking on the phone and then picking up the prescribed vaccines from your mailbox. (These vaccines are given by mouth; you don't have to know how to inject your cat with a needle.)

What Are the Dangers of Standard Vaccinations?

On the covering page of this chapter, I gave a few of the passionate comments against orthodox vaccinations sent me, unsolicited, by holistic veterinarians. Cat breeder Celeste Yarnall in her book *Cat Care, Naturally*[1] found many other holistic doctors damning these vaccinations. She cites, for instance, Richard Pitcairn, D.V.M., whom I know as one of the earliest holistic veterinarians in this country and one of the earliest to specialize in homeopathy—and who also, she points out, has a Ph.D. in immunology (the medical specialty that includes vaccinations). Yarnall cites the doctor as saying that the majority of problems facing veterinarians today stem from vaccinations. (There's that same idea again!)

Checking to see if I could find a major holistic veterinarian to balance all these strong statements against standard vaccinations, I talked to Dr. Tiekert, founder and director of the American Holistic Veterinary Medical Association, whom I consider a conservative holistic veterinarian. By that I mean he doesn't express his knowledge in terms of black and white, and he takes pains to back up empiric evidence with controlled scientific research. I asked if he agreed with the strong statement that traditional vaccinations are one of the two major causes of modern-day illness and death in pets. "I think that's still to be proven per se," he said, indicating that the mass of scientific studies generally needed before a new medical fact is accepted had not yet been completed. So I had my more conservative viewpoint, I thought for a split second. Then he added, surprisingly, "But I *do* agree with that statement."

Dr. Tiekert went even further to talk about another fact I'd heard several times recently: that even orthodox veterinarians are showing increasing signs of turning against overvaccination. (Yarnall states that many veterinarians have told her that they no longer believe in vaccinating *at all* but are afraid to buck the system.) "I think," Dr. Tiekert says, "there's certainly enough evidence coming up within the conventional world saying that we've been way overvaccinating animals, that academia is going to be radically changing the suggestions of how often animals should be revaccinated. There is no longer a huge amount of controversy that we've probably been advised not only to overdo the frequency of vaccinations but also the amount of diseases we vaccinate for—particularly at the same time."

Indeed, holistic doctors consider the harm that standard vaccinations can do to a body as a separate disease in and of itself: They call this medical disorder vaccinosis. Many seriously ill animals who don't respond to other treatments get better when given a homeopathic remedy that's known to combat the damaging effects of vaccines. You might consider this possibility if your cat is sick and veterinarians haven't been able to help him.

Yarnall gives Dr. Pitcairn's list of the possible symptoms of vaccinosis. Even a very shortened list explains how a cat can be assumed to have some other disease: symptoms of cystitis, inflammatory bowel disease, nephritis, aggression, chronic upper respiratory infections, destructive behavior, seizures.[2]

When we allow a cat to be vaccinated with the standard vaccines, we are putting into his system a small amount of the virus we want to protect him against. The idea is that this will produce antibodies against the virus, and the antibodies will protect the cat if he's exposed in the future. One problem with this hope is that if the cat doesn't already have a strong immune system, the injected virus may produce the very disease we were trying to protect him from.

Some holistic veterinarians go just about ballistic when you mention *multiple* vaccinations: that is, when a number of viruses are put into one needle and shot into the cat all at once—as is often done with standard vaccinations. "This confuses the immune system" is how one veterinarian expressed his objection. *Confuses* it? As if the immune system had a mind? Elsewhere in this book I give an explanation of how the immune system works, based partly on a video of a magnified immune system actually at work. It's composed of cells that act for all the world like well-disciplined army battalions, each with its own job to do, and each capable of sending out signals when the "soldiers" need help. (Those signals were actually visible on the magnified video.) To explain simply the *confusion* that multiple vaccinations can cause: Let's say your cat's immune system is healthy, and all the battalions are resting. Suddenly a red alert goes out: "Incoming invaders!" The battalions come to attention: "Is it *my* enemy, or another battalion's enemy?" Under normal circumstances, only one type of virus enters the body at a given time, so the battalion that is best equipped to fight the virus quickly rushes to battle. But with a multiple vaccination, the immune system realizes that "It's many different enemies all at once!"

You can see how the various battalions can now become *confused*, to use the veterinarian's word—getting in each other's way as they race to defend their entity's body, and losing their normal elegant organization. The problem is now more complex than the immune system is used to: Which enemy should we attack *first*?

The above scenario, remember, was for a *healthy* immune system taking care of its cat. But if we send all these invaders at once into the body of a cat whose immune system is already weak, we may virtually destroy that immune system—and the cat.

All the above possible havoc becomes compounded because we are told to repeat some multiple vaccinations often throughout an animal's lifetime. The quote from *Current Veterinary Therapy* on the covering page of this chapter gives an indication of how unnecessary many of these revaccinations may be.

Holistic veterinarians also object strongly to the additives in vaccines, which can include—among other objectionable items—pus, blood, urine, feces, aluminum, antibiotics, acetone, and formalin[3] (a preservative that's so strong that undertakers use it a lot). How are substances like pus, urine, feces, and formalin supposed to help our cats resist disease?

As if all this weren't bad enough, the more we vaccinate, the more we may be opening the way to have viruses mutate and change into new viruses. Did you know that there is now a brand-new form of AIDS? Yes, I'm about to tell you what my question has just made you fear: AIDS is now attacking cats. Yarnall cites Jeff Levy, D.V.M., as believing that feline leukemia evolved because of vaccinating for panleukopenia. (The two viruses look a lot alike under a microscope.) "And then with the vaccination for feline leukemia, the cat just came up with a different disease . . . feline AIDS," says Dr. Levy.[4]

I know full well I've just given you a whole new, and awful, disease to worry about in your cat. Not only that, but—as I write this, anyway—orthodox veterinary medicine has not yet developed a vaccine for it. (Although perhaps we should be thankful for that.) Let me remind you that your cat will most probably never get AIDS if he's on the diet his body evolved to thrive on. Also let me assure you that in the chapter on infectious diseases, I detail a very successful therapy for feline AIDS from a holistic veterinarian, Jack Long, V.M.D., who also has noted the similarity between feline leukemia virus and feline AIDS. He'd already had years of experience successfully treating feline leukemia, and he made some minor adjustments in that therapy.

Yarnall details a number of frightening facts about how specific standard vaccines can do more harm than good.[5] I'll mention only one vaccine. In 1903 the United States military went to the Philippines and started vaccinating for smallpox—although the disease had always been virtually unheard of there. Two years later, the Philippines had a major epidemic of smallpox. Australia banned the vaccine when two children died after being inoculated, and in the next decade and a half after the smallpox vaccine was unavailable, the continent had only three reported cases of smallpox. Here in the United States, we continued to vaccinate for smallpox until 1966, when Dr. Henry Kempe convinced Congress that "fewer people were dying from the disease than from the vaccination," according to Yarnall.

Are Homeopathic Vaccinations (Nosodes) Effective? Are They Safe?

"I've got to be honest with you," Dr. Fudens tells me. "Since I've been using the nosodes, for some ten to twelve years, I have never to my knowledge had one animal break out in any way, shape, or form." As well as cats and dogs, Dr. Fudens treats horses holistically and vaccinates them with nosodes. "I've never had one animal I know of come down with a sickness, disease, or germ that was vaccinatable." He admits that "It may have happened, and I didn't hear about it." But he adds that he feels owners wouldn't hesitate to "let me know and complain" if a pet had come down with a disease they'd had the pet vaccinated against.

Michael Lemmon, D.V.M., writing in 1996 in *Animal Guardian* (Vol. 9, No. 3), notes that "nosodes have a long history of effectiveness in South America, England, and Europe." One fact he cites is that in 1974 a meningitis epidemic in Brazil left many thousands of victims. The nosode against this disease was "highly successful" in preventing thousands of others from being affected by the epidemic.

Citing technical publications, Dr. Lemmon states that recent research from England during an outbreak of kennel cough showed "far greater protection with kennel cough nosodes than injectable and intranasal vaccines." And in Buenos Aires, doctors routinely use nosodes to prevent people from succumbing to a number of diseases, including influenza, measles, and diphtheria. "After many years of this practice," Dr. Lemmon reports, "they have observed a very high immunization level."

Dr. Tiekert (our "conservative" holistic veterinarian for this chapter) expresses what I've found to be the overall view of holistic veterinarians on the safety of nosodes: "Yes, I think they're completely safe." (In the next section, we'll see that Dr. Tiekert does, however, question how well nosodes work to prevent a few of the diseases some veterinarians use them for.) Of course, standard vaccinations by no means always work either—and no doctor I know of considers them anywhere near completely safe.

How Can You Choose What to Do About Vaccinating Your Cat?

Dr. Fudens expresses the optimal goal I believe most holistic veterinarians share: "You make the animals' immune systems so darned healthy that they blow off any virus or bacteria that's audacious enough to try to attack them. That's the ideal: that you don't vaccinate an animal even with the homeopathic nosodes, and they never get sick." (You may find Dr. Fudens' statement surprising, in view of the fact that in this chapter he has been such a champion of homeopathic nosodes. However, he is now talking about his optimal goal. And, like other full-fledged holistic veterinarians, he likes to tamper as little as possible with an animal's body—and he doesn't want to charge owners for unnecessary services.)

Although I strongly recommend you don't follow the above route of no vaccinations at all without talking to a holistic veterinarian about your individual cat, I do know that the above goal is not just utopian. Many years ago, I took in a homeless tabby cat, Puddy, who adopted my husband and me off the streets. I didn't know about holistic veterinary medicine then, so I took her immediately for standard vaccinations. Soon I learned about the new field, and I switched her to a natural diet and gave her no more vaccinations. (I would have considered homeopathic nosodes, but they were virtually not in use then.) Puddy lived with us for about two decades, completely free of any symptoms of illness, until she died in an accident.

I must stress that Puddy was an indoor cat, who never came in contact with any of her peers who might have been carrying feline diseases.

Dr. Tiekert not only strongly advises that you consult, if only by phone, with a holistic veterinarian about your individual cat— but that the veterinarian be one who practices in *your area of the country*. "For instance," he says, "Lyme disease is a significant problem in my area [Bel Air, Maryland]. We've had quite good luck with nosode protection for this disease." So if Lyme disease is a problem where you live, you might use nosodes to vaccinate your cat against it.

But if you have a dog who can be exposed to parvo, you might do best to use the standard parvo vaccination along with the nutritional help at the end of this chapter to ward off negative effects. Why? Dr. Tiekert says: "If you talk to a number of holistic practitioners, and look at the scientific data, you'll see that we don't do so well with preventing parvo. I've known a number of litters that have died from this virus after receiving nosodes."

Another thing you should discuss with holistic veterinarians when setting up your cat's individual vaccination program is your companion's personal lifestyle. For instance, does she get to roam around outside part of the day? Or does she spend her nights snuggling in her own little bed (or your bed) and her recreation time watching her "television" (looking out the window)? Dr. Tiekert says that "even many, many, many conventional veterinarians don't vaccinate 'inside' cats for feline leukemia. They can't justify the risk. Although we don't know the full extent of that risk, a lot of orthodox practitioners simply say 'There's no real reason for me to assault this cat's immune system with a vaccination when the cat never goes outside.' " He stresses though, that in his area, "You see a fair amount of cats who develop feline leukemia if they go outside without having been vaccinated."

Dr. Tiekert indicates that if your cat never goes outside, there may be other vaccinations she doesn't need.

Dr. Fudens, like Dr. Tiekert and every holistic veterinarian I questioned, believes that often "less is better," as I mentioned earlier. And he agrees that treating your cat as *an individual*, rather than as *a cat*, will lead to a healthier, longer life for him. "When I have virgin kittens or puppies come in," he says (that is, animals who have never been vaccinated), "I start them off with nosodes for the first one, two, or three years, depending on their lifestyle. I'm absolutely against giving the standard initial vaccinations. After that we evaluate the cat's health and how well the client is taking care of him and the exposure the cat may have to any disease or contamination. And then—depending also on the owner's perspective—we may continue some of the nosodes, or we may stop them completely."

Perhaps oddly, Dr. Fudens indicates that sometimes his clients "cannot make the break with vaccinations for whatever reason," and he has to coax them not to continue using nosodes when he finds them unnecessary. "I just try to convince them: 'Don't even use the nosodes anymore; you'll just be wasting your money. Susan or Sam or Max will never get sick from a virus or bacteria.' "

Giving another example of not overusing even the homeopathic vaccines, Dr. Fudens says: "A lot of technicians who work with conventional veterinarians use me as the veterinarian for their own pets. And they worry a lot about bringing diseases into their animal's home from all the sick animals where they work. When they first bring their pets to me, this is of course a very legitimate concern. But," Dr. Fudens goes on, "I detoxify that animal and put him on a constitutional homeopathic. Then, if I find his health is as high as possible, I tell the owner, 'Hey, he doesn't really need these nosodes because he'll never get sick on you.' " The veterinarian adds: "And this has worked out very well."

In summary, the bottom-line recommendation from holistic veterinarians is that if you use standard vaccinations at all, use a very limited program. Don't use them for diseases for which effective nosodes exist. Never vaccinate for more than one disorder at a time, and don't keep repeating the vaccinations. Also, if you must use a standard vaccine, protect your cat nutritionally against its dangers, as detailed at the end of this chapter.

How to Give Your Cat Homeopathic Vaccines When You Don't Live Near a Holistic Veterinarian

Before I tell you how easy it is to surmount this seemingly insurmountable problem, let me say that I've seen detailed published instructions on how to make your own nosodes. The instructions I happened to read weren't written by veterinarians, and the authors didn't indicate that they'd been working closely with doctors. I sincerely hope you won't try to help your cat that way. Even assuming the instructions are 100 percent accurate, they seem to me to require you to learn critical aspects of a medical field without an instructor to guide you or check you for accuracy. I wouldn't trust myself to be able to do that—especially since in homeopathy minuscule differences in ingredients are crucial.

So what *can* you do? First of all, maybe you live a lot closer to a holistic veterinarian than you think you do. Check the list at the back of the book.

If you do live uncomfortably far away, remember that an overall recommendation of this chapter was to call and discuss your cat's individual vaccination needs with a holistic veterinarian. After a holistic veterinarian helps you work out your cat's specific needs for homeopathic vaccinations, the doctor will simply *mail* you the specifically chosen nosodes to administer to your cat yourself.

If you're still thinking of homeopathic vaccinations as being much like standard vaccinations, you're now saying, "But I don't know how to inject *vaccine*." When I was also in a primitive state of knowledge about nosodes, I put myself in your place and took this "problem" to Dr. Fudens. "No, no, no," he "explained" to me. "The nosodes aren't injected into the body by needles. You just put them into your cat's mouth.

"We don't just send the nosodes through the mail and leave

clients to their own devices," Dr. Fudens continued. "We send three little bottles and give them specific instructions on how much to put in their pet's mouth. And," he adds, "if owners have questions about the simple instructions, I stick with them. I'm available to them on the phone."

How to Minimize the Negative Effects of Standard Vaccinations

In case, for any reason, you must opt now and then for a standard vaccination, I'm giving in this section easy steps you can take to prevent the two major shortcomings of standard vaccinations: the fact that they sometimes cause the disease they're meant to prevent, and the fact that they sometimes just don't work to prevent it.

First, don't vaccinate your cat when he is showing any signs of illness. If your pet is already ill, his immune system may not be able to produce the antibodies the vaccination is supposed to stimulate, and he stands a chance of being overwhelmed by the small amount of virus in the vaccine and succumbing to the illness he's being vaccinated against.

Second, make sure your pet receives the following supplements for two to three weeks before and after vaccination:

- **Vitamin A.** 2,500 IU a day for the adult cat (less for a kitten)
- **Vitamin E.** 200 IU a day for the adult cat
- **Vitamin C.** 2,000 mg a day. Start at 250 mg a day and increase every second day until 2,000 mg is reached. Give the dosage in stages, two to four times a day. (Introducing large amounts of vitamin C suddenly can sometimes cause diarrhea.)

Third, realize that *vaccinations do not take effect overnight*. Don't take your cat to a groomer, kennel, or other animal gathering place for two weeks after the vaccination shot.

And don't let yourself be talked into any of those multiple-vaccination injections—or into the idea that vaccinations require lifetime repetitions.

Summary

Please get the advice, at least by phone, of a holistic veterinarian who practices in your area and who knows the infectious diseases your cat stands a chance of being exposed to. Also discuss your cat's personal lifestyle (indoor or outdoor), his medical history, and his diet.

Now let's move on to investigate ways to keep your cat in prime health during special times in her life, such as kittenhood, pregnancy, and old age (although if you are reading this while your cat is a kitten, she probably will live many, many years without ever becoming old).

References

1. Celeste Yarnall, *Cat Care, Naturally* (Charles E. Tuttle Co., Inc., Boston, 1995), p. 22.
2. *Ibid.,* p. 23.
3. *Ibid.*
4. *Ibid.,* p. 35.
5. *Ibid.,* p. 24.

Chapter 4

Special Diets for Special Times in Your Cat's Life

"Dead mothers and dead babies: We seldom see them anymore if the mother is fed a natural diet with supplements."
—*John E. Craige, V.M.D., Richard J. Kearns, D.V.M., and many other holistic veterinarians*

"Many people come to us with old, degenerated pets for whom other veterinarians have told them there is no hope. When the owners see how their pets become young again—and recover from the 'hopeless' disorders—they start taking themselves and their families to nutritionally oriented physicians. They realize, 'If nutritional medicine can work wonders for my pet, it can work wonders for us, too.' "
—*Robert Goldstein, V.M.D., and Marty Goldstein, D.V.M. (in 1981)*

"What we're all looking for, when we try to have our patients fed good nutrition and when we treat with alternative medicine, is for the animals to enjoy a very high quality of life and to live this life as long as possible. Everybody knows there are two different ways to grow old. Some pets, and some people, live out the later years of their lives as mere shadows of what they were in their younger years. Our goal is to keep your pets vital, healthy, active, and loving until that inevitable day when death comes—and when it does, it comes swiftly and without pain."
—*Phillip Racyln, D.V.M.*

How to Prevent Problems of Pregnancy and Birth

Nutritional veterinarians have found that many of the "non-preventable" pregnancy problems and deaths just suddenly stop occurring when simple nutritional steps are taken for the expectant mother. Forward-thinking M.D.s have for decades been reporting the same sudden disappearance of pregnancy problems and deaths in human mothers, not only in clinical results, but in scientifically conducted studies.

I have read statements by orthodox veterinarians that one in four newborn pets will be born dead or die shortly after birth—and that this is "normal." But as you can see from the statement on the previous page, this high toll definitely need *not* be normal, if only the expectant mother is fed right.

Even if you're quite positive you have had your cat on the optimal preventive diet, as covered in chapter 2, for quite a while, all the nutritional veterinarians I've talked to over the last decade and a half agree that her pregnancy is a time you *must* add supplements. This is a time of extreme stress to the mother's body—something no reader who has borne a child needs to be told. And it's not such an easy time for the unborn babies, either.

It doesn't take much imagination to realize that one body that is now suddenly trying to provide for several more bodies within her own needs some help. Nutrients that have been sufficient to keep one body running smoothly aren't going to become, magically, enough to keep a number of "newcomer" bodies going nicely. Unless more nutrients are given, someone's body is going to have to be robbed—probably both the mother's body and the tiny developing bodies—and everybody is going to suffer.

Orthodox veterinarians, of course, recognize this fact. As a result, they may recommend that the prospective or nursing mother increase her food, sometimes to three or more times her normal amount. However, nutritional veterinarians believe it is not a greater *quantity* the mother is desperately seeking when she wolfs down triple the amount of food, but more *nutrients*. Indeed, most of the holistic veterinarians I asked told me they find that the mothers-to-be in their practice, that are given additional nutrients in the form of a supplement, generally choose to eat only a little more than they normally do.

It will be of optimal benefit to your cat if you divide her food into four or five smaller meals a day, rather than feeding her two larger meals, as was recommended in chapter 2 for the average healthy adult cat. Large meals can overload an expectant mother's stomach, already being crowded by her growing babies, and can cause serious digestive problems. Also, be sure to offer the mother-to-be more water than she normally drinks. It will help to flush wastes out of her kidneys (which are at this time not only flushing out her own wastes, but also those of her fast-forming babies).

With nutritional supplementation, holistic veterinarians and nutritionally oriented breeders report the virtual disappearance not only of dead mothers and babies but also of many birth defects: cleft palates, "swimmers" (newborns who are huge and, as one veterinarian put it, just "lie around, feet sprawled out and helpless"), and animals born with only a thin covering of skin over the brain (usually these babies die when the tiniest pressure touches this part of the brain). As far back as 1981, Dr. Kearns added that when the mother cat has been fed properly and given the right supplements, there is a virtual disappearance of kittens born with malformed legs and tails, spinal curvatures, and other birth defects.

For those of you who like to know about scientific studies behind medical statements, let me point out just a few of the very many studies proving that vitamin deficiencies can cause birth problems—and that supplementation can help prevent them. One experiment deliberately fed too little vitamin A to a number of pigs. One sow thereupon presented to the world eleven baby pigs—all without eyeballs. Other pigs in the experiment produced piglets with too many ears. When experimenters put enough vitamin A back into their diets, the same pigs produced healthy offspring. This study was published, by the way, in an orthodox medical journal—in 1933.[1]

A number of studies have been run concerning birth problems and wheat germ oil, which has a high vitamin E content and contains another natural substance, octacosanol. I have read scientific studies going back to 1926 on cattle, branching off to studies with humans in 1937, and continuing on to more modern studies. Some of the results of the studies on humans show premature births reduced to *half* their previous level when wheat germ oil was given, babies' deaths in emergency resuscitation *entirely eliminated*, miscarriages *almost halved*, and only 20 percent of the "usual" number of babies born dead.[2] I saw those studies reported in 1970.

One reason I've mentioned how long ago all the above-mentioned studies were conducted is to indicate how many years it can often take for research on nutrition to get disseminated into the offices of most doctors who don't focus on nutrition. Remember that a little earlier I mentioned that holistic veterinarians for many years now have seen the virtual disappearance of kittens born with only a thin covering of skin to shield their brains? Those kittens had what is technically called a neural tube defect. In a book I recently published on nutritional help for mental problems *(Healing the Mind the Natural Way)*, I noted that established medicine had finally listened to years of studies showing that if expectant mothers took a small amount of the nutrient folic acid, there was a dramatic drop in the number of babies with neural tube defects. These defects include brains outside the skulls and spinal cords outside the spines—if there is any brain or spinal cord at all. Finally it is officially recommended that women take in a certain amount of this vitamin that nutritional M.D.s have been recommending to their patients for years. Who knows how many babies suffered these tragic defects—needlessly—in the years established medicine ignored the scientific studies? (The natural diet you feed your cat contains folic acid, and the multivitamin/multimineral supplement holistic veterinarians recommend contains it, too. But just in case a specific brand doesn't contain it, check the label before you choose your cat's supplement.)

Your cat may be happily nursing her little ones and suddenly develop muscle spasms, a high temperature, and convulsions—symptoms of eclampsia. She may die. The least that can happen is that the new mother's milk production stops and she rejects her babies. I have found some orthodox veterinarians estimating that every time a cat has kittens, she has one chance out of twenty of developing this condition. Yet innumerable holistic veterinarians over almost two decades have reported to me that they have yet to see *one case* of eclampsia in a cat on a proper nutritional program. A major reason these animals don't suffer this disorder may be the fact that their natural diet contains magnesium, and so do the multivitamin/multimineral pills we've recommended.

Why am I mentioning magnesium here? For over sixty years, obstetricians have considered injections of large doses of the mineral to be the preferred way to stop convulsions in a woman with eclampsia. Yet it was only a few years ago that it occurred to researchers that maybe magnesium in small doses could help *prevent* eclampsia. Donald R. Davis, Ph.D, reported in my *Healing the Mind* book in 1995 that finally such studies had been run. And they had found that supplements of small amounts of magnesium during pregnancy help to prevent not only eclampsia but the full syndrome of preeclampsia, of which convulsions are only a part. (The list of symptoms of preeclampsia takes up formidable space in medical dictionaries. A shortened list includes extremely high blood pressure, kidney disorders, blood cell destruction, eye damage, fluid in the lungs, and bleeding in the brain. So you can see how lucky we are that research on nutrition has found that all this havoc to our cats can be easily prevented.)

Also, as long ago as 1981 nutritional veterinarians such as Dr.

Kearns reported rarely finding litter runts. Whelping time was cut in half; pets who could never breed suddenly could breed, even with the same mate; and uterine atony had virtually disappeared. Atony is a weakening of the uterus during the birth process that traps the tiny kitten in the uterus without oxygen while it is trying to help it-self be born. Obviously the kitten dies, or at best survives with se-vere brain damage. Isn't it painful to think of all the kittens and puppies over all the years who have died needlessly in this way only because their mamas weren't offered a natural diet and a daily supplement?

Cesarean operations are often done in a last-ditch attempt to save the mother's life and/or the lives of her little ones when birth com-plications result, just as such operations are performed on human mothers. In the early 1980s, Dr. Belfield reported that he offered his clients with newly pregnant animals a choice: "You can pay a few dollars for some vitamins now or pay $250 or more for a cesarean operation later on." With the simple nutritional supplementation, Dr. Belfield reported he had cut the number of cesarean operations he had to perform by at least 95 percent.[3] Other holistic veterinari-ans have reported similar results to me.

Now, what can you do to save your cat and the little ones still sheltered in her body from the horrors we've been describing? While you may have started this chapter thinking you'd have to be God to have this kind of power, I believe you've seen by now that you don't have to be anything but a human being with up-to-date knowledge about nutrition. We're not talking about miracles; we're talking, as we always do in this book, of the scientific fact that nutri-ents control every biochemical reaction in the body.

Before I give information on how you can prevent the previously mentioned strong possibilities of death, deformity, and pain—for your cat, her babies, and yourself—I think I should say a few words to those who fear you can't take the time, or don't have the money, to feed your pregnant cat a natural diet. First, I'd like you to care-fully read chapter 2 regarding how quick and easy it can be to feed the optimal diet, and how it can actually save you substantial money. If you're still convinced you can't feed a natural diet, I'll give you the suggestion of Dr. Racyln, who worries about people who won't, for whatever reason, feed their cat a raw-food diet. In recent years, Dr. Racyln says, a number of good prepared diets have come out that are especially made for the pregnant or lactating mother cat. "The real key," he says, "is to use only an all-natural prepared food."

But then Dr. Racyln presents some of the same quandaries other holistic veterinarians gave in chapter 2. (Please, for your cat's sake, particularly note in that chapter that even the best prepared foods don't contain enzymes, which are absolutely crucial for good health.) For instance, Dr. Racyln says, "You can't believe a label just because it states that the products are all natural. They still might use by-products." Chapter 1 details that by-products include such "natural ingredients" as tumors discarded from slaughtered animals and the remains of cats and dogs who have been euthanized. Dr. Racyln adds a few problems not even covered in chapter 2. "The quality of the grains of some products that are labeled 'all natural' may be really poor," he notes, for instance. He also points out that when people read that a product contains brewer's rice, they tend to assume that the product contains rice. But, he says, brewer's rice has very little nutrition in it compared to the brown rice recommended by nutritional M.D.s and holistic veterinarians.

So Dr. Racyln leads us back to the recommendation given in chapter 2: If you feel you *must* (and we all hope you *don't* feel you must) feed a prepared food as the mainstay of your cat's diet, make phone calls and consult with several holistic veterinarians for recommendations of the most *closely* "all-natural" prepared foods for your pregnant or lactating cat available at the time you read this. Dr. Racyln adds that if you use these prepared foods, it's "definitely" a good idea to use a high-quality multivitamin/multimineral supplement, adding the extra vitamins C and E in the dosages recommended a little later in this section. And, if the most closely "all-natural" food recommended to you has the real truth printed on its label, you'll see that you should supplement the food with enzymes and essential fatty acids. (There goes some of the money you were hoping to save.)

For those of you who already know how easy and inexpensive it can be to feed a truly natural diet to your cat, here's how to prevent the possible disasters we've discussed during and after your darling's pregnancy: Simply keep her on her natural diet but increase the proportion of fat and protein above that recommended in chapter 2. And buy a bottle of cat multivitamin/multimineral pills from a health food store, your own veterinarian, or a pet store. As already mentioned, make sure the supplement contains magnesium and folic acid. Buy the pills already in powdered form, or mash them up in her food.

Give the pills as directed. Do not double or triple the recommended amounts at your own discretion. As discussed in chapter 2, it is possible to overdose your pet—and yourself—with vitamins and minerals. It is even more possible to throw out of whack a delicate *balance* between two or more nutrients if you decide to add a little more of "this" or a little more of "that."

However, as also discussed in chapter 2, the cat multivitamin/ multimineral pill you buy will most probably contain no vitamin C at all and will probably contain too little E for your pregnant pet and her soon-to-be offspring. As I touched on briefly, vitamin E has been shown to be especially helpful for preventing problems connected with pregnancy and birth—and cats have an abnormally high requirement for this nutrient. The nutritional veterinarians I surveyed over many years give the following recommendations: Unless you have a super-giant cat, add to the supplement 1,500 mg a day of vitamin C and 200 to 400 IU of vitamin E a day. Most nutritional doctors recommend a small amount of selenium when vitamin E is given, because they both work better together than when either is used alone.

Dr. Limehouse reminds us that if a cat has not been taking vitamin C, she can get diarrhea if you suddenly give her large amounts all at once.

Foods and Supplements for Lactating Cats

Holistic veterinarians give the same recommendations for basic diet, vitamins and minerals, and number of feedings that they gave in the previous section for the pregnant cat. This short section covers only the variations you should make once your cat has given life to her kittens and is now involved in feeding them.

Oats should be a high proportion of the "working mother's" whole-grain allotment, because this food helps produce breast milk. So do goat's milk and grated raw carrots, so they may play a larger role than usual in her weekly allotment of protein and vegetables. For those of you interested in herbs: The marshmallow plant and fennel will also help mothers produce milk. A bit of garlic in mama's food will pass itself along in her milk to help prevent in her babies the all-too-common problem of worms.

Special Information for Feeding Orphaned, Unweaned Kittens

I certainly don't expect your cat to die during or after childbirth if she's been on a natural diet with the recommended supplements, but just in case you come upon an orphaned kitten in some other manner, I want to ensure you know how to give him the best of care if he hasn't been weaned.

Cow's milk, the milk you get at all supermarkets, is not an acceptable substitute for the milk of a mother cat, who does not produce cow's milk any more than a mother dog (or a human mother) does. Goat's milk, preferably raw, is the top recommendation of many of our veterinarians, since it is much closer in nutritional composition to the milk of cat mothers than is cow's milk. Goat's milk is most easily available in health food stores. It should not be diluted.

For optimal health of your orphaned kitten, fortify the milk with the following, recommended in the first edition by the veterinarians Marty and Robert Goldstein: To 2 ounces of goat's milk, add ¼ teaspoon cold-pressed sesame oil, ¼ teaspoon unfiltered raw honey, and 1 raw egg yolk (*no* egg white). Dr. Kearns recommended adding thymus extract. *Give everything in drop (liquid) form for preweaned kittens.* For this edition, Dr. Racyln recommends strongly that you add probiotics.

Why are you being asked to add anything to the goat's milk? Certainly, mother cats don't add anything to *their* milk. No, but Mother Nature does: Most notably, the mother's protective antibodies are passed along in the milk to the kittens. (This is why orthodox and holistic M.D.s alike recommend that human mothers breast-feed their babies.) Thymus extract and sesame oil are natural ways to build a strong immune system. The egg yolk adds fat and protein, and the honey adds simple sugars to bring the goat's milk closer to cat's milk.

If you can't get goat's milk, you can get special formulas approximating cat's milk from veterinarians. Call a holistic veterinarian (see the list at the back of this book) to make sure the formula your orthodox doctor recommends actually has all the nutrients your foundling kitten needs. Dr. Aloro recommended for the first edition preparing the following formula, which has more of the desirable protein and fat than cow's milk: Blend 4 ounces evaporated milk, 4 ounces water, 1 egg yolk (no egg white), and 1 tablespoon raw honey. Keep refrigerated, and don't heat before using.

Food should be given every two hours during the first four days of the kitten's new life; every three hours up to two weeks; and every three hours during the day, but only once at night, between the ages of fourteen and twenty-four days.

The doctors Goldstein have stressed the following point: "Feed the kitten until the abdomen is slightly larger than the chest. *Don't overfeed.*" Actually, the veterinarians not only underlined those last two words, but used three exclamation points to emphasize how important they feel this point is.

Michael Kreisberg, D.V.M., added several helpful tips on feeding the orphan. "Wake the kitten before mealtime and let him eliminate." (To this, Dr. Aloro added that "sometimes, to help elimination, it is necessary to massage lightly the area around the anus with a soft cloth wet with warm water.") Dr. Kreisberg advised that you place the baby "on his stomach when you feed him. Don't let him nurse too rapidly from the bottle, because kittens can get colic just as easily as babies can."

Weaning of the kitten can start *gradually* at three or four weeks.

Now that the orphan is weaned, and you have a firsthand appreciation of what new mother cats have to go through every day, let's move on to discussing how to keep the little fellow healthy until he's an adult. (At that time, you'll need the information in chapter 2 until he enters his "golden years.")

The Optimal Preventive Diet for Kittens

Until your cat begins weaning her babies, relax and leave all feeding worries to her. After all, she'll be feeding her little ones with the same natural food she would be feeding them in the wild. In other words, the new kittens in your home are now getting off to the same natural start as their ancient ancestor, Ruff, did. Of course, I'm assuming you're feeding mama her natural diet so that the milk she produces will have a minimum of poisons and a maximum of nutrients and antibodies.

Once the kittens are weaned, you should be giving them five small meals a day, including at least two meat or fish meals. (Remember as always to vary all foods, and especially don't give fish more than twice a week.) Raw goat's milk, raw cow's milk, or yogurt, as we've discussed, is preferable to pasteurized (cooked) milk. But remember, if one of the kitties suffers from diarrhea, try eliminating milk products from his diet.

Your newly weaned kitten still has his baby teeth; it's not until he's an ancient seven months old that he'll get all his strong adult teeth. So don't ask your baby cat to struggle with a whole slab of meat; mince it up for him so he won't be in danger of choking to death.

As for the amount of food given at each of the five meals, two teaspoonsful of food should be about right. Increase the amount gradually as your kitten gets bigger. Keep in mind that you should feed the kitten only until its abdomen is slightly larger than its chest. If the kitten still seems greedy for more food, picture the size of his stomach before you're tempted to throw a few more teaspoonsful of food on his plate: At ten weeks, the little guy's stomach is only the size of a walnut! So you can see that even an additional "treat" of one extra teaspoonful could extend that walnut-sized tummy almost to the point of bursting.

By the end of three months, you may feed your kitten only four times a day. By now the intensive demand of his body for protein will be reduced somewhat. Now is the time to start adding a small proportion of *mashed* vegetables and *cooked* grains to the diet, inching the kitten toward the diet (chapter 2) that holistic veterinarians recommend for healthy grown cats. Also, by now you don't have to mince the meat into tiny pieces; just chop it into small chunks.

When your kitten gets to be four to six months old, reduce the number of meals to three, cutting down on the amount of milk rather than on the quantity of meat and grains.

How many calories should you feed younger kittens? Again, there is no such thing as *the* right amount because every little body is unique. However, kittens may need as much as three times the adult caloric requirement per pound of body weight. In chapter 2, veterinarians recommended somewhere in the vicinity of 75 calories for grown cats per pound of body weight, so a three-pound kitten might require as much as 675 calories a day.

Of course, our recommendation in chapter 2 to cut down on calories for the healthy adult cat if he starts to gain weight won't hold true for your kitten. After all, if he *doesn't* gain weight, something is pretty drastically wrong.

You might ask your veterinarian to give you a healthy weight range for your particular kitten's breed at each stage of growth. Then step up or cut down on calories if he slips out of that range.

By the time your kitten is six months old, you might try two meals a day, and you might begin letting him eat as much as he wants at each meal. Remember our rule of thumb to check whether the cat is too fat or too thin: You should be able to *feel* his ribs (he's not too fat), but you shouldn't be able to *see* them (he's too thin).

Even those few nutritional veterinarians who believe supplements aren't really necessary for a healthy adult pet who is receiving his natural diet recommend a multivitamin/multimineral supplement during the first year of a cat's life. When your kitten is full-grown, the nutrients he eats will be used to keep his cells, bones, and organs as they are, but in this first year he needs a lot of extra help so that those bones and organs can grow at almost breakneck speed.

Nutritional veterinarians recommend a multivitamin/multimineral supplement formulated especially for cats to help the kitten through all the physical stresses of growing. These doctors suggest you add vitamin C to that supplement in the following amounts: one to six months—250 mg; six months to one year—250 mg, eventually to 500 mg. Add 100 to 200 IU of vitamin E, depending on the age and size of your kitten. If that sounds like too much, remember that cats have a particularly high need for vitamin E.

Do not give tablets whole to kittens or grown cats. Buy the supplements in powdered form or crush the tablets and spread them over food. There is a danger of choking on a whole tablet.

One other step you must take to protect your charges: Dr. Kearns stressed that it is vitally important to check with your veterinarian regarding the proper temperature climate for them.

When it comes time to get good homes for some or all of your naturally raised kittens, I'm assuming you'll have no trouble doing that because the little ones will have such beautiful coats, bright eyes, and sweet dispositions that people will fall in love with them on the spot. At this point, you have the chance not to let all your good work go for naught and not to let your kittens down at the last minute. Impress upon the kittens' new parents the importance of a natural diet, and give them a copy of this book so they can have the same details you used.

If you sense you're talking to someone who, for whatever reason, isn't going to sincerely try to keep your kitten healthy with a natural diet, you might opt to find a healthier home for him. Or get the person to promise that, in return for your gift of this beautiful, healthy kitten, he or she will at least read the early chapters of this book.

The barest bottom line I suggest you tell such a new parent is to realize that *any* sudden change in a pet's diet can make him sick; and that if the kitten is suddenly changed to commercial foods after being on a natural diet, the person should expect such symptoms as vomiting and diarrhea. To prevent this, they should keep the kitten on his natural diet and only gradually add in the fake commercial foods.

I'd like to make this point—that *any* sudden drastic change in diet can make a pet sick—very solidly, because it may apply to your pets in many different situations. Suddenly changing a cat from commercial foods to a natural diet can do just as much harm as suddenly changing him from a natural diet to a commercial one. I once received a phone call from a distraught woman, Claudia, from Hawaii, who as much as accused me of poisoning her kitten with "your raw foods." They're not *my* raw foods, of course, but Claudia had been following the recommendations of holistic veterinarians from the first edition. "The poor little thing hasn't stopped vomiting since I brought him home from the pet store." Claudia had taken the kitten to a veterinarian who didn't specialize in nutrition, as holistic veterinarians do. "When I told the veterinarian what I was feeding him, she asked me how *I* would like it if somebody made *me* eat raw meat every day."

I overlooked the fact that, according to Claudia, the veterinarian didn't know that cats are carnivores and we aren't. Instead, I zeroed in on the fact that the little fellow had recently been fed at a pet store, and had almost surely not been given a natural diet. I asked the new owner if she had immediately started the kitten on a natural diet. "Yes, because I was so beguiled by your book . . ."

I asked if she remembered that the book called for a *gradual* changeover of diets. Yes, but she had been so eager to get her new charge off to a healthy start.

I suggested that the sudden change might be the cause of the kitten's problems. Since I am not a veterinarian, I legally cannot—and I ethically will not—prescribe therapy. But I urged Claudia to call a holistic veterinarian and discuss the kitten's short medical history in detail. I said to be sure to tell the doctor of the sudden change from a poor diet to an all-natural one.

Claudia graciously called me back a few months later. "The veterinarian agreed with you," she said. "And not only hasn't Snowflake vomited once since I followed your book's suggestion of a *gradual* change, but his hair has fluffed out beautifully. And he doesn't cringe anymore every time I lift my hand, as if he expected me to hit him." Claudia indicated that she had thought Snowflake's "awful-looking hair and scaredy-cat personality" when she brought him home were just part of his basic makeup. "Now," she told me, "I think those problems might have come from a toxic diet and a nonloving environment early in his life."

The Optimal Diet for the Older Cat

As I said in the introduction, it is my greatest hope that you will not destroy your cat ("put her to sleep")—no matter *what* is wrong with her—until you have given holistic veterinary medicine a chance to work its natural wonders. This holds true not only for cats diagnosed as dying of the disorders we'll cover in later chapters, but also for pets falling apart in general from the problems of old age considered "normal" in cats fed poisonous commercial pet food.

Dr. Kearns, some decade and a half ago, when holistic veterinary medicine was much more primitive than it is today, told me about Chloe, a fourteen-year-old cat who was saved from a battery of problems generally considered normal in an aged pet (and in aged humans). These problems began to disappear within two weeks after a fairly simple, natural regimen of diet and supplementation was begun.

When Dr. Kearns first saw Chloe (who had been fed all her life on commercial foods), she was weak. She wobbled when she walked. She was having trouble going up and down stairs. She had a form of anemia that Dr. Kearns described as "nonregenerative and usually incurable using orthodox therapy." She was fat. Her coat was scruffy. She had above-average blood sugar, partial kidney failure, and uremia (excessive amounts of waste products in the blood). She was having trouble hearing and seeing.

In short, there was very little that *wasn't* wrong with poor Chloe.

Dr. Kearns put the cat on a diet of brown rice, turkey, liver, and vegetables. He supplemented this with sesame seed oil, vitamins A,C, E, and B complex, and bioplasma tablets (Schuessler's tissue salts).

In only two weeks, Chloe's "normal" old-age problems had begun to disappear. Sight, hearing, and walking had improved. Her blood sugar was now normal, and her kidney function tests were now basically normal, too. The "usually incurable" anemia was improved. She was acting sprightly and had regained a long-lost interest in her world. Dr. Kearns described her overall behavior not as that of a healthy cat, but as that of a "healthy kitten." In another five months she was also the proud new owner of a beautiful coat of hair and a svelte figure.

A miracle of rebirth? No, Dr. Kearns said. "I feel that the treatment just flushed her system of all the built-up poisons, and that there was enough basic healthy tissue left to promote a healthy body environment."

Several months ago, Dr. Racyln told me of an elderly cat brought to him who was in "really, really bad shape. His people were going to put the cat down because the orthodox veterinarians had been unable to do anything. But they brought him to me as a last resort." Then, echoing the statement every holistic veterinarian or M.D. sooner or later expresses to me, Dr. Racyln said, "I usually *am* the last resort." The fact that many people don't try natural therapy until orthodox medicine has failed saddens many holistic doctors. Although they manage to save a very high proportion of animals and people deemed "hopeless," they agonize over how many more lives they could save—and how much more easily—if they had seen the cat, dog, or person earlier.

But let's get back to Dr. Racyln's "doomed" elderly cat. "I acupunctured him," the veterinarian said, adding that "quite often, acupuncture used alone really brings dying cats and dogs back to life." But this cat was so near death that Dr. Racyln also had to use "lots of supplements, including Chinese herbs." Dr. Racyln also noted, "The cat is not only still alive, but he's doing really well. And by now, he's twenty years old."

What Not *to Do for Your Senior Citizen That You Are Normally Told to Do*

It's often considered just about axiomatic that you should cut down on your cat's calories when he gets into his later years. One basic reason is that today's fake-food-fed pet starts to slow down at that time; he hasn't the energy or strength to exercise the way he did when he was a youngster. The reduced exercise, of course, leads to reduced caloric expenditure; and lower caloric expenditure without lower caloric intake equals overweight. This, in turn, can lead to heart disease and other life-threatening disorders, the same as it can in people.

However, if you have been raising your cat for several years on the natural diet proposed in this book, I would urge you *not* to cut down arbitrarily his caloric intake as he grows older. Chances are he will still have the physical energy and the psychological outlook of a kitten, and curtailing his calories might result in an emaciated cat who wonders why he is suddenly being punished by not being given enough food.

A few holistic veterinarians I interviewed for this updated edition worried if I'd recommended, sixteen years ago, less protein for the older cat, because it was a common thought in those days that you should give an older cat less protein. No, I hadn't recommended less protein, because even that long ago, this idea was discounted by veterinarians who specialized in nutrition. However, when I heard that this idea might still be floating around, I looked at the labels of some present-day pet foods for "seniors" and found them declaring that one reason their "senior" food will help your pet is that it has lower protein.

Several months ago, Dr. Racyln talked to me in detail about this issue. "A lot of people, including those who put out some of the so-called highly nutritious prepared foods, are still saying that you have to cut down protein for older cats. This is based on two theories," he said. "One is that all older cats have some sort of low-grade kidney disease. And the other is that when you have low-grade kidney disease, low protein helps."

How scientifically solid are those two theories? "The original studies that were done on the association between kidney disease and normal-protein diets," Dr. Racyln said, "were done on something like six laboratory rats. And when they were fed a normal-protein diet, they already had kidney *failure*—not minor kidney disease. But the experimenters concluded, on the basis of that handful of rats, that you shouldn't use a normal-protein diet in animals with low-grade kidney disease." And remember that the other false assumption is that all older cats have low-grade kidney disease.

"I think," the veterinarian went on, "it's stretching it quite a bit to conclude that normal, healthy older animals need low-protein diets. I don't think that's true at all."

Dr. Racyln added that, although the few high-quality prepared foods he occasionally recommends put out special formulas for the geriatric pet, he keeps his patients on the adult formulas.

The veterinarian stressed that he was talking here about—just as he said—the normal, healthy older cat. "You should know what your animal's kidney function is before making a decision about what type of diet the animal needs." This may be a good time to remind you that this entire chapter is written for *preventing* future disease in *healthy* animals at special times in their lives. If your cat is ill, read the chapters on disorders for suggestions to help her recover.

Dr. Limehouse expressed the same ideas as Dr. Racyln a bit differently: "It's no longer considered true that you should give an older cat less protein just because he's an older cat. If his blood tests show he doesn't have kidney problems, you should not reduce the protein levels." The veterinarian explained that animals (and people) need protein to build muscles. "And the older any of us gets, the harder it is for us to make muscle mass. So if we cut down on protein, our muscles can get quite thin and scrawny." So maybe the myth that we should cut down on all older cats' protein can be contributing to the fact that it is normal for older cats fed fake diets to become progressively weaker.

What You Should *Do to Keep Your Older Cat Healthy*

As mentioned in chapter 2, some holistic veterinarians consider a multivitamin/multimineral supplement optional for the healthy adult cat, while others think this supplement should be given as a matter of course. If you took the option not to use a supplement, you should start your cat on one as she enters her later years. Chances are that as she grows older, her body will be able to utilize a smaller proportion of the nutrients she takes in. As is true for cats of all ages, a multivitamin/multimineral pill formulated especially for cats should be used, preferably obtained from a health food store.

Holistic veterinarians recommend you add to the supplement 1,000 to 2,000 mg of vitamin C, depending on your cat's size and exercise level. Your older pet's ability to produce vitamin C in his own body may be diminishing. Also add to the supplement 400 IU of vitamin E. Both C and E are antioxidants, which means they slow down oxidation—the process that's mainly responsible for aging. Even that yellowed (aging) picture in your photo album got that way through oxidation.

I'm aware that we've just recommended for your cat, who is diminutive compared to you, multiple times more vitamin E than the recommended daily allowance for humans. But I've never known a holistic M.D. who considers the RDAs nearly high enough. Also, remember that cats have an inordinately high need of vitamin E even in the early years.

There are several different forms of vitamin E, and Dr. Limehouse states, "We like the natural form, d-alpha-tocopherol." The form of E should be listed on the label of any supplement you're considering.

While the holistic veterinarians I have consulted over the years often suggested a very light role in supplementing for the healthy adult cat being fed a natural diet, every doctor stressed supplementing your older cat with antioxidants. If you keep up with nutritional news for humans, you've been hearing a lot about antioxidants in recent years, particularly for people of advanced age.

Agreeing that you should "definitely" supplement your older cat with antioxidants, Dr. Limehouse states that he particularly prefers the recently discovered coenzyme Q-10. "Give a cat about 5 mg a day of that," Dr. Limehouse recommends. Dr. Racyln uses this coenzyme and other antioxidants "in all my older pets."

Another newly discovered and studied antioxidant, as I write this, is Pycnogenol. I asked Dr. Limehouse about this antioxidant. "We like that," he answered. Dr. Limehouse points out that some of the Pycnogenols are made from pine extract, and some are made from red grape seeds. He cautions that if your animal lives in an area with pine trees, he may have developed an allergy to pine. "Then you have to be careful to use the grape seed extract."

Grape seed extract also tends to be cheaper than the pine extract.

You might also ask a holistic veterinarian about adding the natural substance lecithin to your cat's diet. Lecithin helps prevent heart attacks and can help dissolve blood clots.

Dr. Limehouse, who recommends digestive enzymes for cats of all ages, says, "The older a cat is, the more I think he needs these enzymes." Digestive enzymes help the body to *use* the nutrients it gets; this is one of the many abilities that often decrease with age. The veterinarian recommends about ¼ teaspoon a day.

Dr. Limehouse also supplements the older cat (as well as younger cats) with omega-3 fish oils (essential fatty acids)—at least if they're not getting natural sources of fish twice a week, as recommended in chapter 2.

Dr. Racyln, speaking of herbs he commonly uses for older pets, says he focuses on tonic formulas of Chinese herbs.

"We also use fatty-acid supplements in older pets," Dr. Racyln continues. "Holistic veterinarians have known for a long time that fatty acids are essential for a good skin and coat. But more recently we've learned that fatty acids are good for cardiac output, so we use them in all older pets, especially those with cardiac disease. These nutrients are also wonderful for joint pain, so we use them in conjuction with other supplements for arthritis and general old-age stiffness.

"So," Dr. Racyln sums up, "if I get an old, stiff cat walking into my clinic—who has, say, the early stages of heart failure and his liver isn't functioning well—the first thing I do is to put him on Chinese herbs, coenzyme Q-10, antioxidants, and fatty acids." Dr. Racyln adds that he would also immediately start to change the cat over to an all-natural diet. In several decades of reporting on nutritional medicine, I haven't found one M.D. or veterinarian who didn't stress that a healthy basic diet was of prime importance for recovery, as well as for prevention.

If your cat has spent much of her life on commercial foods, she may have lost many of her teeth. You can—and should—help her by cutting up her meat for her, as you did when she was a kitten. Half-chewed food will be half-digested food, which means her body won't be utilizing many of the nutrients she takes in. And there is always a possibility of choking to death on half-chewed food.

Feeding a Half-Starved Stray Cat

The cat you find wandering about the street may appear to be half animal, half skeleton. If you absolutely cannot take the starving entity home with you, at least until you can restore him to health and try to find him a home, *any* food you may be carrying with you—or can get your hands on quickly—may help keep the animal alive long enough so that he can find an adoptive parent.

If you can take the unfortunate animal home, don't succumb to what might easily seem like the "commonsense" idea of letting your half-starved foundling eat unrestrainedly. Give small feedings, four to eight times a day at first. And gradually add just a little bit more food at a time. "It may take as long as ten days before a half-starved cat or dog can be trusted not to harm himself by overeating," Dr. Aloro told me.

If you do let him eat, right off, all he seems to want, you could be leading him, as Dr. Kearns once pointed out, to protein poisoning, inhalation pneumonia, convulsions, and other problems.

Dr. Kearns recommended that raw honey and fluids are of prime importance when you first get the cat home. "Solid foods can always wait," he said. You might at first also give a little yogurt.

The fluids that Dr. Kearns recommended are vitally important because the animal may be dehydrated, or in danger of becoming so. Today, Dr. Racyln explains that "the idea with raw honey is to get some high-quality simple sugars into the cat or dog." While Dr. Racyln doesn't recommend commercial foods as a mainstay of a healthy cat's diet, he does say there are a few commercial products that are "a bit better than just raw honey" for a half-starved stray. As this book is written, this veterinarian would recommend Nutrical because it gives "not only the simple sugars and carbohydrates but also many vitamins and minerals." He would also recommend Hills AC (for acute care) and Purina CV. "The CV stands for cardio-vascular," says Dr. Racyln, "but it's also good for cases like this."

Agreeing with Dr. Kearns that "you should certainly keep the cat off solid foods to begin with," Dr. Racyln adds that you shouldn't do this for too long. When you introduce solid foods, "start him off with something light, like one of the three commercial foods,* and then *slowly* start mixing in some better-quality foods. And you certainly want to give some probiotics at this time, because the cat's intestinal flora are sure to be unbalanced. Give the probiotics *between* his small meals, not with them." (See the index for more information on these fascinating natural products.) Dr. Racyln adds that "if you're into Chinese herbs, you can certainly add some tonifying herbs."

Probably the easiest, least expensive, and healthiest solid diet you can start your stray on when he's ready for regular foods is a diet of cooked chicken or turkey and brown rice. (As mentioned in chapter 2, don't feed heavy proteins like the first two foods at the same time as carbohydrates, such as brown rice.) Fowl and brown rice are particularly high in nutrients and are easily digestible. We can assume the unlucky fellow is likely to have problems digesting things for a while to come. (Well, he *was* unlucky, but now he has you.)

We're suddenly recommending *cooked* chicken or turkey since raw foods are not recommended for your stray pet, partly because they would probably be a sudden drastic change of diet for him.

*Dr. Fudens disagrees strongly that commercial foods should be used.

Chances are his previous owners didn't feed him the delicacies of a natural diet; and who knows what he has been managing to dig out of garbage cans to keep himself alive? As discussed earlier in this chapter, any sudden change of diet—even a change for the better— can cause digestive upset even in a healthy cat; and now we're trying to help a cat whose digestive system is probably already in much distress.

Do give a *powdered* multivitamin/multimineral supplement daily to your new pet. I call him your new pet, even though you may be quite sure you are just keeping the abandoned animal a few days until you can find somebody else to take him off your hands. If you're like many of us, you'll end up looking back over the years and realizing that he became your new pet the moment you saw him looking at you, with sad eyes, for help on the street.

In this regard, Joe and I took in a stray cat that we were just going to feed and keep out of the cold overnight. She was so contented with her newfound luck of a meal and a warm domicile that she fell asleep purring. We had had no experience with cats and had no idea that a cat would purr while *asleep*. So, one hour after targeting us as her adoptive parents, Puddy had carved out a major niche in our lives. This niche ended some two decades later when—as some would say—her spirit decided it was time for her to move on.

I might add, though, that in all those years she never deigned to purr in her sleep for us again.

References

1. Fred Hale, *Journal of Heredity,* March 1933, p. 105.
2. Carlson Wade, *The Rejuvenation Vitamin* (New York: Award Books), 1970, p. 122.
3. Wendell O. Belfield, D.V.M., and Martin Zucker, *How to Have a Healthier Dog* (Garden City, New York: Doubleday and Co., Inc.), 1981, p. 110.

PART 2

Natural Ways of Curing the Mildly Ill, the Very Ill, and Even the "Incurably" Ill

Chapter 5

New Help for Crippling Disorders

"Although I've been a holistic veterinarian for many years, I'm still amazed to see how cats with crippling disorders respond to natural therapy. We know that dogs start to get better in about two weeks, but very often cats respond in three days."
—*Norman C. Ralston, D.V.M.*

"I think the nutrients glycosaminoglycans must be included in any treatment of arthritis, hip dysplasia, or any other crippling disorder, because of their invaluable influence in healing those problems. These substances help produce healthy tendons, ligaments, joints, bones, and cartilage. They are safe for cats, dogs, and humans.

"The omega-3 fatty acids are also invaluable: For one thing, they are natural antiinflammatories that are a lot safer than the antiinflammatory drugs commonly used."
—*Robert J. Silver, D.V.M.*

"Many times, conventional therapies fail to work for pain or chronic degenerative diseases, or are contraindicated because the animal has another disorder. When this happens, the veterinarian has two choices: either to destroy the animal—or to use an unconventional technique. Acupuncture has a very high success rate with crippled animals whom conventional therapies have not helped."
—*Sheldon Altman, D.V.M. (specialist in veterinary acupuncture)*

Writing in 1981, in Veterinary Medicine/Small Animal Clinician (p. 1307), veterinary acupuncturist Sheldon Altman, D.V.M., pointed out that "until recently, chronic pain and chronic degenerative diseases in animals were seldom treated. Because of economics, inconvenience, and concern for suffering, the usual solution to these problems was euthanasia." Euthanasia is, of course, a "nice" word for killing the animal before he may have chosen his own time to die. Unfortunately, we can't ask the cat if he himself has given up on living.

Since orthodox veterinarians have started treating more animals for crippling problems, they have been using, in part, the following drugs: painkillers, muscle relaxants, tranquilizers, antiinflammatories, and corticosteroids. Nerve blocks and neurectomies are also used for large dogs. "In many cases," Dr. Altman says, "these therapies are unsuccessful or are contraindicated because of the presence of some other disease." The veterinarian says that when these treatments don't work or are contraindicated, practitioners must then either use an unconventional therapy or destroy the animal.

In the same year Dr. Altman wrote the above (1981), holistic veterinarians were detailing to me their alternative therapies for crippling disorders and were reporting good to excellent results in the majority of cases, even those who didn't respond to orthodox techniques. In this edition, holistic veterinarians tell you of the new therapies developed since the early 1980s that offer even more help.

Cats don't tend to be as susceptible as dogs are to developmental bone disease, such as hip dysplasia (a particular curse for large-breed dogs), because of cats' "small size and the lower impact of gravity on their bodies," says Robert J. Silver, D.V.M., M.S. He adds that "most of the arthritis that we see in cats is usually in the very aging members of our feline population—cats from, say, eighteen to twenty—or it's secondary to trauma." As Dr. Silver discusses later, one trauma that commonly leads to arthritis is orthopedic surgery. Ironically, that's the type of surgery that's conventionally used to treat the disorders covered here. We'll see that a holistic veterinarian who must resort to surgery will also use natural techniques to ward off arthritis.

While the fact that cats aren't as prone to some crippling problems as dogs is good news for cats in general, I assume you're reading this chapter either because your cat does have a crippling disorder, or you suspect he does. As I mentioned earlier in this book, I've talked often to M.D.s who work with various "rare" disorders. Many have expressed the idea that if someone you love has only a 10 percent chance of getting a disease—and *gets* it—then for you that 10 percent statistic is 100 percent.

The following is general information on what holistic veterinarians suggest you do—*and don't do*—to help your cat with a painful problem that's started to, or already has, crippled him.

First, *don't* give him aspirin or other "human" painkillers unless you call a holistic veterinarian (see the list at the end of the book) and get an okay for a specific painkiller for your individual cat. Many of the usual analgesics can be very toxic to cats.

Actually, cats have a worse reaction than dogs to several nonprescription drugs (including Pepto-Bismol, which I've seen *recommended* by orthodox veterinarians for dogs, along with the stern admonition, "Don't give to cats."). *The Doctors Book of Home Remedies for Cats and Dogs* okays buffered aspirin for dogs but says "Aspirin can be dangerous for cats," adding that other painkillers like ibuprofen can be dangerous for both cats and dogs. And as for ace-tominophen (Tylenol), the book states flatly, "One extra-strength Tylenol can kill a cat."

With that strong warning about Tylenol, you may be tempted to take your cat immediately off a drug she has been *prescribed*. It is true that virtually any drug has potentially serious side effects. Cortisone, for instance, as Ihor John Basko, D.V.M., once pointed out, may produce in some patients "weakening of muscles, includ-ing the heart; stress on the kidneys; suppression of the immune sys-tem; and decreased healing." Also, while cortisone can cover up the pain of a crippling disorder, it does nothing to heal the disorder it-self. So your cat may take to using the still-diseased joint (which he wouldn't do if the pain were not being artificially covered up), thus causing further degeneration to the joint.

Yet I talked to some fifteen holistic veterinarians about taking your cat off a prescribed drug, and they all agreed that you should phase these drugs out gradually and then only under the super-vision of a veterinarian. So make that a point you take up when you phone or visit a holistic doctor.

As with most drugs, there are safer, and usually less expensive, natural alternatives. For instance, vitamin C has been known for many years to be an effective deadener of pain. As Phillip Racyln, D.V.M., pointed out to me in a recent interview, omega-3 fatty acids are now known to help joint pain, "so they're part of what I always use for arthritis and general old-age stiffness."

S. Allen Price, D.V.M., is also careful to keep the salt content of the diet extremely low, since salt can increase pain. This veterinarian once also told me: "I have very good success in pain alleviation with castor oil packs over the joints. This is quite simple to do. Just soak cotton in castor oil, wrap the cotton around the affected limb, and secure it with bandages. Leave the cat's toes outside the bandage; the pet will continue to walk as long as he can feel his toes touching the ground." The castor oil decreases the inflammation that causes pain. It also increases circulation, and increased circulation pro-motes healing. Thus, the oil is working not just to mask the symp-tom of pain, but to alleviate its causes.

Dr. Silver gives a case history of Fluffy, a nineteen-year-old domestic long-haired female cat whom he had just rescued "from death's doorstep, so to speak," because of end-stage ("terminal") kidney failure. Fluffy was now quite healthy, except for a new concern: She could no longer jump up on the windowsill where she used to love to sun herself all the time. Often, in a cat Fluffy's age, a symptom like this is considered normal. But doctors and pet owners with experience in holistic medicine know better than to "settle." Actually, one of the tenets of holistic medicine for animals and humans is that the *normal* state of the body is a healthy state: There is no such thing as a normal state of ill health even in an elderly animal.

Dr. Silver says, "Fluffy, because of her kidney disease, was already getting several nutrients that also help crippling disorders: the B-complex vitamins, vitamin C, and omega-3 fatty acids. So I suggested to the owner that we add the nutrient glucosamine sulfate, which is particularly helpful for crippling disorders. And in about forty days, she called to tell me that Fluffy was now jumping easily up on that windowsill, and was once again able to enjoy her days with her favorite pastime."

Basic Suggestions for Treating Arthritis and Other Crippling Disorders

As is the case with most disorders, any printed therapy—orthodox or alternative—can be used only as suggestions for your particular pet. Every individual body chemistry is unique—a concern that is one of the major tenets of holistic medicine. For instance, my miniature poodle, Shiki, remained symptom free for sixteen years of what a veterinarian at one of the country's most esteemed orthodox medical centers had diagnosed as a case of arthritis for which nothing could be done. (She died peaceably, with no suffering, a natural death of old age about fourteen years later than the orthodox veterinarians predicted we would find we'd have to put her—unnaturally—to sleep. In other words, following an idea I put forth early in this chapter, Shiki chose her *own* time to die. My husband and I didn't choose it for her.)

The therapy we found for Shiki was simple: the use of a natural diet, the addition of a multivitamin/multimineral pill, and a bit of apple cider vinegar spread over her food every day. (This form of vinegar adds acidity to the body's basic acid/alkaline balance.) However, I would not dream of guaranteeing that these three steps alone would achieve a similar control for your particular pet. For one thing, Shiki was only a year old, so she had youth on her side; for another, she had been on the harmful commercial foods for only that year, and they hadn't had much time to wreak a general degeneration of her entire body. She also happened to have had an indominately spunky, devil-may-care spirit that left her particularly unsusceptible to psychological stress.

It always worries me when I read short articles that seem to promise that they contain all the information readers need to treat their cat or dog, or themselves, on their own. As mentioned in earlier chapters, many holistic veterinarians are available these days for phone consultation if you don't live near them. (See the list at the end of the book.) Hopefully, you'll use the following information as inspiration to help your cat holistically, and as a groundwork for drawing up your own specific questions for a holistic veterinarian and for understanding what this doctor prescribes for your cat.

The box beginning on page 129 gives basic suggestions for an all-out attack against arthritis and other degenerative problems such as hip dysplasia. Much of the information was supplied for the first edition by Robert Goldstein, V.M.D., and Marty Goldstein, D.V.M., who are particularly successful in treating these problems. For this edition, I checked with other holistic veterinarians who tell me this information is still valid after all these years. But, as you might expect, advances have been made that *add* to the chance that your cat can have a complete recovery without surgery or harmful drugs. I detail these advances immediately following the box.

The doctors Goldstein pointed out that they modify the following for each pet after scientific testing of individual body chemistry through urine and hair analyses, blood analysis, and so on.

Basic Suggestions for Fighting Arthritis and Other Degenerative Problems

- **Phase out drugs.** Gradually withdraw drugs, *under the supervision of a veterinarian,* as the natural therapy begins to take hold.
- **Phase out old diet.** Gradually eliminate chemical-filled processed foods and replace with a natural diet over a period of one or two months.
- **Feed a natural diet.** This diet differs somewhat from the preventive diet in chapters 2 and 4. That diet is designed to maintain health in an already healthy animal. Now we are dealing with a cat who has different requirements to rid him of a disease. The new diet should contain: 30 percent finely chopped fruits or vegetables; 35 percent flaked grains (cooked brown rice, millet, or oatmeal, soaked in hot water until soft); 35 percent organic beef or other red meat (lightly steamed), raw milk or yogurt.
- **Offer only pure water.** Offer pure steam-distilled water only. Distilled water helps remove undesirable mineral salts from the joints. (If your cat is highly toxic, check with a veterinarian since distilled water may remove toxins too fast for him.) Do not allow your cat access to water during the meal or for one hour before or after.
- **Fast your cat.** This gives the digestive processes a rest and allows the body to eliminate stored toxins. The doctors recommend a twenty-four-hour fast weekly. The fast consists of removal of solid foods and the offering of steam-distilled water, fresh carrot and celery juice, or a broth made by adding the skin of four potatoes to one quart of distilled water and simmering for fifteen minutes. *A fast should be administered only under the supervision of a veterinarian experienced in monitoring animals during fasts.*
- **Supplement cat's diet.** For a fifteen-pound cat, based on two meals a day, supplement with the following: brewer's yeast, 1 teaspoonful per meal; kelp, ½ teaspoonful or 1½ tablets per meal; whey (preferably goat's), 1 teaspoonful per meal; vitamin C, 750 mg per day; vitamin E, 100 IU per day; pantothenic acid, 100 mg per day; eggshell, ½ tablet per meal; cod-liver oil (cold pressed), ½ teaspoon per meal; wheat germ oil (cold pressed), ½ teaspoon per meal; lecithin (granules or liquid), ½ teaspoon per meal; vitamin A, 2,500 IU, 1 capsule per meal; vitamin D, 200 IU, 1 capsule per meal. As the cat improves, these dosages can be adjusted downward to minimum daily maintenance dosages.

- **Massage cat.** Finger massage of affected joints will increase circulation and therefore help promote healing.
- **Exercise cat.** If your cat happens to be leash trained, a twenty-minute walk outdoors twice a day is recommended—or shorter walks if you go up and down *small* hills. (Avoid steep hills.) If he isn't leash trained, share with your pet several daily play sessions with an active toy, such as a ball or a pull toy.

In addition, for the first edition the doctors Goldstein and other veterinarians such as S. Allen Price, D.V.M., stated that they often found SOD (superoxide dismutase) helpful. SOD is an enzyme produced naturally in the body that helps destroy harmful free radicals that contribute to degenerative diseases such as arthritis. In other words, it's an antioxidant. (If you've been following the news on human nutrition over the last decade or so, you've heard that antioxidants can help the body in ways that would have been considered "miraculous" until recently.) The doctors Goldstein stated that improper diet can deplete the body of its natural supply of SOD, and external SOD supplementation may be necessary.

Working with me in 1997 on updating, Dr. Silver said, "SOD was considered pretty innovative when you wrote the first edition, and nothing has happened since then to put it in disfavor. There's nothing wrong with still recommending SOD. But there are many other antioxidants we can choose from these days. I've got a list of new antioxidants an arm long.

"All these new antioxidants are fine to use, from the viewpoint of the animal's health," Dr. Silver continued. "But I think it's best to keep things simple, and try to keep everything as inexpensive as possible for people. I don't think we should get carried away with telling people they have to buy expensive, fancy, hard-to-get, hard-to-administer antioxidants."

Using those criteria, this veterinarian's major recommendation from among the new antioxidants is grape seed extract, which other holistic veterinarians recommend strongly elsewhere in this book. Dr. Silver said that, while the antioxidant SOD recommended for crippling problems in the first edition "was the antioxidant of the '80s, grape seed extract is probably the antioxidant of the '90s."

Pointing out that the simplest antioxidants to use are vitamins C and E—already recommended in the boxed information—Dr. Silver added that another antioxidant, selenium, should always be used when you give vitamin E. "We're finding that E and selenium work together in harmony even better than each of them works alone," Dr. Silver said. "I, personally, would never give vitamin E without also giving selenium." Other holistic veterinarians—and all the related new studies sent to me by research institutes—back up Dr. Silver's use of selenium with vitamin E.

Dr. Silver added that vitamin C is "only one small part of the big picture in terms of collagen production and repair." Important coworkers with that vitamin are the minerals manganese, calcium, and magnesium, which are recommended in the box in the form of kelp. "And lately," the veterinarian said, "we have found that other very important coworkers are the minerals boron and copper." He noted that the more we learn of the interrelationships between various nutrients and the workings of the body, "the more we understand how complex these interrelationships are." He also noted that "there is a simple solution" to the complexity of taking in all the right nutrients needed to keep all body processes healthy: "Eat real, unprocessed foods." If you have read only part of one chapter elsewhere in this book, you have already read of holistic veterinarians' passion for a diet of the cat's natural foods.

Glucosamine Sulfate

Dr. Silver also offered details about the glycosaminoglycans, especially glucosamine sulfate. From the beginning of the chapter, you may remember Fluffy, the aged cat who could no longer jump to her favorite perch. For many doctors and owners, it might have seemed that, because of her age, her jumping days were simply over for good. It was glucosamine sulfate that Dr. Silver prescribed for Fluffy, starting her out at 500 mg a day, that helped her easily to regain her "forever lost" ability to jump.

So, that nutrient was all Fluffy needed for her lameness? No. Since the relationship between nutrients and biochemical reactions can be so intricate, there is often no one "magic bullet" that can cure an existing disease. (Isn't aspirin, say, a magic bullet when it alleviates the pain of arthritis for a while? No, because it's just covering up the *symptom of pain*. It's not destroying the *disease of arthritis*. Nutrients work to restore healthy biochemical reactions that get rid of the underlying *causes* of diseases.) You may remember that when Dr. Silver prescribed glucosamine for Fluffy, she was already receiving, to keep her free of her previously diagnosed "terminal" kidney disease, several nutrients that work well with glucosamine for crippling problems: vitamins C and B complex, and the omega-3 fatty acids. (These fatty acids are also called marine lipids and EPAs. In my experience, it's EPA that's often featured on the label.) Dr. Silver said that "All my clients get my lecture about these fatty acids because they're so very valuable globally for keeping the body healthy. Just two of the properties they have that specifically help crippling disorders," he said, "is that they're anti-inflammatories and antioxidants." He added that he has found that these extremely important nutrients are "across the board either not present in the diet, or—because they are easily destroyed by light and heat [as in commercial processed foods]—are destroyed before the animal gets to eat the food containing these nutrients." Dr. Silver specified that the omega-3 fatty acids are found only in cold-water fish, such as salmon, halibut, and cod. (The diet given in chapter 2 to *prevent* these disorders recommends that you give your cat all her foods except grains raw—and that you feed her fish a few times a week.)

Dr. Silver said that the glycosaminoglycans are compounds that he thinks "must be included in any treatment of arthritis, hip dysplasia, or any other crippling disorder because of their invaluable influence in healing these disorders." He added that glycosamine sulfate is "safe for cats, safe for dogs, safe for humans"; and that it is no problem to give to a pet because it can easily be added to their food, and it's tasteless. Even if your cat is finicky about the taste of her food, she won't know you've snuck a medicine into her bowl.

Dr. Silver explained how glycosaminoglycans work: "They are molecules that are combinations of sugars and amino groups. And they're used by the fibrocytes, which are cells that produce fibrous tissue and collagen. Fibrocytes also produce what is called the ground substance, which is what all the cells sit in that holds the cells together."

As Dr. Silver explained, one of the substances that fibrocytes produce from glycosaminoglycans is collagen, a protein substance. How important is collagen? It acts as the body's cement; it is connective tissue that literally holds the parts of your body together. Frank L. Earl, D.V.M., once gave me a vivid description of animals with severe collagen problems: "They look like they've become unglued. They look like they're falling apart before your eyes." Actually, without collagen we would all—people and animals alike—*literally* fall part. Our bodies would collapse into hundreds of uncoordinated, unconnected pieces.

Collagen helps form tendons, ligaments, bones, and cartilage—all very important parts of our bodies that must be strong and healthy if we're not to become victims of a painful crippling disorder, or if we are to recover from one of these disorders.

Many of us—and many of our pets—are walking around (or trying to) with various stages of collagen disorders. These disorders in humans include rheumatoid arthritis; rheumatic fever; and a condition characterized by anemia, hemorrhages into the skin, and bizarre central nervous system symptoms (thrombotic purpura).

The body normally creates its own glucosamine sulfate from glucose and the amino acid glutamine. But if a metabolic defect prevents utilization of these raw materials, the body won't be able to produce enough glucosamines; and in turn the fibrocytes won't be able to produce healthy cartilage, tendons, ligaments, and bones.

Dr. Silver explained that by adding glucosamine sulfate directly in the diet, "you can be certain that you are giving the cells of the joint the material they need so they can create healthy cartilage," even when the body cannot make its own glucosamine sulfate.

I would like to share with you Dr. Silver's case history of Cosmo, a one-year-old domestic shorthaired cat. One reason I want you to know about Cosmo is that I think Dr. Silver's treatment plan gives a good example of blending the best of alternative medicine with the best of orthodox. As I say often in this book, by entrusting your cat to a holistic veterinarian, you are giving your pet a good chance of not needing toxic drugs or surgery. At the same time, you are not depriving him of orthodox techniques when they will be to his best advantage. And you are letting him have medical care that offers additional techniques to prevent side effects that may be common with the conventional therapy.

Cosmo had gotten through his first year of life with no noticeable problems. But one day his owner came home and found that a heavy piece of furniture was knocked over, and Cosmo was limping. Probably assuming that the furniture had fallen on the cat and caused a short-term injury, the owner took him to Dr. Silver. "But when I examined him," Dr. Silver said, "I found that Cosmo actually had a developmental bone disease, a ligament disease called buckling patella, which means that the kneecaps go out of joint. (A developmental bone disease is one that starts while the kitten or puppy is still growing.) "This was probably something Cosmo had been compensating for well in his year of life, but the injury from the falling furniture caused the problem he'd been able to manage to become clinically active."

Although Cosmo was limping on only one leg, when Dr. Silver examined his rear legs, he found both knees had similar problems. "The only difference was that the kneecap on the leg on which he was limping never went back into place, while the kneecap on the other leg would go in and out quite easily," he noted. Dr. Silver treated Cosmo with acupuncture, Chinese herbs, chiropractic manipulation, and glucosamine sulfate. "And we were able to get Cosmo feeling a lot better and walking with a barely noticeable limp."

Dr. Silver added, though, that "this type of condition—with the severity that it was in Cosmo—is really best treated with surgery on the knee. That's the only way you can correct some of the bone angles that contribute to the pulling out of the kneecap from the knee joint." The veterinarian added that the bone angle contributing to the severity of this problem in Cosmo was the fact that "the cat was bowlegged. The tendons on the patella are supposed to pull it straight up and down through the knee joint when an animal walks. But because Cosmo was bowlegged, the patella was being pulled to the inside—and his kneecaps were pulling out inside the knee."

The veterinarian pointed out that "anytime we surgically invade a joint capsule—no matter how excellent our surgical techniques are—we are definitely opening the door to the later development of arthritis." But, he said, some scientific studies show that supplying the body with a high amount of glucosamine sulfate helps to improve the repair process following orthopedic surgery. "So we're keeping Cosmo on his glucosamine, vitamin C, supportive trace minerals, and good-quality diet before surgery, and he'll be on the same formula after surgery. I believe that this will prevent the otherwise almost inevitable degenerative joint disease arthritis."

How Can Acupuncture Help Your Cat?

Acupuncture is a nondrug, noninvasive technique of healing that has virtually no side effects. It is sometimes assumed to be a new therapy (and therefore, to skeptics, an *unproven* therapy) by those in this country who have not taken the time to learn much about it. The truth is that this "new" therapy of acupuncture has been practiced for five thousand years in the East and since the 1700s in Europe. But surely, you may think, using acupuncture to treat *animals* must be a brand-new idea. Not true. For instance, recently a treatise was discovered that gave specifics for how to use acupuncture to treat elephants. It is estimated that the veterinary acupuncturist—or whatever he may have been called in those days—wrote that advice three thousand years ago. It wasn't until the 1950s that acupuncture slowly began to be accepted into medical practice in America. By

1984 there were some four hundred veterinarians in this country who regularly used acupuncture as part of their practices.

Acupuncture is often erroneously thought to be of value only in alleviating pain. Even if that were *really* all that acupuncture could do, you can see that it might be of great value to your cat with a crippling disorder, since pain is such a debilitating part of these disorders. But acupuncture also helps other problems associated with crippling disorders. Actually, Sheldon Altman, D.V.M., states that the majority of animals referred to acupuncturists suffer from arthritis and various forms of paralysis or neuropathies (inflammation and wasting of the nerves).

Also, controlled investigations on animals have shown that acupuncture can have beneficial effects in treating shock, ulcers, and abnormal heart rhythms. Case studies have shown that acupuncture can be of value in a wide variety of nervous, reproductive, urinary, digestive, respiratory, and circulatory problems.[1] The National Association for Veterinary Acupuncture noted as long ago as 1977 that "acupuncture has been used to treat a number of other conditions, including certain eye problems, dermatitis, deafness, general debilitation of old age, and epilepsy. In fact," they stated, "about the only thing that acupuncture is not recommended for is acute infections."[2] Dr. Altman adds that acupuncture can sometimes even bring animals out of comas and respiratory arrest.

HOW DOES ACUPUNCTURE WORK? Traditional Chinese medicine explains acupuncture in terms that often sound weird to the Western ear: *yin* and *yang*, the negative and positive; *chi*, the life force. Dr. Altman, quoted in the *Journal of the American Veterinary Medical Association* in November 1992, says: "The Chinese terms scare us. We understand the sympathetic and parasympathetic nervous systems, but if we call them *yin* and *yang*, we're going to raise eyebrows." He says, though, that our physiology is simply traditional Chinese medicine "being looked at from a different point of view."

I, too, find concepts like *yin* and *yang* rather mystical, so I'm giving this brief explanation of how acupuncture works in terms of the more scientific (if you will) research done since acupuncture has been incorporated into Western medicine. We have documented quite well that one reason acupuncture controls pain is that the needles release endorphins and other hormones that are well known to lessen the brain's perception of pain. We have come up with *theories* about additional ways that acupuncture alleviates pain—through various neural mechanisms. But I think details of these are better left to a textbook.

Effects of acupuncture other than pain alleviation are believed to be mediated via the autonomic nervous system. As the journal article explains, nerves from certain acupuncture points overlap with nerves from various organs in the spinal cord. Stimulating these acupuncture points causes a reflex arc, which results in autonomic nerve responses. This explains why an acupuncture point for a specific organ may not be directly over that organ.

For treating crippling problems, an acupuncturist will stimulate specific acupuncture points that lie over nerves, muscle/tendon junctions, or motor points.

DOES ACUPUNCTURE RELIEVE ONLY THE SYMPTOMS, AS DRUGS OFTEN DO? No. The idea behind acupuncture is that symptoms and diseases are the result of disturbances in the normal strength and pattern of energy through the body. As Dr. Basko explained in the first edition, "We run tests to determine the underlying *causes* of the symptoms. The chosen acupuncture treatment is designed to correct this underlying cause. Acupuncture actually returns the body to a healthy, balanced state—*where it will heal itself.* Since the healing comes from within, it is self-perpetuating."

The doctors Goldstein reminded us here of the pervasive importance of a natural diet: If the condition being treated is due to a degenerative metabolism caused by poor nutrition, acupuncture will give only temporary relief *if the diet is not improved*.

IS ACUPUNCTURE EXPENSIVE? The rule of thumb I've been given is that the price of an acupuncture treatment is approximately equal to the cost of a regular office visit plus one vaccination. Yes, but how many treatments might your cat need; is acupuncture one of those therapies (like insulin for diabetes) that has to be maintained for life? Of course, I can't specifically answer the first part of that question, but your cat definitely won't require lifetime acupuncture treatment. Remember Dr. Basko's statement above: Since acupuncture helps the body to heal itself, the healing is self-perpetuating. Consider also Dr. Altman's study, detailed a bit later, in which he had a high rate of success with, usually, a *maximum* of eleven treatments—on animals most of which had been found incurable with orthodox treatments and were also well up there in years.

However, as I've just hinted, acupuncture is often successful in cats who are considered "hopeless" and are set for euthanasia. (Dr. Altman reports that the majority of animals referred to him for acupuncture treatment have failed to respond to conventional therapy.) A course of acupuncture treatments will cost more than putting your cat down. (Since putting your cat permanently "to sleep" is a simple, one-step procedure, it's relatively inexpensive.) Acupuncture will cost more in dollars, that is. It will, of course, cost substantially less in guilt and sorrow.

You may be able to cut down the number of acupuncture treatments necessary by applying acupressure. Ask your cat's doctor to show you this technique. Acupressure is based on the same principles as acupuncture but is done with the fingers rather than with needles, so the only training it requires is learning which parts of your cat's body you should touch to help the specific disorder. It is less effective than acupuncture, but often can be used as a helpful adjunct.

WILL ACUPUNCTURE HURT OR FRIGHTEN YOUR CAT? Since one of the major uses of acupuncture in animals, and people, is to deaden pain—it is even often used as the only anesthesia during surgery—it would hardly make sense that acupuncture is painful. As for the needles frightening your pet, cats do not tend to have the apprehension of needles that we do. Both Dr. Basko and Dr. Altman have reported that often while the acupuncture needles are inserted in place, the animal will snatch the opportunity to take a nap. (Imagine you or me snatching a nap after getting a needle at the dentist's.) Dr. Altman tells me: "About the only time my patients get emotional is when I have accustomed them to a treat after therapy and then don't give them this treat after one particular session. *Then* they put up a fuss and a racket."

WHAT ARE THE CHANCES THAT ACUPUNCTURE MIGHT HELP YOUR PET? As we have said previously, acupuncture has an impressive success rate with a number of disorders. Dr. Altman has done a rather large study of acupuncture as treatment for a number of cats and dogs with crippling disorders. Most of the animals in Dr. Altman's study had been treated by conventional methods for a long time—unsuccessfully. Further weighting the study toward potentially poor results, the veterinarian didn't reject any patients, even if improvement seemed unlikely. And the average age of the animals was eight and a half years, so they were hardly youngsters. Dr. Altman treated most animals with acupuncture eleven, or fewer, times. Some of the veterinarian's results follow:

- **Paresis in the small dog and cat:** Eighteen of twenty-seven animals treated had 75 to 100 percent improvement, while only four showed 0 to 10 percent improvement. Paresis includes partial paralysis, tremors, and seizures.
- **Paralysis in the small dog and cat:** Eleven of twenty-seven animals treated had 75 to 100 percent improvement, while ten had 0 to 10 percent improvement.
- **Pain (cervical disk) in the small dog and cat:** Of eight patients treated, five had 75 to 100 percent improvement; only one had 0 to 10 percent improvement.
- **Central nervous system disorders, such as ataxia (muscle incoordination) and chorea (uncontrollable and ceaseless jerky movements):** Of twelve animals treated, one had 75 to 100 percent improvement, four had 50 to 75 percent improvement, and only four showed little or no improvement.

- **Chronic arthritis:** Of nineteen animals treated, five had 75 to 100 percent improvement; two had little or none.
- **Miscellaneous pain syndromes:** Eleven of twenty-five animals showed 75 to 100 percent improvement, while three had little or none.
- **Traumatic peripheral nerve injury:** Six of ten animals treated had 75 to 100 percent improvement; two had 0 to 10 percent improvement.[3]

Please remember how this study was more weighted toward failure than toward success. Another important point is made by the National Association for Veterinary Acupuncture, of which Dr. Altman is a member of the board of directors: The technique and other treatments are not mutually exclusive. Thus, your pet may benefit *even more* by acupuncture used with another therapy.

For instance, Dr. Basko commented that the Association's reported results for arthritis and intervertebral disk syndrome can be improved by 20 to 40 percent when Chinese herbal therapy is added to the acupuncture. Since the Association reported a 60 percent success rate in animals with chronic cases of intervertebral disk syndrome *that had not responded to either surgery or conservative treatment*,[4] Dr. Basko's estimate would bring the success rate for these "hopeless" animals to 80 to 100 percent, just by adding one more natural therapy.

Dr. Basko was commenting in 1981 on the Association's 1977 statistic. Remember that this book reports the great strides made in holistic veterinary medicine since then.

If you want to try acupuncture for your cat, you are much luckier than readers of the first edition, because so many more holistic veterinarians have discovered the effectiveness of acupuncture and have been trained in this therapy. Check the list of holistic veterinarians at the back of the book to find the nearest one who uses this therapy.

With acupuncture, there are a few problems that you don't have with most other natural therapies: Holistic veterinarians cannot send you this therapy through the mail, as they might send you, say, homeopathics or vitamin and mineral supplements. And you can't ask your orthodox veterinarian to learn to use acupuncture over the phone from a holistic doctor, because acupuncture is a hands-on therapy that can't be learned by just listening to words.

If you don't live near a veterinarian who uses acupuncture, ask yourself: Am I *sure* I can't spend the time or money to travel to the nearest veterinarian who is trained in acupuncture? If your answer is yes, try calling holistic veterinarians near you. Discuss your cat's medical problem. You may find that these veterinarians have other therapies that can help your cat, and because so many holistic veterinarians keep adding acupuncture to their areas of expertise, you may find that a nearby veterinarian has been trained in acupuncture since I wrote this book. And be sure to ask the doctor if acupuncture's cousin therapy, acupressure, wouldn't be almost as helpful as acupuncture.

Additional Ways to Help Crippling Disorders

Norman C. Ralston, D.V.M., details his basic approach to arthritis and other crippling problems: "The first thing we do," he says, "is to find out what's *causing* the problem. Then we go back and correct the cause," rather than attacking the symptoms. To find the cause, Dr. Ralston uses contact reflex analysis, or kinesiology.

"We often find that the cause is a malfunctioning thyroid gland or adrenal gland due to nutritional deficiencies," the veterinarian says. "So then we know we have to add the nutrients that naturally keep that gland healthy. We also try to *remove* anything from the body that would interfere with healing. For that, we use a lot of homeopathy."

Dr. Ralston adds that he finds that cleaning the cat's teeth can also be very helpful in healing crippling problems. (He does this without anesthetizing the cat with drugs, by the way.) I'd be surprised if you weren't questioning what cleaning the teeth has to do with helping a crippled cat. Dr. Ralston explains that tartar from teeth can break off, enter the cat's body, and be deposited around the joints.

Although Dr. Ralston is hardly new to the "miracles" of holistic therapy—he has been practicing for several decades—he tells me that "it's amazing . . . how these cats respond. We know that dogs start to get better in about two weeks, but very often cats improve in three days."

Dr. Ralston explains a basic way he judges how to modify initial therapy as the cat starts to get better. "One key we use is when the animal just refuses to take the medicine he's been taking until now without complaining about it. We feel that the cat knows best— after all, it's *his* body and *his* spirit—and so we ask the owner to let us test the cat again at this point. What we usually find is that the cat was right: The dosage he needs has gone way down, and he shouldn't be taking the original dosage anymore."

I asked Dr. Ralston to comment on the use of intravenous vitamin C, which was once the treatment of choice for serious cases of some crippling disorders. "While that's no longer the usual preferred treatment these days," he said, "it *becomes* the preferred treatment if the animal's body *says* it is."

Ruptured Disks

Symptoms of ruptured disks can include paralysis in the hindquarters and legs and inability to control bowels and urine. The daily addition of vitamins C and E, as suggested in chapters 2 and 4, will help prevent this problem. As long ago as 1981, Wendell O. Belfield, D.V.M., reported that even in the more serious cases, it usually took only three to five days to bring an animal "back to its feet." He recommended that you try nutritional therapy before taking the pet for expensive and risky spinal surgery.

However, Drs. Robert and Marty Goldstein have added a cautionary note: "We feel that this is a very delicate decision for an owner to make. In those cases in which the ruptured disk is putting a lot of pressure on the spinal cord (those cases in which surgery would definitely be beneficial), waiting days to see if a nutritional program helps could lead to permanent paralysis."

Dr. Price recently told me that he finds chicken cartilage to be very helpful for ruptured disks. "I may also do a little spinal manipulation." He uses vitamin C, usually orally, as well.

Dr. Ralston—who, like Dr. Price, was one of the pioneering holistic veterinarians—told me, "I have a completely different idea about ruptured disks than I used to have. Cats will develop some gout along their spine, but it's usually deposits of toxins. And very often they are due to a deficiency in the thyroid gland." As mentioned earlier, Dr. Ralston finds that deficiencies in this gland are behind many cases of crippling disorders. Here he points out that in bringing this gland back to health, he doesn't use a synthetic thyroid drug. Instead he uses a prostaglandin. Prostaglandins are nutrients that act in the body as short-term hormones; the thyroid gland's major function is to produce the hormone thyroxin. The veterinarian notes that the prostaglandin "causes the gland to be able to work well on its own." He adds that "when we unnaturally supply something from outside that the body needs to be supplied from inside the body, we can get into trouble. We're *substituting* something for what nature had in mind. So we don't do that: Instead, we use the prostaglandin, which causes the thyroid gland to produce on its own what it's supposed to."

Summary

If you haven't found your cat's diagnosed crippling disorder mentioned in this chapter, this is by no means an indication that holistic veterinary medicine doesn't successfully treat the problem. It is instead an indication that holistic doctors use as guidelines for crippling problems the overall nutrients mentioned early in this chapter—and it's an indication that holistic veterinarians treat what's off base within the individual cat's body, rather than treating a diagnostic disease label.

I'll close with the story of Windsor, a male Persian cat, who was nine years old when he was brought in to Neal Weiner, D.V.M., in 1995. The cat had lost a lot of weight, and the muscles in his hind legs were thinning. Orthodox blood tests also found that Windsor had early kidney failure.

"I put him on a natural diet, of course," Dr. Weiner told me in a 1998 interview. "I also gave him blue-green algae, a natural viamin-mineral mix, and digestive enzymes. I used the homeopathic remedy Nux Vomica to detoxify his body." Windsor also got vitamin E, cod liver oil, the B complex, vitamin C powder, and a kidney glandular (Renafood).

Windsor's muscle, weight, and kidney problems all responded very nicely. "Three years later, Windsor's still doing quite well and thriving and prospering," Dr. Weiner told me. "And he looks radiant."

References

1. M. J. Shively, D.V.M., M.S., Ph.D., *Dog Fancy,* December 1981, p. 17.
2. *Guide to Acupuncture for Animals,* The National Association for Veterinary Acupuncture, Fullerton, CA, 1977.
3. *Veterinary Medicine/Small Animal Clinician,* September 1981, pp. 1307–1312.
4. *Guide to Acupuncture for Animals,* op. cit.

Chapter 6

Problems of the Eye

"I'm always amazed at the ability of the eye to repair itself, if you just give it the natural support it needs. . . . I recently treated an animal born with one of his eyes incompletely developed. I started him on the nutrients he tested out to be deficient in, and now the eye has developed very nicely."
—*Norman C. Ralston, D.V.M.*

"I find homeopathic phosphorus and the antioxidant glutathione to be of great help in treating glaucoma. . . . Glutathione used with several other antioxidants also greatly improves the eyesight of most cats with cataracts. Even if the cataracts are very advanced when I see the animal, his vision may improve. Seldom do cats with very advanced cataracts get any worse."
—*S. Allen Price, D.V.M.*

"I just don't have a problem treating corneal ulcers, period."
—*Richard J. Kearns, D.V.M.*

A Plea Not to Put Your Blind or Otherwise Handicapped Cat "Out of His Misery"

Before we go into ways you can help your cat with eye problems, let me put in a plea on behalf of your blind or otherwise handicapped pet—who can't put in his own plea in words you understand: Please don't put him to sleep. (I dislike that phrase, because I think it is a euphemism that sometimes lulls veterinarians and owners alike to do less than they might be able to, to help an animal.) I'm not in a position to tell you, of course, that there is never, ever a case where putting your pet "to sleep" isn't kinder than letting him suffer through a painful, hopeless existence. However, as this book shows over and over, there are countless pets deemed hopeless who can be easily and inexpensively helped by the newer field of holistic veterinary medicine.

You may think that you are putting your cat who is blind, deaf, or lacking a limb "out of his misery" by having him euthanized. If this were really the kind thing to do, wouldn't we be putting blind or deaf children permanently to sleep? And yet cats are not devastated psychologically by handicaps such as blindness in the way that people often are. In addition, our pets actually *need* their eyesight less than we do. For instance, your cat's whiskers act as sensors, alerting her to the slightest change in air pressure around her face. She can "see," partially, through her whiskers. Even in the dark, an increase in air pressure around her whiskers tells her: "Big object to my left, don't walk into it, could get hurt."

As John E. Craige, V.M.D., once told me, blind animals "get along quite well. They can . . . do almost everything a sighted animal can do. They don't have any psychological traumatism as do blind people."

I would like to quote another statement pointing out that not only should you let your handicapped cat live out his life, you might even relax and stop feeling sorry for him. The following is a quote from a book by Pat Widmer, an animal nutritionist. Widmer has rescued numerous abandoned animals, and so she has ended up caring for many handicapped cats and dogs.

"My so-called 'handicapped' pets have never demonstrated any overwhelming problems and have in many instances proved that they can be just as obnoxious as anyone else," Widmer says.

"Blind cats and dogs have no difficulty, provided you don't move all the furniture every day. . . . In particular, my blind street cat (picked up at six months of age at a construction site . . .) is the toughest cat I have. He was born blind with congenital cataracts. . . ." But this has "not deterred him in the least. One amusing note: He has obviously learned that when he hears [note: *hears*] the light switch turned off, the other cats are at a momentary disadvantage while their eyes adjust. It is at this very second that he will attack another cat. I have dealt with this situation by warning him *not* to attack anyone as I turn out the light. Also, I note the other cats all watch him as I reach for the switch. No dummies there. . . .

"Lameness or lack of a limb is meaningless to animals," Widmer continues. "My fastest-moving cat has four legs and three feet, probably from birth. He is named Flash because he always flashes by. His motto is 'Don't walk, *run!*' "[1]

In short, let your handicapped pet enjoy the rest of his life. And stop making yourself unhappy by assuming he would choose to commit suicide if he could (or be put to sleep), because he somehow knows he isn't quite "right" by our terms.

I think of all the animals who devote their lives to helping handicapped humans. Seeing Eye dogs come most readily to mind, but even many monkeys spend their lives using their specialized training to become their handicapped persons' eyes, ears, or limbs. These animals don't give up on their people because they don't seem quite right.

Let me add one more thought before we go on to natural therapies for eye problems: I hope you always keep in mind, as you read about successful natural therapies anywhere in this book, that holistic M.D.s offer similar hope for us humans.

Glaucoma

Glaucoma is too much pressure behind the eye's cornea. The pressure is caused by a blocking of the normal flow of the fluid in the space between the cornea and lens (intraocular area). As you probably know, if not successfully treated, glaucoma will cause blindness.

S. Allen Price, D.V.M., says: "To reduce intraocular pressure, I use homeopathic phosphorus, a strength of about 30C, usually once a week. And I use glutathione, an antioxidant that is most abundant in the intraocular area when that area is normal. I've found these two nutrients to be a big aid in cats and dogs with glaucoma."

"Of course," Dr. Ralston adds, "vitamin A is our eye vitamin, and we always check if the animal with glaucoma is deficient in it." The relationship between healthy eyes and vitamin A has been established for a very long time.

Like Dr. Price, Dr. Ralston also uses the nutrient glutathione, which "cleans the eye from behind." That doesn't mean this nutrient has to be inserted behind the eye by surgery. If you put a natural substance into the body, it will find its own way to where it's naturally supposed to go. And remember that glutathione is abundant in the space behind the eye. "As soon as you've cleaned up that eye," Dr. Ralston says, "the animal's vision will improve."

He adds that this use of glutathione is based on research going back to the 1920s that has been validated and enhanced over the years since.

"Once I've got the animals cleaned up and straightened out," Dr. Ralston says, "I put them on a multivitamin/mineral supplement that covers all the bases. And then I check up on them every two or three months to make sure they're still doing all right."

Cataracts

By now you certainly know that holistic veterinarians consider a poor diet to be a major factor behind all disorders. "We see cataracts more in dogs than in cats," Dr. Ralston comments. He adds that "cats are able to get a little more varied diet, even if they have to eat bugs. They're more finicky eaters than dogs, and they're more likely to leave some of their fake food on their plate and catch a few cockroaches instead." If you think you didn't correctly understand Dr. Ralston, you probably did. He finished his statement with "A cat may get more nutrition out of a cockroach than he can get from some of the commercial foods." If this idea still sounds outlandish to you, remember that bugs are a natural part of the diet cats evolved to thrive on. Commercial pet foods are not.

What *are* cataracts? A medical dictionary will tell you that they are a filmy sort of substance in the lens of the eye that prevents animals and people from seeing clearly. As the substance grows thicker, it becomes opaque, so that the victim can no longer see at all. But what is this mysterious substance *made* of? "Cataracts are basically accumulations of toxins in the eyes," Richard J. Kearns, D.V.M., once told me, reminding us that "a natural diet has few or no toxins."

Thus, as Dr. Ralston now indicates, the less unnatural food your companion eats, the less likely he is to get cataracts. Dr. Kearns also pointed out that if an animal has had cataracts successfully dissolved by natural therapy, they are likely to come back again if you keep your pet on toxic foods.

You will note that Dr. Kearns mentioned that natural therapy *dissolves* cataracts. The common cataract surgery *cuts* cataracts out, after giving pets potentially very dangerous anesthetics to cover the obvious great pain of having something cut out of their eye. Also, a cataract operation removes the lens of the eye (the cataract is in the lens, remember), so that normal eyesight is really never restored.

Dr. Ralston says, "I don't recommend the cataract surgery. In my orthodox veterinary schooling, I was trained in that surgery, and I did it one time and said, 'That's enough; I'm not doing that anymore.' It was not successful, and when I later referred animals to veterinary ophthalmologists for the surgery, they didn't have the success I wanted, either." Dr. Ralston states that using glutathione to clean up the eye has much more success than surgery seems to, and without the risks or expense.

Dr. Price uses glutathione and vitamin A (mentioned previously as "the eye vitamin"), as well as the antioxidants selenium and vitamins C and E, which were used for cataracts in the early 1980s. "We've had a considerable number of cats in which one or both eyes have substantially improved so they can see much better," he says. "In most of the others—who have more advanced cataracts—they don't get any worse."

Other Problems of the Eye

In addition to the eye problems covered previously and later in this section, holistic veterinarians have successful natural therapies for other problems, including dry eye, conjunctivitis, and chronic blepharitis (inflammation of the eyelid).

You might be interested in an overview of a holistic approach to all eye problems. A number of doctors have told me that they have found an ancient teaching of Chinese acupuncturists to be true: that liver problems play a prominent role in eye disorders. Thus, stimulating the acupuncture liver point often helps heal the eyes. As Marty Goldstein, D.V.M., once told me: In acupuncture, it is believed that the energy forces feeding the health of the liver are the same forces feeding the health of the eyes. "I believe," Dr. Goldstein told me, "the majority of eye problems are not primarily eye problems, but rather secondary reflections of disorders of the liver. As a matter of fact," he added, "I have rarely seen a pet with a chronic eye problem who tested out to have a normal liver function." Dr. Goldstein comments that "in actuality, vitamin A is of great importance in preventing and treating eye problems because it helps the liver perform its detoxification chores." The liver's master plan in our animals' bodies, and in ours, is to filter out poisons from the system.

Interestingly, glutathione also helps the liver detoxify our bodies.

Agreeing that the health of the liver is of prime importance in eye health, Dr. Ralston adds that "the eye also needs energy that comes from the brain stem. So do the ears. Once we find out what's causing the problem in the individual animal, we can correct the liver problem or the brain stem energy by supplying the proper nutrients."

Although we're covering here common therapies for eye problems, the bottom line—as always for holistic veterinarians—is to treat whatever tests out to be amiss in the individual animal's body. "People ask me what do I use to treat so-and-so disorder," Dr. Ralston says. "And I say I really don't know. I have to ask the animal's body first. If you override what the body tells you, you're really just *guessing* what the animal needs.

"There were times when I felt sure the animal needed this or that nutrient," Dr. Ralston adds, "but when I tested the animal's body, it told me no. Then, maybe two or three weeks later, the body would say yes. In other words, when I first thought the animal needed the nutrient, it was attending to something else that was more important."

With all that in mind, the following covers therapies that most usually fill the individual needs of animals with one of several eye problems.

Macular Edema

Macular edema is an abnormal pooling of fluids (edema) in the macular area of the eye's retina.

"For this problem," Dr. Price says, "I've recently been using shark cartilage, about one gram daily for every ten pounds of body weight." He explains that shark cartilage works by way of "cutting down on the blood vessels that are getting in the retinal area, rupturing, and causing that edema."

Abscesses inside the Eye

Abscesses are holes filled with pus, surrounded by swollen tissue. They're caused by infection. Obviously, you don't want them anywhere on your cat's body—and certainly not inside her eye. Dr. Marty Goldstein once told me of a veterinary eye specialist who asked him to help treat an animal with abscesses inside the eye. The pet had already lost one of his eyes to the same problem, and two years later the animal had developed abscesses inside his remaining eye. The ophthalmologist was aware that his orthodox medical approach was not helping the eye the unfortunate animal still had and asked Dr. Goldstein if acupuncture could help. Dr. Goldstein told me that it took only two acupuncture treatments before the problem was "completely controlled." The veterinarian added that he treated the animal at the acupuncture liver point.

Corneal Ulcers

Ulcers on the cornea of the eye are a serious condition, and books on orthodox veterinary medicine have warned that without early treatment, the pet may end up having to have his eye cut out surgically. However, as long ago as 1981, holistic veterinarians such as Drs. Robert and Marty Goldstein were telling me that "a lot of times corneal ulcers that are incurable with standard drugs will heal with natural therapy." And Dr. Kearns said, "I just don't have a problem treating corneal ulcers, period." He and other early veterinarians were using vitamin E and the herb eyebright.

The veterinarians working on this new edition indicate that the information in the above paragraph is still valid, but you must keep in mind that newer therapies are also now in use that can be of even further help. We have already covered these newer therapies.

Today, Dr. Price tells me that cats with ulcers of the cornea usually respond to a homeopathic remedy, Ledum Paluste, 30C, given orally—crushed and put on the tongue. "Topically," he writes me, "I use vitamins A and E, all in the eye, and I keep the cat in a dark environment." The veterinarian adds that if the ulcer perforates, surgery is necessary.

When the case called for it, Dr. Kearns would also sometimes start off with an orthodox technique: a simple operation that brings the third eyelid up over the ulcer. The third eyelid is that membrane you can see in the inner corner of your cat's eye if she'll let you poke at her like that. Why bring this eyelid up over the ulcer? "There is no blood supply to the cornea," Dr. Kearns explained. "That is why corneal ulcers are generally so hard to heal, because there is no way for any healing substance you put into the body to get circulated into the cornea. The third eyelid does, however, have circulation; and, when placed over the ulcer, it will lend part of its circulation to the ulcer." In other words, the third eyelid will help bring the medicine to the ulcer.

John S. Eden, D.V.M., added that this simple operation also protects the ulcerated area from irritation caused by the outer lids passing over the ulcer when the animal blinks. As he stated: "This can be of considerable value, when you consider that the lids blink thousands of times a day."

I once had occasion to learn too well, firsthand, what an animal with an injured cornea can suffer. I was stupid enough to stick my own finger into my own eye while gesturing dramatically to make a point in an argument. I had managed to give myself an abrasion of the cornea. You want to talk about pain? Orthodox eye specialists, after admonishing me to try to learn how not to stick my finger in my eye, simply taped an eye patch over my eye so I couldn't blink. The pain immediately disappeared. You can see that the eye patch was the equivalent of the simple third-eyelid operation. Why give me an eye patch, and a cat a mini-operation? The doctors felt they could count on me not to use my paws to scratch the eye patch off.

Reference

1. Patricia P. Widmer, *Pat Widmer's Cat Book*
   (New York: Charles Scribner's Sons), 1981, pp. 49–50.

Chapter 7

Problems of the Skin and Hair

"I suppose we veterinarians who do a lot of work with skin and hair problems ought to thank the commercial pet food manufacturers for all the business they create for us."

—*J. Keith Benedict, D.V.M.*

"For some cats, just giving them the vitamin B complex is all they need to produce in their bodies a natural element that repels fleas.

For the infectious skin disease pyoderma, a good diet, a nontoxic shampoo, and a short round of antibiotics will usually be all that's needed. But if the animal is put back on a poor diet, the pyoderma will return—no doubt about it."

—*Nino Aloro, D.V.M.*

"If your cat is short haired, and doesn't go outdoors, sometimes all you might need to get rid of a flea infestation is to use a flea comb."

—*Michael W. Lemmon, D.V.M.*

$\mathbf{L}$*et me tell* you about Bella, a mixed Siamese. She suffered many spiritual and physical problems, including a severe case of a skin disorder, pyoderma, that is often fatal when treated only by orthodox techniques. One reason I want to share Bella's story with you is that it provides a case history in which an orthodox therapy (antibiotics) played a big role, but the additional *natural* therapy prevented negative side effects and made a complete recovery possible. I stress often in this book that holistic veterinarians, who have been thoroughly trained and licensed in orthodox techniques, will not deny standard treatments if they are best for the animal—and that these veterinarians rely most heavily on standard therapies added to natural treatments when the animal is presented to them in very dire straits. Bella was presented to a holistic veterinarian in such straits.

Those of you who are especially interested in an entity's *spirit* might see in Bella's saga the story of a cat who started out in life with a rotten karma that changed radically when she and a certain person met. But first let me tell you about Bella's medical problems.

"Bella was about a year and a half old when she was brought to me," Nino Aloro, D.V.M., told me in a recent interview. "She was skinny, she had fleas, and she had a terrible case of pyoderma." Pyoderma is a skin disease in which eruptions on the body ooze pus. "Bella's body was pretty much covered from head to tail with pustules oozing junk, for want of a better word," Dr. Aloro said. She had been fed, in her short lifetime, only a cheap commercial dry food; and she had just given birth to kittens, which had further depleted her body. (Although cats always need top nutrition to stay in good health, they particularly need it under the stress of sharing their nutrition with kittens rapidly growing within their bodies. See chapter 4.)

Bella was a stray and had never received the honor of becoming a house cat. Yet apparently she stuck close to the two people who were showing her the only human kindness—food, albeit poor quality—she had ever known. These people brought her in to Dr. Aloro because they were being transferred to another part of the country, had a dog, and didn't want to take Bella with them. On the other hand, they didn't want to leave her behind as a stray with no one to feed her. They hoped Dr. Aloro could find a home for her.

"Yes, fine," Dr. Aloro said, ironically expressing to me the enormity of what they had asked. "How could I expect anybody to adopt her when she was so sick and looked like that, with pus oozing from all over her body?" he asked me rhetorically. *I* certainly didn't know. "It took about six months to get her completely well," the veterinarian said. "Advantage [a product we talk about later] got rid of the fleas; and eventually the pyoderma disappeared with the nontoxic shampoos, the antiobiotic, and the change from the junk foods to a chemical-free diet."

Dr. Aloro added that "after two or three months, the most amazing thing happened." (You may see elsewhere in this book that holistic veterinarians, using their expertise in natural medicine to achieve results that seem like miracles to many, are sometimes surprised themselves by these results.) "Bella's fur assumed a different look. She was part Siamese and part striped (tabby). When she came to me, the tabby was on the face, feet, and tail. The rest of her body was rather uniformly beige. The Siamese part of her coat was sparsely developed. But as the treatment went on, her coat changed to nice, silky, and full. And the tips of that coat became like seal point—the seal point of a Siamese." (Later in this chapter we discuss long-ago research showing that nutritional therapy can change hair color.)

Bella also gained weight, so she would no longer scare a prospective adoptive parent because she looked like a small skeleton; and,

Dr. Aloro says, "she became more sociable. When she was first brought in to me, she didn't know what awful things people might be going to do to her next." Now she no longer feared the worst. She had found some reason to hope that any new person might treat her nicely.

So, finally, Bella was in good enough shape to achieve her lifetime ambition of having her very own caring person. She was now a fine-looking, healthy, sociable young cat with all that pretty sealpoint hair. She was very adoptable. But as Dr. Aloro brought me to this point in Bella's karma (if you will), I was also aware that he had treated her medically and spiritually for six months. "Dr. Aloro," I asked, "is Bella your own personal cat now?"

Yes, it was Dr. Aloro who became Bella's permanent adoptive parent. So Bella, seemingly doomed to a lifetime of despair—and a short lifetime at that—has now snuggled in to a probably long life with her very own person, who is uniquely able to give her high-quality medical care and to know how to nurture her spirit.

Actually, it was Dr. Aloro who named this cat Bella. Sounding like a proud papa, the veterinarian told me, "She grew to become what I knew from the beginning she could become—a *bella*." Dr. Aloro is Italian, and *bella* in Italian means, of course, beautiful.

A major holistic therapy for all skin and hair problems is to start the cat on a natural diet. If you have read chapters on other disorders, you've seen that a natural diet is a basic treatment for *all* disorders, since holistic veterinarians consider poor diet to be a prime *cause* of all disorders. As Dr. Aloro puts it: "Very little works to help an animal if you don't give a good diet."

As detailed in chapter 3, the overuse of vaccinations has been found in recent years to be, along with poor diet, a major factor in just about every kind of chronic disease in cats. "No matter what skin or hair problem the cat has when he comes in," Dr. Lemmon states, "I start off by getting his history of vaccinations." The effects of overvaccinating can be helped by administration of a specific homeopathic preparation.

Many veterinarians have told me that problems of the skin and coat are the most common disorders they see. That would be good news if these problems were as inconsequential as they might seem to be: only "skin deep." But many veterinarians estimate that 90 percent of skin disorders are merely outward manifestations of something physically wrong *within* the body. And many skin problems are life threatening in and of themselves.

That's the bad news about skin disorders. Here's the good news: Since natural therapies rebalance the total biochemistry, other, seemingly unrelated disorders often disappear along with the skin and hair problem. And as far back as 1981, Wendell O. Belfield, D.V.M., in his book *How to Have a Healthier Dog,*[1] stated that 70 percent of skin problems could be cleared up simply by putting a pet on a chemical-free diet and adding vitamins and minerals. Remember that holistic veterinary medicine was in its infancy in those days.

Some Basic Suggestions for Treating Skin and Hair Problems

Please see the text of this chapter for important details

- **A natural diet as described in chapters 2 and 4.** Initially, however, a diet of lamb and well-cooked brown rice may be tried. (The lamb and rice should not be served at the same meal.) This diet is free of foods that commonly cause allergies in pets—and food allergies are frequent causes of skin disorders in cats.* Additional foods may be added to the diet one at a time; if any one addition results in a flare-up of the skin problem, it may be an indication that your cat is allergic to that particular food.
- **A multivitamin/multimineral supplement formulated for cats**
- **Additional vitamin C:** for a ten-pound cat, 250 mg twice a day
- **Additional vitamin E:** for a ten-pound cat, 200 units a day
- **Additional B complex with B$_{12}$:** 10 mg per meal

* Dr. Aloro points out, though, that individual cats may be allergic to lamb.

- **Additional selenium:** 10 mg a day
- **Additional zinc:** 5 mg a day
- **Cold-pressed oil (sunflower or sesame):** initially, 1 teaspoon for each of the cat's two meals
- **Wheat germ oil capsules:** ½ a day
- **Kelp:** ½ teaspoon a day
- **Nontoxic shampoo**

An initial fast, with distilled water only, may be helpful in aiding the body to rid itself of stored-up toxins. *A fast over twenty-four hours must be done under medical supervision.* Do not fast a cat—even for twenty-four hours—who has diabetes or any other chronic disorder without checking closely with a veterinarian who is experienced with fasting animals. Michael W. Lemmon, D.V.M., adds that besides an initial fast, he will often suggest a twenty-four-hour fast once weekly.

You'll note that the boxed information calls for *cold-pressed* oils. Dr. Lemmon warns that just because the label states that the oil is cold pressed does not mean that it has not been subjected to heat and light, which rob the oil of nutritional value. He states that "manufacturers can call the oil cold pressed if it just starts out cold. But then the presses can be very hot, and of course they heat up the oils." A giveaway might be that if the product is not packaged in a dark or black container, to keep out the light, the manufacturer may not have worried much about keeping the product from heat and light before packaging, either. If it is in a dark container, and the label states the date on which the product was pressed, as well as the date by which you should use it, you can be rather confident you're buying a truly cold-pressed oil.

Since most readers will study only the chapter on the disorder that concerns their cat, I feel that there are one or two facts I should repeat in every disorder chapter. Although this section offers suggestions (and remember they are only *suggestions*) that holistic veterinarians often give for skin and hair problems, these doctors will always tailor the therapy to the individual cat. So if you contact a holistic veterinarian who doesn't do things the way they're mentioned here, don't assume that the doctor is in any way wrong. Although, in line with the new communication people expect to have with their doctors, you might want to ask *why* the veterinarian isn't doing something you expected.

For instance, Dr. Lemmon says that the suggestions in the box "are important and certainly can be of help. So when a client comes in who has been using those suggestions, I'll say, 'That's fine.' But if the cat has not been completely helped, we'll modify that treatment. On the other hand, if the client has not been giving the cat any treatment, I won't necessarily use all those suggestions." Then, echoing the individual approach so central to holistic therapy, the veterinarian adds that "it just depends on the case."

One way in which Dr. Lemmon would often use a different approach to get the same result would be in the suggested use of vitamin B complex in supplement form. "I'm not real big on the B complex in synthetic form. My own feeling is I'd rather give those vitamins in natural form: from the green concentrate herbs, such as spirulina or barley grass, or from the organ meats, or perhaps high-quality yeast—if the animal can handle that." (As stated elsewhere in this chapter, a number of cats are allergic to yeast.)

Dr. Lemmon discusses other natural therapies he will often use for skin and hair problems. "Depending on the situation, I might use raw glandulars, such as raw adrenal concentrates." As you might expect, adrenal concentrates will be used when the cat's problem is traced in whole or in part to a malfunctioning adrenal gland.

"Another substance I might use is evening primrose oil, because it contains gamma-linolenic acid, which is helpful for inflammation, allergies, and other problems that go along with many skin and hair disorders," Dr. Lemmon continues. He adds that for a ten-pound cat he might start out with one-fourth of a capsule a day and increase to one capsule daily.

The veterinarian adds that he may work on the specific cat's problem from a homeopathic standpoint, doing a classical homeopathic workup on the cat to find the best remedy. (These workups are painless and noninvasive.)

Depending as always on the individual case, Dr. Aloro will often use a number of herbs combined in one capsule that help rebuild the immune system. Some of the herbs are propolis; barley green; echinacea; red clover tops; suma; American, Korean, and Chinese ginseng; ginger; chlorophyll, dandelion; burdock; spirulina; peppermint; and blue-green algae. Remember that these are all combined in one capsule; you don't have to get them into your cat in some twenty different "shifts."

Dr. Aloro says that this combination of herbs has proven so useful that it has "greatly changed" his practice in the last few years. The combination is prepared by an herbalist in the veterinarian's area.

Before we discuss specific skin disorders, let me give just a brief "taste" of some of the medical research throughout the years that has shown how nutrition can prevent—and cure—skin and hair problems. While I might have chosen to list *new* research, I opted instead to give a sampling of studies from the 1930s and 1950s, so you'd have an idea of how long these problems have been linked with nutrition. The veterinarians I cite in this chapter have been using the *newest* research, which has often used this old research as a mere stepping-stone.

Human volunteers kept on diets just slightly lacking in one vitamin (B2) developed overly oily hair and skin.[2] The reverse problem, skin that is too dry, has been caused in humans by giving too little vitamin A or C, linoleic acid, or any one of several B vitamins.[3]

Imagine the following mystery happening to your body, and you might conclude that only a miracle could help you. You're a fair-skinned person, but your skin begins turning dark. (This condition can be caused by exhausted adrenal glands, as in Addison's disease.) Eventually, your skin becomes nearly black. It was shown many years ago that an adequate nutritional program could reverse this process and restore your natural skin tone.[4]

In 1950, a study showed that 4 to 8 tablespoons a day of the natural food substance lecithin healed even the most severe cases of the skin disease psoriasis within five months.[5]

Gray hair? Once you've got it, the only way you can get rid of it is with dye, right? It's just God's or nature's will. Or it's just part of growing old. Yet gray hair was produced in various studies before 1965 by giving too little copper, too little folic acid, too little pantothenic acid, and too little PABA—all nutrients. And hair was restored to its original color sometimes by giving only PABA.[6] If you thought the hair color change in Bella, the cat whose true story opened this chapter, was hard to believe, maybe you're reconsidering?

So much for an extremely sketchy discussion of how medical research has been for at least six decades linking skin and hair problems to nutrition. Now for information about how all these decades of research can help your cat.

Fleas

Some Suggestions for a Do-It-Yourself Nontoxic Flea Treatment

The following is a nontoxic treatment suggested by a number of holistic veterinarians for a cat with a moderate case of flea infestation. (See the text for important details.) *If your cat is bleeding or chewing excessively, consult a veterinarian, at least by phone.*

- In certain situations, a flea comb may be all that's needed.
- In some cases, just the use of the B-complex vitamins will help the body produce a natural flea repellent.
- Bathe your cat in a nontoxic shampoo and dry him thoroughly.

- Apply a natural healing ointment (vitamin E, A, or D) to the reddened areas and deter your pet from licking it off.
- Give an adult cat one teaspoon of brewer's yeast a day.
- Add half a clove of fresh garlic per day to your cat's food. Use a garlic press or chop the garlic finely.
- Flea collars? See text of this chapter for details.
- Sprinkle brewer's yeast onto your pet's coat and skin every two to three days during heaviest infestation. Then use once every two weeks.
- Gradually change the diet to a chemical-free diet. See chapters 2 and 4.

Putting your cat on a natural diet, supplemented with a multi-vitamin/multimineral pill, will help rebuild the total health of your pet. Fleas are parasites, and as such their role in life is to scavenge the blood of sick bodies—and sick bodies only. (Remember we said earlier that more often than not skin problems are a sign of internal sickness?) When you have rebuilt your companion's overall health, he will no longer fit the category of a sick host. At that point, your cat will probably be able to come into contact with fleas many times (from other animals, from the yard, from newly hatched eggs hidden in your house), and the fleas will snub his body as being "an unfit place to live."

To the abbreviated suggestions in the boxed material, Dr. Lemmon adds that you should try to make sure the brewer's yeast is of high quality. And remember always that a number of cats (and, by the way, people) are allergic to yeast.

Commenting on the suggestion of using garlic, Drs. Aloro and Lemmon stated that it sometimes is very helpful and sometimes doesn't help at all. Again, we're back to the fact that, while specific nutrients often help certain disorders, cats have individualized biochemistries.

Dr. Lemmon says that if your cat is short haired, a flea comb can be of great help. "First of all, it can be an easy way to find out if the cat *has* fleas," he says. "And it can be useful in helping to get rid of them. Actually, if your cat doesn't go outdoors, the flea comb used alone will usually get an isolated flea infestation under control."

Dr. Aloro states that in some cases just giving the cat a B-complex supplement will be all that's needed. While he has found that to be true over the years in terms of actual results, he doesn't believe the biochemical rationale has been discovered yet. His theory is, though, that some bodies produce a substance that is a natural repellent to fleas. "As you know," he says, "some people are eaten up by fleas, while others in the same yard or room are unaffected. I think some of my patients don't have that particular element in their bodies, and the B complex given on a daily basis helps to produce the natural repellent."

Dr. Aloro points out that brewer's yeast, mentioned in this chapter as being helpful in controlling fleas and in aiding other skin and hair problems, is a good source of B vitamins.

Nontoxic rinses are also helpful for controlling fleas. Holistic veterinarians point out that—unlike unnatural, chemical rinses—you can use nontoxic ones every day, thus increasing their effectiveness. These rinses can not only help get rid of fleas but can also soothe irritation from the scratching that fleas cause. And since they don't contain poisonous chemicals, your cat won't be harmed while she does "her thing" of grooming her hair to keep it pretty.

What about Flea Collars?

In some cases it's possible to bypass flea collars, whose drawbacks we discuss below, with the simple, inexpensive use of brewer's yeast and/or raw grated fresh garlic in your pet's food. Both these substances give the cat's skin a smell that nobody notices—except fleas, who can't bear it. The garlic and yeast also contain nutrients that are extremely healthful for our pets—provided, as always, that your cat isn't allergic to yeast. As a matter of fact, some veterinarians recommend that brewer's yeast and garlic be a part of your pet's daily diet—fleas or no fleas.

Or you might dust brewer's yeast directly onto your pet's body, a good ploy for a cat who may take forever to accept strange new objects that appear in his food bowl. In grooming himself, your cat will lick up the yeast on his coat and will thus benefit not only from the good external effects, but also the good internal effects of the yeast.

If your cat goes outside as a matter of course, it's best to put him outside for a while after the "dusting," because the yeast is not a poison and therefore does not kill the fleas (or your cat), as poisonous flea collars can. It merely sends the fleas scampering off your pet's body.

"As far as I know," Dr. Aloro says, "there is no flea collar that is effective, including the ones that the companies guarantee will kill fleas for months. I had one that guaranteed to keep working for a full year; but when I saw that the fleas were just, say, having a nice time frolicking right there under that collar, I gave up the idea of dispensing any flea collars."

In the first edition, veterinarians often recommended herbal flea collars as being not only safe but also much more effective than the poisonous collars. They work not by killing fleas—and therefore potentially killing the cat—but by giving off an herbal aroma that fleas hate. So they abandon the pet's body in search of another cat who doesn't smell so awful.

But Dr. Lemmon now tells me that he doesn't push herbal flea collars. "I'm not opposed to them if the client has already used one, and it's worked out for the cat," he says. "But I have found that some pets do have problems with these collars."

New Flea Controllers

Dr. Lemmon believes that many veterinarians are turning away from flea collars in favor of two new flea controllers, both known as recreation regulators. In other words, they work to stop new fleas from being born. These two products came out only a few years ago. One is called Program, and the other is called Advantage. Program is given by mouth, and Advantage is put directly on the skin.

"Apparently they work quite well," Dr. Lemmon says. "And when a client tells me he or she has already been using one of the products, and the animal has shown improvement and hasn't had any side effects, I say, 'Sure, go ahead using it.' But I'd prefer not using them if I can avoid them." Dr. Lemmon's concern is that not enough time has elapsed since they were put into use for us to have full knowledge of any possible harmful effects.

Dr. Aloro adds that these two products "are supposed to be nontoxic. But until millions and millions of cats use them without any problem, how can we really be sure that they're not toxic?"

However, both veterinarians see indications that these new products work to control fleas. Dr. Lemmon says that he has had some clients tell him, "My pet used to have problems with fleas all the time. I just put one drop on his skin, and he doesn't have any problems anymore."

Dr. Aloro suggests, though, that you read the labels thoroughly. One of the products specifies "in the small print that even some doctors don't read" that you must still use shampoos and treat the house. "If you can't eliminate the source of fleas in the cat's environment, you will have an endless flow of fleas onto the cat, and the product will be just a worthless added expense."

It's impossible for me to know how long after I write this book you will actually be reading it. Call one or two holistic veterinarians (see the list at the back of this book) to get updated information. Ask how these products have withstood the test of time regarding effectiveness and lack of toxicity.

Getting Rid of the Source of Fleas by Cleaning up the Environment

If you have successfully gotten rid of fleas that were tormenting your cat, and they have come back, first make sure you have been maintaining her on a natural diet. Second, consider that the fleas that left your cat's body simply took up residence elsewhere in your house until the "medical threat" was over. You may have to take steps to get fleas out of your cat's domicile. (Actually, as mentioned previously, some flea products say you have to do this as a matter of course.) Dr. Lemmon says that "very often, just really good cleanliness can be enough to get rid of the source of fleas: really good vacuuming, cleaning up the beds, getting rid of hair and other debris, that type of thing." When that doesn't work, Dr. Lemmon says that he recommends cleaning with 20 Muleteam Borox or Flea Busters because they are relatively nontoxic and have worked very well over the years for his clients. These two products consist basically of boron, an essential nutrient.

Fleabite Allergy (or Flea Allergy Dermatitis)

Fleabite allergy is an extension of the general problem of flea infestation. This disorder shows itself in bald spots and in swollen, inflamed (and painful) skin, the result not only of the fleabites but also of the afflicted cat's sometimes desperate biting and scratching to try to make things better. Just as we do when we are in constant discomfort, your cat may lose her appetite and change from a sweet, happy being to an irritable, mean one.

"We can pretty well eliminate fleabite allergy these days," Dr. Aloro says. He specifies, of course, that changing to a natural diet is of crucial importance. "And we have to ascertain that the kidneys are in good working order and use natural therapies as necessary if they're not. Also, now we have better shampoos than we used to have to treat fleas and other skin conditions."

Dr. Aloro will often use Advantage, mentioned in the previous section. "You just put a few drops on the back of the neck, not the entire body. And that kills about 98 percent of the fleas within twenty-four hours and will keep working effectively for the next month. Then you just keep repeating the few drops once a month."

Dr. Lemmon adds that acupuncture is sometimes helpful for fleabite allergy.

Hair Loss

"You have to determine what is *causing* the hair loss," Dr. Benedict told me many years ago. "But no matter what is causing it, it is imperative that you improve the animal's nutrition." George M. Thue, D.V.M., like Dr. Benedict, stated that he will check for such things as hormonal deficiency, parasites, and pressure wounds that might be causing the hair loss. "When there is no indication for specific treatment, I will occasionally use cider vinegar, in addition to a natural diet plus supplements," Dr. Thue told me. "Daily application of cider vinegar rubbed in thoroughly on small areas of hair loss can do wonders to stimulate dead or weak hair follicles and restore natural hair growth."

Today Dr. Lemmon tells us that "a lot of what I do today is similar." He particularly stresses the importance of the unsaturated fatty acids. As always, they should be cold pressed. Dr. Lemmon adds that flaxseed oil and primrose seed oil in capsule form are particularly helpful in treating hair loss.

To sum up: Hair loss in your cat should be checked out by a veterinarian to find out its exact cause. Remember that skin and hair problems are very often signs of something amiss within the cat's body. However, no matter what the cause is, you can help your cat by making sure his nutrition is optimal, as detailed in chapters 2 and 4.

Skin Ulcers

Holistic veterinarians often treat skin ulcers with vitamin E. One case history, reported in a personal communication to Dr. Wilfrid E. Shute (one of the world's major pioneers in work with the vitamin), told of a young animal with skin ulcers[7] whose coat was restored to beautiful condition after about ten weeks on the vitamin. This was despite the fact that the pet had been in such trouble that literally half his body was bald. The owners had dragged the animal to half a dozen veterinarians, none of whom could help him, for two years. You can imagine how much that cost the owners in dollars—and how much it cost them and the pet in stress. At the end of those two years, the owners had been told to give up and put their companion to sleep. (By the way, the owners were able simply to give the vitamin E by mouth at home.)

Other veterinarians have reported success with vitamins C and A—depending, as always, on which of the nutrients that are generally helpful for a disorder are most deficient in the particular animal's body. Jan Bellows, D.V.M., has specified that he often found the mineral zinc to be helpful.

Dr. Thue added that he used a medicated shampoo and ointment for skin ulcers and shaved the affected area to keep it clean. He also gave B complex and vitamin C. Then he had the owners continue giving their pet multivitamins with additional C and E.

Dr. Lemmon recently said, "That information is certainly fine. But I'd like to add that I will also usually investigate the animal's problem from a classical homeopathic point of view."

Red (Demodectic) Mange

This skin disorder usually affects cats and dogs under two years of age. At first, hunks of hair disappear from around the muzzle and the eyes. The bald areas are red and a bit swollen. If you see these symptoms, you should obtain immediate veterinary aid for your pet. Red mange can spread quickly. A chemical insecticide may be needed to kill the mites that cause the disorder. Be absolutely certain to increase your cat's nutritional supplementation at this point, to help detoxify the insecticide.

For generalized red mange (that is, red mange that has already spread over the body), every source I turned to—whether orthodox or orthomolecular—while working on the first edition offered mainly despair. I persisted, however, until I found holistic veterinarian Dr. Bellows, who gave details of a combined orthodox-nutritional therapy that, he said, "works on almost all cases." The veterinarian stated: "First the pet must be supplemented with vitamins to get him in a positive nitrogen balance, using megadoses of the B complex, C, and E. Also, any infections must be cleared up with antibiotics. Then amatraze (an insecticide) must be used as a rinse."

Animal nutritionist Pat Widmer added that in her clinic all animals with generalized red mange tested out to have very low levels of zinc in their bodies. "With the use of zinc," she said, "we have seen the entire coat grow back within a week." Widmer also stated that relieving stress is very important. "When I find a pet has a very stressful home situation," she told me, "I persuade the owner to let the animal stay with me at the clinic, where I make sure to give him a calm environment and a lot of loving attention."

The first edition's new offers of hope for mange stopped there. Now, as you might expect, holistic veterinarians have additional natural ways to help animals with this problem. These include herbs that support the liver in detoxifying the body and combinations of nutrients that improve the immune system. Homeopathic remedies are also helpful.

Holistic veterinarians now also have more effective rinses and shampoos to use externally. But their main concern continues to be treating what is wrong *inside* the body that is causing the problem that may look only "skin deep."

Remember I said that initially I had met with nothing but hopelessness about treating an animal once red mange had spread over the body? Please keep that in mind as you read about Snowball, a Persian cat whose plight upset my whole neighborhood. (I might add that during Snowball's plight, our neighborhood bonded together to worry about him. After that, our neighbors went back to calling the police on each other for broken fences and the like.) Snowball wasn't remotely a friendly cat, so you can't say everybody's love for him came from a feeling of camaraderie. We all loved him just because he was so darned beautiful, especially his luxurious, silky hair. (I used to fancy that he knew just how beautiful he was, and that's why he was so snooty.)

We all knew Snowball because his people let him roam free all day and part of the night. Many of my neighbors were afraid that the cat would be hit by a car, attacked by a stray dog, or would meet with some other disaster that can strike an animal left out on the streets unattended. People came to my husband, Joe, and me, entreating us to "have a stern talk with your tenants," Snowball's owners. We said that we had indeed suggested they not leave the cat out on the street unattended, but they had ignored us. And, after all, we were their landlords, not their parents—and Snowball wasn't our cat.

Then a terrible thing started happening to Snowball. Every time anyone in the neighborhood saw him, he had less and less hair. His beauty was disappearing—and, we all feared, so was his life. We bombarded Snowball's people with requests to take him to a veterinarian, but they replied that "cats just naturally shed."

Finally, Snowball no longer looked like a luxurious-haired Persion cat, or indeed a cat at all. He looked like the skeleton of a cat. At this point, I finally got his people to admit to themselves that something must be wrong, and they took him to a veterinarian. I waited for them to come back from the doctor that day with the same anxiety I might have had waiting for Joe to return with a verdict about our own cat, Puddy.

When Ryan answered my knock at his door, I could tell from his face that the news was awful. "The veterinarian said it's generalized red mange. He doesn't think anything can be done. We should put Snowball to sleep."

I had, of course, pleaded with Ryan to take Snowball to a holistic veterinarian in the first place, but he had been adamant about "paying money to a quack." That night I pleaded again, but now he was thoroughly convinced that nothing could be done "because the doctor said so."

Overnight, I wrestled with my guilt about not being able to convince this man of the best way to try to help his cat. The next evening Snowball himself gave me the new inspiration I needed. When I came home that night, Snowball was lying, uncharacteristically, at the foot of the stairs to our house. When he saw me, he stood up, looked me firmly in the eye, and uttered a very loud and plaintive "*Meeee-owwwww*!!!" My own cat had led me to understand that this elongation of the more common word mee-ow meant "I'm in big trouble, and I need you to help me." Then Snowball lay down again, put his head between his paws, and continued to stare me in the eye, seeming to ask if I had understood what he was talking about.

Snowball had never tried to make any connection to me, or to anyone else in the neighborhood as far as I could tell. All my years of dealing with death, karma, spirit—or whatever words you might like to substitute—led me in that moment Snowball had created to think that, somehow, this cat had divined that I was his only real chance to go on living.

I am not by nature an aggressive person, but what I felt Snowball was telling me that night led me to bang loudly on Ryan's door. It was late. Would I wake him up? I suddenly didn't care. Frankly, I don't remember what I shouted at Ryan. I do remember it was one of the most impassioned speeches of my life—and it worked.

The next morning, Ryan and his roommate, instead of taking Snowball to be euthanized, consulted a holistic veterinarian.

Not long afterward, Snowball was strutting around the neighborhood again, letting everyone admire (from afar) his beautiful, silky hair. You may have guessed that now Snowball and I had a special relationship. But you'd be wrong. He never again acknowledged my existence.

I can't say that bothered me, though. Just seeing him alive—let alone strutting and healthy and beautiful again—was my reward. And after all, Snowball—in that moment he created for us—just asked for my help. He didn't promise me his friendship.

Pyoderma

This is the disease that severely afflicted Bella, the mixed Siamese cat whose case history led off this chapter. Pyoderma, a staph infection of the skin, attacks young cats. Eruptions appear on their bodies and start oozing pus. The standard treatment is antibiotics and steroid cream, but this treatment works slowly for pyoderma—when it works at all. It is not uncommon for cats on this standard treatment to end up having to be destroyed.

For the first edition, J. Keith Benedict, D.V.M., stated that antibiotics used alone are not the best way to treat pyoderma. "You've really got to get the nutrition up," he said emphatically. "As a matter of fact, there is no contest between the standard antibiotic treatment and the combined antibiotic-and-nutrition therapy." He stressed high amounts of vitamin E, which helps promote healing and prevent scarring.

One reason antibiotics used alone are not the best solution for pyoderma was given by Drs. Robert and Marty Goldstein. The substances that come out through the skin in the pus "are built-up toxins within the body. Antibiotics stop the elimination of these toxins. This, of course, causes a buildup of toxins within the body and eventual recurrence of the pyoderma. Therapy must include some detoxification in order to achieve a cure. This detoxification is a nutritional program." Since I, like you, am a person owned by animals, I can well understand that if antibiotics used alone stopped that awful pus from oozing out of your cat's body, you would consider the cat cured. And, if the cat came down again with pyoderma, you would consider this a normal part of the disease. But, for holistic veterinarians, a return of any disease is not normal.

John S. Eden, D.V.M., stated many years ago that he used antibiotics "only in severe or intractable cases." Besides diet and supplementation, Dr. Eden stressed cleansing of the skin, using either an iodine-based or chlorhexidine shampoo. "I recommend that the owner, while bathing the pet, open the pustules and remove scabs to allow the shampoo (surgical scrub) to get at the bacteria," he stated.

Commenting on the preceding paragraph for this new edition, Dr. Lemmon said, "To treat the animal externally, I might use iodine or chlorhexidine, but only if the problem is very severe. Otherwise, I would treat the animal with herbs. There are a number of herbal bases, including witch hazel, that have the power to disinfect and to kill the bacteria." He adds, as he does elsewhere for skin and hair disorders, that homeopathy can also be helpful.

As Dr. Thue once pointed out, vitamin C is especially valuable in helping skin to heal. "For instance," he told me, "I've done surgery on animals whose bodies simply couldn't heal the skin. Two whole weeks after surgery, there would be no healing whatsoever. Then

I've given vitamin C, and in another week or two the skin was completely healed."

Dr. Aloro recently noted that he is still using antibiotics "for severe cases of pyoderma. But diet is crucial for treating pyoderma, as it is for any type of skin disorder. Because if the diet is the kind that causes allergy, any skin outbreaks will become infected, will become pyodermic. So a round of antibiotics lasting from a few days to a few weeks usually takes care of the pyoderma—as long as people change their diet. But," Dr. Aloro adds, "if they put the cat back on a harmful diet, the pyoderma will come back. No doubt about it."

References

1. Wendell O. Belfield, D.V.M., and Martin Zucker, *How to Have a Healthier Dog* (Garden City, New York: Doubleday and Co.), 1981, p. 205.
2. W. H. Sebrell *et al.*, *Pub. Health Rep.*, 53, 2282, 1938.
3. V. Ramalignaswami *et al.*, *Brit. J. Derm.*, 65, 1, 1953.
4. Adelle Davis, *Let's Get Well* (New York: Harcourt, Brace and World, Inc.), 1965, p. 155.
5. P. Gross *et al.*, *NY State J. Med.*, 50, 2683, 1950.
6. Davis, *op cit.*, p. 166.
7. Cited by Belfield, *op cit.*, p. 205.

Chapter 8

Infectious Diseases: Distemper, Pneumonia, AIDS, and More

"The only time I use an antibiotic for respiratory diseases is when the client insists on it. With drugs, the animal has less of a chance of being cured than he has with natural therapy. Also, even in those cases where the drug does cure, the poor cat or dog can be suffering for a week or two; whereas with vitamin C and other nutrients, he can be well in three days."
—*Richard J. Kearns, D.V.M. (in 1981)*

"I don't agree with orthodox thinking, which considers feline AIDS a terminal disease. Using natural therapies, I have found that AIDS in the cat is a very treatable disease."
—*Jack Long, V.M.D. (in 1998)*

"Bacteria and viruses do not attack a healthy body. Most doctors worry about the bacteria and viruses. I do not treat them. I treat the animal."
—*Numerous holistic veterinarians (from 1981 to 1998)*

If you're starting this chapter as a die-hard skeptic, you will read some facts that may seem much too good to be true. But I believe that if you read with an open mind, you will finish this chapter with new knowledge that can save your cat's life.

You will read that even if your veterinarian has told you that there is nothing to be done for your cat in the final stage of an infectious disease, she may be back to all her old mischief within days after administration of a natural therapy. You will read of two diseases (feline leukemia and feline AIDS) generally considered "terminal" when diagnosed—even if diagnosed so early that the cat has no symptoms—that holistic veterinarians consider quite treatable.

No, I am not claiming that holistic veterinarians can work miracles. Although the recoveries may often *seem* like miracles, the therapies these doctors use are built virtually always on modern medical research—or at the very least hundreds, sometimes thousands, of years of actual proof.

For instance, you will see that vitamin C is basic to the therapy for infectious diseases—and the "miraculous" results of this vitamin in dealing with these diseases have been documented in medical studies since at least 1937.

Keep in mind that every disease was once incurable—until medical science found a cure for it. Keep in mind also that it took a number of years for many of today's totally accepted cures to come to the attention of most doctors and even more years before most doctors accepted them. This book covers new cures and controls for pet disorders that are presently caught in that unfortunate limbo.

Let's investigate the history of vitamin C, since it is so basic to the therapies used by holistic doctors to effect their sometimes "impossible" cures of infectious diseases. Adelle Davis cited medical studies going back to 1937 that show the "new notion" that vitamin C can kill bacteria.[1] Dr. Fred R. Klenner, chief of staff at the Memorial Hospital in Reidsville, North Carolina, began his work in the late 1940s. Dr. Klenner's work, published extensively in the medical literature, was often done with human patients who were by all rights supposed to die. Many of them had been previously treated with penicillin, Aureomycin, and other antibiotics with no success. Often these terminally ill people, with fevers of 103 to 105 degrees, had a normal temperature within a few hours after administration of vitamin C and were able to enjoy the next meal offered at the hospital. Two or three days later—when they otherwise would have been lowered into the earth—they walked out of the hospital in good health.[2]

The diseases Dr. Klenner successfully treated with vitamin C included hepatitis, herpes simplex, measles, chicken pox, mononucleosis, meningitis, encephalitis, polio, viral pneumonia, and lockjaw.[3]

The books of nutritionist Adelle Davis were published in the 1950s and 1960s and were so popular with the public that, the last I checked, they were still in print. I believe she was the first strong voice in getting information about nutritional therapies out to the public. Her books were popular despite the fact—or maybe because of the fact—that they were heavily weighted by her fervor for giving proof of every fact with details from technical medical research. Backing up Dr. Klenner's work, Davis cited a number of other studies, conducted in the years from 1938 to 1960, that reported that vitamin C is deadly to all types of bacteria and viruses.[4] Why *all*? Because vitamin C doesn't waste its time racing through the body trying to attack the viruses and bacteria per se; it rebuilds the immune system.* And the rebuilt immune system kills the viruses and bacteria—just as it does, when it is strong, many times in the course of a normal day.

---

* Dr. Long adds that this vitamin has also been documented to kill viruses *directly*.

If your veterinarian doesn't have expertise in nutritional medicine, he or she may wonder how vitamin C can help a cat, because cats (unlike people) *naturally* produce vitamin C in their own bodies. This argument overlooks the fact that what the animal can produce does not approach the high amount necessary for a therapeutic dosage. Dr. Klenner's excellent results with people, for instance, were sometimes achieved with well over four thousand times the recommended daily allowance of vitamin C.

Holistic veterinarians add that if the animal is to *naturally* produce vitamin C in his body, he must have a *natural* diet. And the commercial foods that many cats are fed are by no means a natural diet. (See chapters 1 and 2.)

A Basic Therapy for All Infectious Diseases

Jack Long, V.M.D., advises that the information from the first edition remains accurate. But, as always, so many advances have been made in alternative medicine since 1981 that holistic doctors now have numerous additional therapies from which to choose the optimal treatment for your individual cat. Dr. Long specifies: "I'm using more herbal medications than I did in those days—particularly echinacea and garlic." Echinacea, for instance, as Robert Goldstein, V.M.D., points out, stimulates the immune system by increasing the number of white blood cells and phagocytes. For infectious diseases in general, Dr. Long will often use five drops three times a day for a cat or small dog weighing up to twenty-five pounds. "And when the client okays it," Dr. Long adds, "I always try to include a homeopathic analysis in the work."

Holistic veterinarians still use high dosages of vitamin C, often in the form of sodium ascorbate, as a central part of their therapy for all infectious problems. In times of crisis, the C will be given intravenously, often at the rate of half a gram or more per pound of body weight, twice a day.

The difference between intravenous vitamin C and a vitamin C tablet can very probably be *the* difference between life and death for your cat with a very serious infectious disease. Nutrients given intravenously, rather than through the mouth, bypass the digestive system. This allows them to go directly into the blood and begin circulating immediately throughout the body. Also, because intravenous medicines bypass the digestive system, you can give much higher amounts without toxicity.

The preceding paragraph gives only one reason that I urge you not to make up your own treatment for your cat with a severe infectious disease. (Maybe you would never dream of doing that, but I worry about the people who do believe that natural, nontoxic therapies can always be used without the help of a doctor.) Once your cat is past the crisis, lesser amounts of the nutrients will be needed, and you can give them to her yourself by mouth.

Often, in crisis cases, intravenous fluids also will be administered to offset existing dehydration, a common killer for humans and animals alike in acute illnesses. And solid foods will be withheld.

Nutritional veterinarians also use thymus extract. The thymus gland is a major part of the all-important immune system; and, as Dr. Kearns once told me, "The amount of thymus gland hormone in the blood can be just about destroyed in twenty-four hours by infectious problems."

Calcium and the B complex and other vitamins also are often used as part of the natural therapy for infectious diseases.

To combat phlegm, discharge, and lung congestion—common problems with many infectious diseases—various herbs and homeopathic remedies are helpful. However, holistic doctors point out that if these discharges are not adversely affecting the cat, they should not be stopped, because they are the body's natural way of getting rid of toxins. In other words, what's coming out of the body in these gunky discharges are substances that *should* be coming out, and holistic veterinarians believe it's not their job to hamper an animal's body as it uses its innate wisdom to try to heal itself.

Vitamin A not only helps rebuild the immune system but also helps directly in problems of the mucous membranes common in such serious diseases as pneumonia and distemper. While the original form of vitamin A is fat soluble (which means it can accumulate in the body and be toxic if used in extremely high doses), by 1981 a water-soluble form, which does not accumulate in the body, was being used. This allowed veterinarians to use massive amounts of the vitamin to flush out poisons very quickly—and to do so without toxicity.

Today, John Fudens, D.V.M., writes me that instead of vitamin A he prefers the more newly discovered beta-carotene. This is the precursor to vitamin A—which means it is the substance that the body naturally converts to make its own supply of the vitamin. The veterinarian comments that the body will convert beta-carotene to the amount of vitamin A that it needs at the time, and any extra will be excreted naturally—even in a sick body. (However, he warns, if the cat has liver damage, "you still have to be very careful of toxicity.")

Dr. Fudens sums up: "In my opinion, vitamin A is low on the scale of immune-stimulating factors we have today."

Unlike many orthodox veterinarians, holistic veterinarians often will not try to fight the symptom of fever, unless it is extremely high. Fever is a sign of increased body metabolism; the high metabolism results from the fact that the body is in the middle of intense activity—fighting off its invaders. Also, heat kills bacteria. As you know, that's why we boil contaminated water and why we are warned to cook thoroughly such foods as pork, hamburger, and chicken.

Actually, some holistic veterinarians have told me that, if a cat is brought to them in the final stage of a disease that usually produces a fever and the cat doesn't have a fever, they have much less hope of curing him. They consider fever a sign that the cat's life force is still strong enough to fight.

Feline Distemper (Feline Infectious Enteritis, Feline Panleukopenia)

Several of the orthodox veterinary books I once consulted used exactly the same phrase for feline distemper: "the most deadly of all cat diseases." The death rate was described as "enormous"; one estimate set it at 80 percent. Working now some 17 years later, I asked

Dr. Long if orthodox veterinary medicine had developed a better treatment in the intervening years. "Not really," he said.

Yet in 1981, in sharp contrast to 80 percent mortality, Richard J. Kearns, D.V.M., reported: "I do not lose these cats—unless they are brought to me already in a coma."

Feline distemper takes its toll extremely rapidly. Your cat may start out one morning in apparent good health and may be dead the next morning—unless you know what signs to look for and how to deal with them in a hurry. In this section, I give you this information.

Indeed, the enormous death rate reported by traditional veterinary medicine may be due in no small part to the fact that owners don't get treatment fast enough.

Since this is such a fast-acting disease, the best way to *treat* it is to *prevent* it (which, of course, is true of any disease). So if you're skimming through this chapter while your cat is healthy, give her the recommended preventive amount of vitamin C and the natural diet recommended in chapters 2 or 4, whichever is relevant for her time in life. Vaccinate her against distemper using the information in chapter 3 on homeopathic and standard vaccinations.

Several holistic veterinarians talking to me for other chapters have said that—to save pets and owners the stress of separation, and to spare owners expense—they will send some cats home with an IV drip kit after teaching the owner how to use it. Since feline distemper and a number of other disorders overtake a cat so quickly, you might want to ask your veterinarian for one of these kits while your cat is healthy. Ask the doctor when it would be appropriate for you to start using it on your own, before you can get the cat to a veterinarian. (I have been told that the following is a rule-of-thumb sign that an animal is dehydrated: If you pull up the hair and skin at the back of his neck, and the resulting wad doesn't go back down almost immediately, the cat is dehydrated.)

I said in the introduction that for many problems, if you don't live near a holistic veterinarian, you can try consulting directly on the phone with such a doctor or, better yet, have your own veterinarian consult. But since time is so crucial with this disorder, you can't risk taking an unnecessary step. *Get to your own veterinarian* *immediately.* As a matter of fact, that might be amended: *Get to the nearest available veterinarian immediately.* Show the doctor these pages and ask—or if necessary, demand—that he or she consult with one of the holistic veterinarians listed at the back of the book.*

If you are dealing with this at a time when veterinarians in your area of the country are generally unavailable, try calling a doctor practicing in another time zone—from the other end of the country, or from Hawaii or Alaska.

Symptoms of Feline Distemper

The first sign your cat will give you that he's in trouble is that he will refuse his food. Since I was owned by a cat for about two decades, I'm aware that we cannot rush our cats to a veterinarian every time they turn up their noses at food. However, to be safe, take your cat's temperature immediately when he refuses a meal. If he has distemper, you may find it to be 104 degrees or more. *Take him to a veterinarian right away if he has a high fever.*

Another early telltale sign your cat may give you that he is in serious trouble and needs your help is if he sits hunched up and looks generally miserable.

An hour or two after first refusing his food, your cat will start to vomit violently. Only liquid will be brought up, not solid foods. (The vomit will at first be white in color; later it will turn yellow.) At this point, you must take his temperature—whether you took it before or not. If it is high, whisk him to a doctor immediately. The violent vomiting produces severe dehydration; and very quickly your pet will have lost so much weight that he may be unrecognizable. The progress of feline distemper is so rapid that all I have mentioned—including the extreme weight loss—can happen within several hours.

---

* Dr. Fudens, agreeing with this suggestion, added: "Then the two veterinarians can work together to pull the cat's immune system through."

Holistic Therapy

I hope you have read the preceding section *thoroughly* before reading this one.

In this book's first edition, I detailed the therapy used by Dr. Kearns, because at the time he was reporting more success with feline distemper than the other holistic veterinarians I contacted. (Holistic veterinarians, just like holistic and orthodox M.D.s, have their own individual areas of expertise.) Dr. Long tells me today that, like Dr. Kearns, he, too, finds feline distemper "certainly a treatable disease. With holistic therapy, we pull most of the cats through it."

Dr. Long states that what he is doing is quite similar to what Dr. Kearns was doing in 1981. The following gives Dr. Kearns' therapy along with Dr. Long's comments.

"The first thing we use," Dr. Kearns said in 1981, "is fluids, because the cats are dehydrated. In the fluids we put amino acids, to supply all the amino acids they're missing, and then we add sodium ascorbate (a form of vitamin C) and the B complex. We pass a tube orally down into the cat's stomach, and we give them vitamins A and E that way, and we give them a little egg yolk—so that it all gets optimally absorbed." Some nutrients, including vitamins A and E, must be accompanied by fat, which occurs in egg yolk, in order to be used by the body. "We also give pancreatic enzymes this way."

"While I do use amino acids occasionally," Dr. Long comments, "I don't use them for every case. But every cat does get the vitamins C and B complex, as well as fluid replacement, intravenously." Adding that veterinarians must start to use the stomach tube "as soon as the cat can handle anything on his stomach," Dr. Long says that he uses the same nutrients through the tube as Dr. Kearns did.

The only major difference between Dr. Kearns' 1981 therapy and Dr. Long's 1998 therapy for feline distemper is in the first veterinarian's use of laetrile, sometimes called vitamin B_{17}. In 1981, I found at least several holistic veterinarians who used laetrile for various diseases, but in 1997 I didn't come across any, except Dr. Price, who says he still uses it in his highly successful therapy for feline leukemia. One veterinarian commented that laetrile was "much harder to come by" at this time. Others told me that they simply had no experience in using it—perhaps because it's now hard to come by? No veterinarian I questioned ventured the opinion that the use of laetrile had been shown to be invalid. Specifically commenting in 1998 on the use of the substance for feline distemper, Dr. Long said that he found the idea of using it "interesting."

Is this a rare instance in which a helpful substance has been lost to holistic veterinary medicine? I don't know. I don't even know that laetrile *is* presently lost among holistic veterinarians, and I don't know if it may be more easily available by the time you read this book. What I do know is that Dr. Kearns felt very strongly that much of his success with feline distemper was due to laetrile. So I will do what I always try to do when there is a medical debate or a question like this one: give the information I have found so that you can make your own educated decision.

The decision you will have to make is: If your cat's veterinarian doesn't use laetrile, should you ask the doctor to call around to holistic veterinarians trying to find one who does? I believe I have made my point about the importance of time in feline distemper strongly enough by now that you won't make the use of laetrile a requirement before getting veterinary help for your cat. Also, do not ask your cat's doctor to use laetrile if he or she is not consulting closely with a veterinarian experienced in using it. Laetrile, if used in too high a dosage, can break down in the intestines, releasing a radical it contains: cyanide. As you know, cyanide is a poison.

Dr. Kearns told me that with laetrile, or vitamin B_{17}, he cured close to 100 percent of the cats brought to him with feline distemper. Without laetrile, he had a success rate of 50 to 60 percent (still very high by orthodox standards).

"I think laetrile was 'made' for cats," he said. "When you get a cat in with distemper, you get tremendously high fever and tremendous wasting. The poor cat is in absolutely terrible shape. Laetrile gets their temperature down, makes them feel good, gives them a sense of well-being—so that they will start to eat. Once they start eating, you can bring them right back to health."

I have just said that a major reason Dr. Kearns used laetrile was to lower the cat's temperature, and you may remember my saying earlier that holistic veterinarians often don't *want* to lower the animal's fever because it is a natural way to fight infection. Contradiction? No. Earlier I said that holistic veterinarians often won't try to lower the cat's temperature unless it is excessively high. With feline distemper, the animal's temperature often *is* excessively high.

Dr. Kearns did say, though, that "laetrile is not in and of itself a cure for feline distemper and is actually a very small part of the total treatment. It might be more accurately called a 'trigger' that turns the cat around."

Dr. Long told me of the latest case of feline distemper he had treated when we talked in late 1997. "Sammy had received nosodes for feline distemper, and so he got a mild case of it." Nosodes are *homeopathic* vaccinations, not standard vaccinations. And, if you're wondering how there could be a *mild* case of feline distemper— after all I've discussed about cats going from seeming to be healthy to being dead literally within a day—yes, the answer probably is in the homeopathic vaccination. (See chapter 3 for more details.) Dr. Long says, "I treated Sammy with intravenous fluids and nutrients and a homeopathic remedy. And in two days he was fine."

Respiratory Diseases (Including Pneumonia and Pneumonitis)

Pneumonia and Pneumonitis

These diseases are characterized by high fever, coughing, rapid breathing, and rapid pulse. In severe cases, there will be a blue cast to the lower eyelid. This is due to the fact that your cat is suffering from oxygen starvation. You may notice your pet trying hard to avoid lying down. He may take up an odd new sitting position, with his neck extended forward and his elbows turned out. This strange behavior is his instinctive attempt to give his constricted chest cavity literally *more room to breathe*.

Following is the basic therapy for pneumonia and pneumonitis as used today by Dr. Long.

Vitamin A (perhaps 10,000 units daily) and, again, vitamin C are mainstays of the holistic treatment for respiratory diseases. Dr. Long adds that "the B complex is very helpful also," and he occasionally uses Arsenicum album (a homeopathic remedy), at a low potency, "for the guys who really have a lot of nasal discharge and painful inflamed eyes."

Sometimes holistic veterinarians use the herb garlic, which has a great mucus-destroying effect. Mucus in the lungs, of course, is a prime problem in respiratory diseases. There are also newer treatments from which to choose. Dr. Long comments that "I use herbal treatment whenever I can. I try to choose it according to the temperament of the cat."

Dr. Long adds: "Of course, I'll use the typical conventional treatment of keeping the cat hydrated. And I'll get calories into the cat the best way I can—orally if the cat is ready for that, or by stomach tube if he's not."

Other Respiratory Diseases

With rhinotracheitis and other respiratory tract diseases, the holistic veterinarians I worked with in 1981 reported a 90 percent cure rate in early cases, but if the animal had been treated with antibiotics and other drugs before they saw him, their success rate dropped to about 75 percent. Why should the antibiotic-treated pet have a lesser chance of being cured? Michael W. Lemmon, D.V.M., explains, "While antibiotics may inactivate or kill bacteria, they also suppress the immune system," the body's *natural* way to kill bacteria. The therapies used by holistic veterinarians improve the immune system, rather than weaken it.

The preceding statements may create a question in some readers' minds: Why in certain emergency situations will some holistic veterinarians use antibiotics? The veterinarians I just quoted were talking about pets who had been treated with antibiotics before coming to them. If holistic doctors feel they must resort to antibiotics, they know which natural therapies can offset the negative effects of the drugs.*

Dr. Long recently wrote me that he will never use an antibiotic for a viral infection. Contrary to popular belief, antibiotics, while they can be effective against bacteria, do not tend to have an effect on viruses. ("Viral infections will cause clear nasal and ocular discharges," he explains, "while bacterial infections will cause cloudy or thick yellow discharges.")

Dr. Long's standard approach to infections of the upper respiratory tract is a combination of nutritional therapy and homeopathic remedies. "I typically will give a multivitamin injection followed by oral supplements of vitamin C (500 to 1000 mg a day), B complex (25 to 50 mg of each B vitamin a day), vitamin A (5,000 to 10,000 units a day), and vitamin E (200 to 400 units a day)," he noted. The veterinarian added that he will, of course, give fluid injections if the cat is dehydrated. "I will often teach owners how to give the subcutaneous fluid injections so that the cat can be treated at home," he wrote. This, of course, saves the cat the stress of hospitalization and saves the person substantial money—as well as his or her own separation stress.

"Most cats respond well to this treatment," Dr. Long said, "with early noticeable relief of symptoms and quick recovery."

Dr. Long wrote me about Myrtle, a nine-year-old cat who was, for him, "perhaps the most difficult case of upper respiratory infection I have ever treated." I have tried to balance the case histories in this book so that it doesn't look like *every* cure comes quickly and easily, so I was happy to hear about Myrtle.

"Myrtle was brought to our clinic after being sick for two weeks with coughing, wheezing, profuse clear discharges from her eyes and nose," Dr. Long wrote. "The mucus was literally *streaming* down her

---

* Dr. Fudens writes me, however: *"I never use antibiotics!!"* He uses only homeopathy first with, for secondary infections, a mixture of herbs that stimulate the immune system.

face and neck." You may see that Myrtle represents a fact I mention many times in this book: that holistic veterinarians often don't get to see a cat until the animal is literally at the brink of death.

Actually, Myrtle was so sick when she was brought to Dr. Long that, he noted, her infection was systemic. That is, the upper respiratory infection had spread throughout her body. So Myrtle's story is really one of how Dr. Long typically treats a cat with a systemic infection. His therapy for infection that has spread throughout the body is basically the same as for infections of the upper respiratory tract, but it is more intense.

Dr. Long gave more details about Myrtle's severe condition when she was brought to him: "Her appetite had gotten worse during the past week to the point that she was refusing all food and water. She had lost two pounds of her body weight and was severely dehydrated. She had a fever of 104 degrees." You won't be surprised to know that Dr. Long summed up his impression of Myrtle with "she looked miserable."

Dr. Long admitted Myrtle to the hospital isolation ward to prevent spread of her infection to other animals. He started her on a fluid replacement drip containing the B-complex vitamins and vitamin C. "Within twenty-four hours her hydration was restored, and she seemed to feel better," he related. "Her fever had gone down to 103. I progressively increased her vitamin C dosage to 1,000 mg *per pound* per day intravenously over the next twenty-four hours." That's much more of the vitamin than he uses for the average case of a cat with upper respiratory infection.

"I also gave Myrtle injections of vitamins A and E every day and I gave her the homeopathic remedy Arsenicum album," the veterinarian continued. "After a few days, Myrtle would eat small amounts of baby food from my finger, but she still had profuse nasal discharge and congestion that blocked her sense of smell." Dr. Long explained that cats often will not eat if they can't smell their food. "After five days, she was still not drinking water, but her appetite had improved to the point that she would eat soupy food, and her nasal discharge was reduced although her sinuses seemed blocked."

Myrtle was first brought to Dr. Long in such dire straits that she was hospitalized for two weeks before she got well—an abnormally long time not only for Dr. Long but for holistic veterinarians in general.

Feline AIDS

Before contacting holistic veterinarians for this new edition, I came across several references to a new disease in cats: AIDS. (The virus causing it is called FIV: feline immunodeficiency virus.) The orthodox books didn't mention a cure—or even a treatment—and neither did the few holistic books I found mentioning FIV.

When I sent out questionnaires to holistic veterinarians, I asked specifically if anyone had experience with treating AIDS in cats. Although many veterinarians checked infectious diseases as one of their specialty areas, no one volunteered to talk about AIDS. I feared that after sixteen years of working with holistic veterinarians, I had finally come across a disease that was hopeless not only for orthodox veterinarians but for holistic veterinarians, too. I now believe I had trouble finding doctors with experience in treating feline AIDS because, at least at the time, the disease was not only new but also relatively rare.

Then I got a communication that embodies what makes the grueling work of compiling a book like this so rewarding. "Yes," Dr. Long wrote me, "I treat feline AIDS, and the cats do quite well."

In an interview, Dr. Long stressed that the AIDS virus in cats is very similar in structure when viewed under the microscope to the feline leukemia virus, and "the disease has similar effects on the immune system." So you can see that Dr. Long is using what might be called medical common sense by using similar therapies for the two diseases.

But, you might say, feline leukemia is, to all intents and purposes, a fatal disease. Yes, it is—in orthodox veterinary medicine. Dr. Long points out that, although an orthodox veterinarian might put the cat on antibiotics for a specific problem stemming from AIDS, "there is no other conventional treatment at this time. Mostly AIDS is handled the same way as leukemia in cats: If they test out positive for the FIV antibody, euthanize them to control the spread of the virus, even before they have any symptoms."

But that's the present *orthodox* "solution" for cats with leukemia or AIDS. In the chapter on cancer, you'll see that even many years ago, holistic veterinarians found feline leukemia far from hopeless— even in cats so riddled with symptoms that they couldn't stand up— and expressed sorrow at the orthodox view of "test and slaughter," as one nutritional doctor called it. In fact, Dr. Long, who has been successfully treating feline leukemia for many years, reports 60 to 70 percent success for that disorder.

So, if your cat has AIDS, she might have as good a chance of becoming healthy again as a cat with leukemia who's treated holistically? No. She might have a much *better* chance. "Although I view the AIDS virus as having *similar* effects on the immune system as the feline leukemia virus does," Dr. Long told me, "these effects seem to be far less devastating. So I find AIDS much more amenable to treatment than many cases of leukemia are."

Dr. Long has found so far a success rate of about 95 percent in treating this "hopeless" disease of feline AIDS. He points out, though, that feline AIDS is uncommon in his area, and is a quite "new" disease. So as I write this, he has treated only some twelve cases. Still, if treated conventionally, we have every reason to assume that all twelve of those cats would have died, either from AIDS or from euthanasia. Only one of Dr. Long's cats with AIDS died— "And I'm not positive that his death was related to the virus," he reported.

Dr. Long gave a case history of a cat named Sylvestor, whom he treated with the regimen he typically uses for cats with AIDS, and who responded as they typically do. "I first met Sylvestor when he came in with an abscess four and a half years ago," Dr. Long said. "The abscess had been treated by another veterinarian, but that doctor was having trouble getting it to heal, and Sylvestor had a persistent fever. So the veterinarian had blood testing done, which found that Sylvestor was FIV positive. I had helped Sylvestor's owner before with a cat who had feline leukemia, so she brought Sylvestor to me to see if we could do anything for AIDS.

"When Sylvestor was first brought to me, the abscess was badly infected," Dr. Long continued, "and he had been for two weeks on two antibiotics to control his fever, but they weren't working. I began treating him as I usually treat a cat with leukemia or AIDS, and soon the wound healed nicely and Sylvestor's temperature was normal. We had taken him off the antibiotics as we replaced them with the more natural therapy." If your cat is on antibiotics—for any disease at all—I pass on to you the urging of many holistic veterinarians: Don't take her off them without consulting, at least on the phone, with a holistic veterinarian. Note that Dr. Long indicated a *gradual* withdrawal of the drugs timed with *replacement* by natural therapy.

After just several weeks, the only problem Sylvestor had was that he developed some acne under his chin, which, Dr. Long noted, was a sign that there was still an immune issue to deal with. Today, Sylvestor's acne is "for the most part under control," Dr. Long reported. "Occasionally he'll have a little pimple break out, but it seems to clear up quickly with the homeopathic remedy I've chosen for him."

Remember that Dr. Long and Sylvestor's lady are—four and a half years after Sylvestor was diagnosed with a "fatal" disorder—now concerned with an occasional little pimple. And that these pimples have been their only concern for over four years. (Sylvestor is now eleven years old.) If you're reading this because your own cat has been diagnosed as having AIDS, I'm sure you would eagerly embrace the chance of sharing the same kind of "luxury" concern with your companion years from now.

I hope the information in this section shows you how you and your cat can have that chance.

But if you're extremely skeptical of holistic medicine, you might be looking at Sylvestor's representative case history the other way around: Why is Dr. Long still spending time—and Sylvestor's lady still spending money, albeit a small amount—on the cat's occasional pimples? First, you have to go back to the facts that the "mission" of AIDS is to completely destroy the immune system, and that acne may be a sign that the immune system is not 100 percent powerful. Second, just as with the AIDS virus in humans, there is no test for the virus itself, only for the antibodies *against* the virus. "So," Dr. Long said, "while I can be sure when I've eliminated the similar *leukemia* virus from the cat's body, I can never *really* be certain that I've completely eliminated the AIDS virus from the body. Although in my other cases I believe we have completely gotten rid of the virus, there is no scientific test that can tell me if I'm right."

In Sylvestor's case, Dr. Long had done the latest FIV test a few months before he and I talked. "It came out a weak positive," the veterinarian said. Although the cat had tested out strongly positive when he was brought to Dr. Long, "I can't tell whether Sylvestor has just a residual antibody or whether there's still a small amount of the virus in his system."

Holistic Therapy for Feline AIDS

As mentioned, Dr. Long uses the same therapy for cats with AIDS as he does for those with leukemia. You'll find that therapy detailed in the chapter on cancer. Summing up the therapy, the veterinarian says: "I use vitamins, minerals, and herbs that are known to strengthen the immune system. I also use acupuncture—at the acupuncture points that build up the immune system—fairly frequently to start with, until everything's under control." He adds that when he does acupuncture on cats, he uses an acuscope, which most cats are more comfortable with than the more usual acupuncture needles.

Those are the basics of his treatment whether the cat is still only carrying the virus, or whether she has already developed symptoms.

Dr. Long points out that it often is difficult to get cats to take echinacea, an immune-building herb that, in liquid form, is part of his regimen for feline AIDS and leukemia. (In recent years, this herb has been in great use by nutritional veterinarians and M.D.s alike.) "Cats just don't like the taste of it—even though, like the other herbs, I dilute it in water and give it by the dropperful." But recently he has found a brand of echinacea (Annimmune) "that has kind of a sweet taste, and cats seem to like that well enough." He adds that this brand is also a lot more powerful than what he was using before.

Dr. Long emphasizes—as every holistic veterinarian has emphasized to me—that he individualizes his treatments for any disorder to the specific needs of the animal. "I will try to target the specific symptoms the animal's body expresses due to the biochemical imbalances the disease is causing in that individual animal."

Answering a Few More Questions You Might Have about Feline AIDS

Is Dr. Long the only holistic veterinarian who has success with feline AIDS? Most probably not. First, let me stress that I by no means contacted every holistic veterinarian in the country. If I had, this book would have come out perhaps sometime in the mid-twenty-first century. Also, by the time you read this, I assume that many more holistic veterinarians will be treating feline AIDS successfully, since it is no secret that the virus is so similar to the feline leukemia virus. Use the list at the back of the book, and call the doctors in your area. If none of them has experience with the disease, he or she may know of others who do. (A late note: As this book was going to the printer, Dr. Fudens informed me that he treats feline AIDS.)

If your cat shares her domicile with a dog, will your dog catch AIDS? Dr. Long says that, at least as known in early 1998, "we haven't discovered an AIDS-type virus associated with the dog." While your cat is still carrying the AIDS virus, might she infect your other cats? Yes. You should make every effort to find a way to separate the infected cat from others in your household. Then check to see if a homeopathic vaccination has been developed since I wrote this.*

How has AIDS entered the feline world? Dr. Long says that "at this

---

* Just as this book was going to press, Dr. Long wrote me that there is, indeed, a homeopathic nosode for feline AIDS now, from the Hahnamen pharmacy in Berkeley, CA.

point, that's not officially known." He mentions, however, that he has heard pioneering holistic veterinarian Richard Pitcairn, D.V.M., say that he has a "strong suspicion" that the feline AIDS virus is a mutated vaccine virus. (Dr. Pitcairn, in addition to having a degree as a veterinary M.D., holds a Ph.D. in immunology.) And in her book, *Cat Care, Naturally,*[5] Celeste Yarnall quotes Jeff Levy, D.V.M.: "I believe that feline leukemia evolved because of vaccinations for panleukopenia [cat distemper]. And then with the vaccinations for feline leukemia, the cat just came up with a different disease, FIV [AIDS]."

Septicemia (Blood Poisoning)

Septicemia is blood poisoning throughout the entire body of the cat. The definition tells you that it can be a very serious disease that is often fatal. Septicemia, for instance, is said to kill many more new kittens than does any other disease. However, even back in 1981 numerous holistic veterinarians were reporting to me excellent results with septicemia.

Since septicemia, like feline distemper, can kill very quickly, I urge you to look at the earlier section on distemper for suggestions on dealing with this disease as quickly as possible.

Symptoms of Septicemia

It is imperative that an owner keep a sharp eye out for symptoms of septicemia, especially in a newborn kitten, because once the disease gets hold of the baby, it can spread like wildfire. The kitten may have started out his new life looking well and nursing well. But then, perhaps a week after birth, he may withdraw from the rest of the litter and even from his mother. His cries become piteous and grow fainter.

When the symptoms start, the animal should get immediate veterinary help, or he will die within twenty-four to forty-eight hours.

Symptoms in the adult cat will be listlessness, poor appetite, and fever.

Holistic veterinarians add a point that they make for all other disorders covered in this book: This dread disorder can be prevented by the natural diet and supplements detailed in chapter 2. However, to stop septicemia from striking your newborn pet, prevention must begin with the mother at the start of pregnancy or before. (See chapter 4.)

Holistic Therapy for Septicemia

Dr. Long says that the therapy commonly used by holistic veterinarians starts with—you won't be surprised to hear—intravenous vitamin C (½ gram per pound of body weight). Also included are garlic and other herbs known to purify the blood, which is of course the task at hand in blood poisoning. Garlic, for instance, is one of the few foods containing inulin, which helps the kidneys remove soluble materials from blood.

All solid foods are withheld until the cat is cured; only liquids are given. Enemas will sometimes be administered to help clear the system faster of toxins, especially if the poisoning is thought to have come from foods.

When blood tests and acupuncture testing reveal an accompanying problem in an internal organ such as the liver or kidneys (both of which filter out poisons from the body), a holistic veterinarian may use vitamin B_{12} injected in the acupuncture trigger point for that organ. Why B_{12}? You may know that Hollywood and sports stars sometimes get B_{12} shots for energy. While this is a gross oversimplification of all that B_{12} can do, the vitamin does act as a stimulant on acupuncture points that are deficient in energy. And obviously, if our cat is being treated for blood poisoning, we want her liver and kidneys to have a lot of energy so they can accomplish their natural, appointed mission of getting poisons out of her body.

References

1. Adelle Davis, *Let's Get Well* (New York: Harcourt, Brace and World, Inc.), 1965.
2. Adelle Davis, *Let's Eat Right to Keep Fit* (New York: Harcourt, Brace and Co.), 1954.
3. Davis, *Let's Get Well, op cit.*
4. Ibid.
5. Celeste Yarnall, *Cat Care, Naturally* (Boston: Charles E. Tuttle Co., Inc.), 1995, p. 24.

Chapter 9

Some Problems of Internal Organs: Diabetes, Cystitis, Stones, Kidney Inflammation, Intestinal Worms, and More

"Many times veterinarians react to diabetes by starting the cat immediately on insulin. Often, if they had just changed the diet to the one that's natural for cats, the animal would never have *needed* insulin shots. Typically, when we holistic veterinarians first see a cat with diabetes, he is already insulin-dependent and we have to treat not only the diabetes but the dependency on insulin. But we still can get the cat's diabetes controlled—to the point where he doesn't need insulin at all—within six weeks or six months, depending on how long he's been on the insulin and the owner's compliance with home care.

"Changing the diet and adding vitamin E and other antioxidants can really help cats with fatty liver disease."

—*Ihor John Basko, D.V.M.*

"I have very good success with chronic kidney inflammation. Even if we don't get to see cats until they already have the usually fatal uremia, we typically give them a much-extended life that is comfortable and happy.

"You can rid your cat of any type of intestinal worms if you restore his normal intestinal balance of bacteria, flora, and fauna by adding a natural probiotic to his food. . . . Probiotics were developed first as a natural therapy for humans. They can help people with such 'mysterious' disorders as chronic fatigue syndrome."

—*Neal K. Weiner, D.V.M.*

"Probiotics can help greatly in treating not only worms but also other problems of the intestinal tract, such as inflammatory bowel disease and colitis. . . . Since intestinal health is so important to the *overall* health, probiotics can help with many other problems in addition to those of the intestines."

—*Jack Long, V.M.D.*

In this chapter, holistic veterinarians discuss therapies for a number of serious problems of internal organs, including the pancreas, bladder, kidneys, and intestines. These therapies involve little or no surgery or drugs and are often much more successful than the more toxic therapies that are in wider use.

If your cat's disorder isn't mentioned in this chapter, or in any chapter of this book, don't despair. As I repeat often, nutrients are behind every biochemical reaction in the body. Call a holistic veterinarian listed at the back of the book and discuss your companion's disorder.

Diabetes

Diabetes overtakes your cat if her pancreas becomes unable to secrete enough insulin to maintain a normal blood sugar balance. Diabetes can cause convulsions and death. Traditional treatment can be successful in controlling the diabetes, at least for a time. But, as will be discussed, this traditional treatment has drawbacks that often lead orthodox veterinarians to suggest that owners consider euthanasia. You will see that the newer therapies detailed here do not tend to have these drawbacks.

Symptoms of Diabetes

It is imperative that you don't ignore the symptoms of diabetes. Not only can diabetes be a killer directly, it can also lead to liver enlargement (the liver can actually double in size), kidney damage, and cataracts, among other serious problems.

Your pet's appetite can be a symptom: He may become a glutton. At the same time he's eating more, however, he may start losing weight. (This does not mean an obese animal cannot develop diabetes. The disease is as common in obese pets as it is in obese people.) He may also develop increased thirst, spending more time at his water bowl, lapping furiously. If these symptoms appear, don't think of them as "odd changes in habits." They could be the only warning you'll ever get that your cat has diabetes.

The Difference between Orthodox and Holistic Approaches to Diabetes

Standard medical treatment involves introducing insulin from *outside* the body for the lifetime of the cat. Holistic vetcrinary treatment involves rebuilding the total health of the body, particularly the pancreas, so that it can again naturally produce enough of its *own* insulin—*inside* the body—just as it always did before it got diabetes.

Insulin shots are expensive and have to be maintained throughout the pet's life. They do not always work. (Some veterinarians have told me it would be more accurate if I wrote that "they *many times* do not work.") Their rigid scheduling can make an owner a slave to the pet's sickness. (Scheduling of nutritional supplements is not so crucial and allows the owner more freedom.) For these reasons and others mentioned in the next paragraph, some orthodox veterinary books for the public have stated that you might be better off putting your diabetic companion permanently "to sleep."

Insulin introduced artificially into your cat's body makes him continually vulnerable to diabetic shock, which can be fatal. This is called an insulin reaction: If you are not around to give your pet immediate emergency help, he may die. (If your cat is on insulin, *please* be sure to have your veterinarian tell you when insulin shock is most likely to occur, what signs to look for, and what emergency help you can give.) This is another fact that leads an owner either to become a slave to a diabetic pet, sometimes rearranging work and sleep schedules to be nearby when diabetic shock might be expected, or to dispose of the pet entirely.

Once a natural therapy allows the cat to be removed completely from insulin, of course, the owner need no longer worry about the possibility of insulin shock.

At its best—when insulin controls diabetes without side effects—it does only that: It controls the diabetes. It does nothing for the degenerative changes in the body that caused the diabetes in the first place, that are still preventing the body from creating its own insulin naturally, and that are probably causing other health problems as well. An overall holistic approach will attack the cause of the diabetes (a chemically imbalanced body), rather than just trying to control the diabetes, which is only a *symptom* of the imbalance. In this way, the body usually will again be able to form enough of its own insulin. You may also very well find that your cat suddenly recovers from other, seemingly unrelated, health problems as well. A number of case histories in this book tell of cats who recovered not only from the problem their people were concerned about, but also from disorders they had no idea could be connected, disorders that were coming from the same imbalances in the cat's body.

Holistic Therapies for Diabetes

In this section, I will focus on therapies presently used by two holistic veterinarians. In some details the approaches may seem different, but in those details the two doctors are using different therapies that have the same results: changing the biochemistry of the body back to its original ability to produce enough insulin on its own.

Ihor John Basko, D.V.M., summarizing his basic therapy for cats with diabetes, says, "I use diet change, acupuncture at the points on the body known to stimulate insulin production, and Chinese herbs." The last two therapies have thousands of years of empiric evidence behind them, and have recently undergone scientific study by Western terms.

"We put the cats on a natural diet," Dr. Basko continues, echoing the words of every veterinarian over the years who has spoken to me about prevention or treatment of any disease. "We give them foods that help stimulate the natural secretion of insulin within the body. We try to get fresh pancreas from the butcher and give it to the cat. We use other fresh organ meats, such as liver, and other meats and some fresh fish. We also give the cats vegetables that help stimulate insulin, such as string beans."

For the herbal part of his treatment, Dr. Basko uses ginseng. "Not ginseng alone," he says, "but in combination with other herbs, which I choose individually according to the individual animal."

Dr. Basko tells of Stuart, a cat with diabetes, who, the veterinarian says, is a typical case history of cats he treats with this disorder. "Stuart had been to conventional veterinarians, and he was having to have increasingly higher doses of insulin. And with the increasingly high doses, his people were getting more and more alarmed." The need to give more and more insulin to keep the cat at "where he used to be" is common when insulin is introduced into the body from outside. "I think that's when most people bring their cats to me," Dr. Basko says. As mentioned in the introduction, the higher success of holistic veterinary medicine can be seen as particularly amazing in light of the fact that these veterinarians often don't get to see a pet until he's very far along in a disease.

Stuart was being fed a popular veterinarian-recommended commercial cat food, and Dr. Basko comments that he wishes more people would realize that these diets "should be treated like a serious disease." He adds that "in many cases, if the veterinarians had just changed the diet, the cat would never have needed insulin shots." (The veterinarian adds that dry foods especially contain improperly balanced carbohydrates that overload the pancreas.)

"But with Stuart," Dr. Basko continues, "we were not only dealing with advanced diabetes, we were dealing also with a problem of insulin dependency. It can take us from six weeks to six months to get the cat over that dependency, depending on how long the cat's been on the insulin, although we usually can do it within six to eight weeks. In Stuart's case, with the acupuncture, the diet, and the ginseng combination, we were able to *start* lowering his insulin dose after a week or two, lowering it 30 percent every two weeks until Stuart was on about one-fourth of what he had been on when he was brought to us. And then we gradually kept on lowering it, until his dependency was completely over. Then we stopped the insulin entirely."

Dr. Basko adds that now Stuart's body is back to producing the normal amount of insulin that it produced before he came down with diabetes—and any need for insulin shots is only a nasty memory for his owners and for Stuart. You might want to know if the continuing holistic therapy that replaced the insulin is as expensive as insulin. There *is* no continuing holistic therapy—except a natural diet, which, as detailed in chapter 2, can be actually less expensive than a diet of toxins.

Remember that Stuart was Dr. Basko's typical case history of a cat treated by insulin before being taken to a holistic veterinarian. Remember also that Dr. Basko's typical case history of an animal treated early by a *holistic* veterinarian would be of a cat receiving a recommended change of diet and being sent home without any other therapy except herbal supplements and minerals.

An important warning: As holistic veterinarians warn elsewhere for other disorders, do not take it upon yourself to remove your cat from an orthodox therapy. Note, for instance, that Dr. Basko *gradually* withdraws cats from insulin shots as holistic therapy increases the cat's ability to produce her own insulin. It is crucial that there be at no time either too much or *too little* insulin introduced from outside the body, to balance the new amount your pet's body is producing. Monitoring insulin levels requires periodic scientific testing.

Norman C. Ralston, D.V.M., once pleaded with me to reemphasize the above point. "I just lost a wonderful cat," he said, sounding almost as pained as if the cat had been his own. "The owner decided to treat her animal herself because what I did seemed so simple. And it *was* simple—but she depended too long on her own treatment, without having the cat's insulin level professionally checked. The cat was rushed to emergency and died."

Complementing Dr. Basko's information, Neal K. Weiner, D.V.M., said, "I certainly try to persuade all owners to get our patients on fresh food diets; and I know what basic vitamins and minerals have been proven to work best for diabetes, but beyond that I tailor my protocol to my individual patient." This is, actually, a prime approach of holistic doctors in treating any disorder; and Dr. Basko, like Dr. Weiner, began his interview with me by saying, "We don't treat one diabetic cat like all diabetic cats. We treat them like individual animals."

"For the herbal part of my treatment," Dr. Weiner told me, "I'll often use Essiac tea, which is a combination of four herbs often used to treat cancer. It's a powerful detoxifier and immune-system strengthener. I show my clients how to brew the tea, and they mix it in with the cat's food. Or I may use a combination of herbs called Nonijuice, which is very, very wonderful for diabetes." Both these products are available, as I write, at some large health food stores. By the time you read this—if the present explosion of knowledge about natural therapies continues—you may well be able to go to the nearest drugstore and get these products.

"What I do before I choose my specific herbs," Dr. Weiner continued, "is to test the cat to find which herbs known to help diabetes have the most beneficial effect on the energy pattern of my individual patient's body, especially the pancreas and kidney." (The latter organ is often damaged in diabetes.) To test how various substances affect energy patterns, Dr. Weiner uses kinesiology, which is relied upon heavily these years by a number of other holistic veterinarians.

Dr. Weiner defined kinesiology—at least as used by holistic doctors: "I put the food or other substance I'm testing on the cat's back, and I have a surrogate touch the cat. The person tries to keep his or her arm straight. If the arm goes down—that is, if it is weakened— the energy of the food is drawing energy out of the cat's body."

Continuing his discussion of how he treats diabetes, Dr. Weiner added that "minerals are really important for insulin metabolism." He stated that he often uses a product called Sea Meal, which contains nineteen different seaweeds that are ground into a powder. This product, he said, "has a vast array of minerals that help in proper insulin metabolism." He recommended that Sea Meal, which is made by a company called Solid Gold, be given "at ⅛ a teaspoon for every fifteen pounds of the cat's body weight."

Dr. Weiner added that, "since diabetes deals with problems of the pancreas, I may put my patient on a pancreatic enzyme supplement to take the stress off the organ." (These enzymes were popular among holistic veterinarians in 1981.) He specifies that he often uses a product called Prozymes.

He almost always puts cats with diabetes on vitamin E, generally about 100 IU a day; 250 mg of vitamin C daily; and cod-liver oil. And he uses kinesiology to see which homeopathic remedy affects the cat's body energy most positively.

Dr. Weiner's reference to vitamin E leads us back to the first edition, in which I cited a number of studies that found this vitamin allowed 80 percent of people with diabetes to go off insulin entirely or drastically curtail its use. I think taking your time to detail this information here would be unnecessary. Any competent holistic veterinarian or M.D. will know of this research, as well as updates. For the same reasons I warned earlier about taking your cat off insulin and self-treating, I make the same strong warning here in reference to vitamin E. *Consult a holistic doctor.*

Fatty Liver Disease

Dr. Weiner told me that fatty liver disease usually occurs in cats who are overweight. "Then they go off their feed," he said, "perhaps because they're ill from another disorder, and all of a sudden they start to lose weight rapidly. The excess fat in their body gets metabolized down into the liver. All this fat tends to shut down that organ, and the cat won't eat at all."

Dr. Weiner said he used to see many cases of cats with fatty liver disease but hasn't happened to have seen any in some four or five years. "You have to tube-feed them, because they won't eat on their own," he said. "The cats that I used to see were all treated traditionally, because I couldn't convince their owners to try holistic therapy, except that I force-fed them a more *natural* diet." Dr. Weiner adds that he found those cats "very hard to treat."

On the other hand, Dr. Basko, who has more recent experience in treating cats with fatty liver disease and who has had the chance to use holistic therapy, has found that "changing the diet and adding vitamin E and other antioxidants can really help cats with this disease."

This veterinarian also blames the cat's "starting point" for fatty liver disease—obesity—on a diet too high in carbohydrates. He mentions two prepared foods very popular with owners who want to give high-quality food without actually feeding the natural diet as detailed in chapter 2. He also blames many cases of diabetes on these two commercially prepared dry foods.

Cystitis, Bladder Stones, Urinary Blockage (Feline Urological Syndrome)

Urological problems involve the kidneys and bladder, since urine is secreted from the first organs and stored in the latter. These disorders are painful and often life threatening. They are among the most common health problems in cats not fed their natural diet. Actually, some veterinarians state they are *the* most common.

With conventional therapy, these problems are expensive to treat. As Dr. Basko points out, the expense comes from the fact that "with traditional treatment, the problem doesn't clear up. The cat is put on antibiotics and various other drugs, and when the drugs are withdrawn, the problem just comes back." He says that orthodox veterinarians do recommend a low-ash diet, which is a correct recommendation, but that "all too often people keep on giving the cats dry foods," which are low-moisture and high-ash diets.

As we will see a bit later, cats treated holistically for urological problems can often be helped easily without drugs, surgery, or great expense. And there are seldom the relapses considered almost inevitable with conventional therapy. Actually, Dr. Basko wrote me that the only times cats relapse is when their owners return them to dry cat food.

First, though, I'd like to talk about prevention, even though I know you're probably not reading this unless your cat already has a urological problem. I have two reasons for this: One of the toughest problems holistic veterinarians tell me they face is to convince owners to use a natural diet; and it will be difficult at best to prevent the common recurrences without this diet.

Holistic veterinarians have told me for almost two decades that they rarely if ever see a case of feline urological syndrome (FUS) in cats raised basically according to the suggestions for a natural diet and supplements in chapters 2 and 4. Dr. Weiner told me, "If all cats were fed a fresh-food diet from very early in their lives, I believe the incidence of feline urological syndrome would probably be reduced 80 to 90 percent." He added that to the best of his knowledge, this syndrome "does not occur at all in the wild."

If you have read the early chapters on prevention, you already know *why* holistic veterinarians believe many diseases don't strike animals eating their natural diet in the wild—and seldom strike domesticated animals eating their natural diet even though the rest of their environment (a human's house) is unnatural. Adding information specific to FUS and dry diets (kibble), Dr. Weiner says that investigators studying cats in the wild have found that these cats "get almost all their moisture from the animals they eat, and so they drink very little water. A cat in the wild who drinks a fair amount of water, they say, already has a weakness in his body.

"So when domesticated cats eat a dry-based diet," Dr. Weiner continued, "they're getting very little moisture. This lack of moisture may weaken the kidneys." Dr. Basko explained further that cats can't drink enough water to supplement what's lacking in dry foods, and the kidneys attempt to work harder to accomplish their natural job of flushing out wastes from the body.

"Dry food is not an appropriate food for cats," the veterinarian states strongly. "I'd say that 95 percent of the holistic veterinarians I know acknowledge that fact." You may have an obvious question here: Then why in the world are there so many dry foods for cats? Dr. Basko has a succinct answer: "Because most of the research is done in veterinary colleges that are supported by money from big pet food companies, and it is convenient and fast to feed."

Dr. Basko's strong words about dry foods led me to a question I asked Dr. Weiner in a later interview: What about the top-quality purer prepared dry foods recommended (reluctantly) by some holistic veterinarians to owners who for various reasons don't feel they can give their cat his natural diet? Would these foods be as likely to lead to FUS in a cat? Dr. Weiner's answer indicated that, while they certainly are less detrimental to the cat's general health than commercial dry foods are, they still have the same problem of lack of moisture.

Dr. Weiner adds another reason, besides moisture, that a natural diet prevents urological problems. "Those cats out there in the wild are eating their kill; they're eating a lot of meat. Meat creates an acid urine, and bladder and kidney stones simply can't form in an acid urine." (In chapters 2 and 4, we pointed out that the healthy pH of a cat's body—to help keep *all* problems away—is acidic.) "But many commercial foods have a lot of grains, and grains create an alkaline urine." An alkaline urine will allow stones to form. In addition, Dr. Weiner points out that, of course, "commercial cat and dog foods have more debris and toxins that the kidneys have to filter out, which can also weaken them."

Symptoms of FUS

Your cat may run to his litter box a lot more frequently than usual. He may strain, trying hard to pass urine—and yet on many of these trips he may pass little or none. The reason for this behavior is that the itching and burning of the urethra, which carries urine out of the body, make the cat think he has to urinate extremely often, when in reality he doesn't.

If this symptom of cystitis is left untreated, the urethra will plug up, and your pet won't be able to urinate even when he has to. Or your cat may forget all his manners about where you have taught him he is supposed to urinate and start urinating wherever he happens to be at the time. There may be blood in the urine. As Dr. Ralston has emphasized, these last symptoms "may be an emergency, and the pet should be rushed immediately to a veterinarian." These symptoms indicate urinary blockage. (For more on urinary blockage, see the section later in this chapter.)

Male cats, because of body structure, may exhibit the earlier signs of FUS for only a day or two before they advance to the emergency state of urinary blockage. So if your companion is a male cat who has been on a commercial diet, keep an eye out for the early symptom of straining without urinating and treat that symptom as an emergency.

Cystitis

For a case history, let me take you back in time to 1980, when I was grappling with early work on the first edition of this book. My literary agent, Denise, called me about her cat, Agnes, who was on her third bout of cystitis. "I have always done what the veterinarian prescribed," she told me. "I gave her the antibiotic once a day for a month and the acidifier twice a day for two months. As soon as I stop the acidifier, she just gets the cystitis symptoms all over again. Now the veterinarian says Agnes may have to stay on the two drugs indefinitely. Do any of the nutritional veterinarians you're writing about have any solutions?"

As you see in this section, today holistic veterinarians have plenty of natural therapies from which to choose the best for the individual cat. But at the time, in 1980, my early research had come across only vitamin C as a simple natural treatment for cystitis. Knowing that this vitamin's use for disorders like cystitis already had decades of research to back up this use, I suggested that Denise ask her veterinarian to consider using it.

Denise called again the next day. "As I suspected," she said dryly, "he doesn't *know* anything about vitamin C and cystitis, and so he doesn't believe in it, and so he won't try it."

At that moment, I knew of only one holistic veterinarian who answered questions by phone, and I knew of no holistic veterinarians who lived close enough to Denise so that she could take Agnes directly to the doctor. (Today the number of holistic veterinarians around the country has grown greatly, and many of them tell me that much, if not most, of their work is done by phone consultation.)

Denise called the one consulting holistic veterinarian I knew about, and that brief call resulted in Denise giving Agnes 500 mg of vitamin C (in the ascorbic acid form) every four hours around the clock, crushing the tablets up in her pet's food, until the symptoms disappeared. Then she gave Agnes, as a maintenance therapy, 500 mg only twice a day.

When I later asked Denise about Agnes, the cat still remained free of the cystitis that had attacked her three times before the simple vitamin C treatment.

"I still can't get over how quickly those vitamin C tablets worked and how much cheaper they are than the drug therapy," Denise told me. When Denise and I counted up what she had paid for both therapies, we found that the cost of the drug therapy, which didn't work, was more than *ten times* that of the natural therapy, which did work.

How does vitamin C help in curing cystitis? This disorder is caused by a virus, and the secondary infections accompanying cystitis are caused by bacteria. As covered in the chapter on infectious diseases, vitamin C is effective against virtually all, if not all, types of viruses and bacteria. Also, vitamin C, in the form of ascorbic *acid*, makes the urine *acidic*, which we have explained is what cats need. (Remember that Agnes kept getting into trouble when the *drug* prescribed as an acidifier was removed.)

For this new edition, however, Dr. Basko warns that vitamin C alone will probably not be enough to prevent recurrence of cystitis indefinitely. "Cats have to have Chinese herbs," he says, referring to a combination of these herbs that, he says, "remove the problem in from the kidney, not just the bladder. They remove predigested products that eventually form stones. They help acidify the bladder and heal the bladder's lining." The veterinarian adds that these herbs, plus the maintenance level of vitamin C that Agnes was being given, will result in a permanent control for cats.

Many holistic veterinarians have expressed concern to me that some owners don't keep up prescribed maintenance doses of nutrients. Dr. Ralston once made this strong warning about cystitis and other disorders: "An owner can become too confident that everything is all right, discontinue maintenance—and end up with a dead animal."

Another word of warning: Although Agnes' treatment seems simple, do not treat your cat yourself until your veterinarian has established that she has cystitis and cystitis only. For the dangers involved, see the section later on urinary blockage. Remember that Denise not only had a clear diagnosis of cystitis, but she also consulted by phone with a nutritional veterinarian for her cat's correct nutritional therapy.

Dr. Weiner gives his therapy for cystitis. Like Dr. Basko and other nutritional veterinarians, he will get the cat off dry foods and on a low-ash diet and will try hard to convince the owner to use the cat's natural diet. "And I definitely get cats on vitamin C, 250 to 500 mg a day. I use cod-liver oil and vitamin E." The oil is a good source of many nutrients, especially vitamin A. Vitamin E, known to prevent scars, is helpful in cystitis because it aids in preventing and healing scarring of the bladder. "I will often give a product called Rentean, which has a number of different herbs that are very good for restoring health to the kidneys. For cats I tend to use herbs in a glycerine base, instead of capsules." As have other holistic veterinarians who talked with me, Dr. Weiner has found that cats take to the sweet taste of the glycerine and will readily eat glycerine-based products, but will refuse a product in an alcohol base, even if it is diluted. The veterinarian will also use various homeopathic remedies chosen for the needs of the specific patient.

Dr. Basko's initial therapy for cystitis includes the Chinese herb combination he spoke of earlier for maintenance therapy. He says that this combination "works like a charm with or without antibiotics and with or without acupuncture." He adds that he uses antibiotics "very rarely, maybe 10 percent of the time." Acupuncture eases the pain that cystitis causes, "and I use oral vitamin C to flush out the kidneys and bladder. I recommend Ester-C, 100 mg twice a day." The veterinarian also uses antioxidant nutrients.

Dr. Basko says that if the cat is refusing to eat, he makes a kind of a "milkshake" of raw liver, tomato juice, and purified water. "I put that in a blender," he says, "and the cat will usually drink that straight out. I may also mix a little bit of fresh carrot juice or wheat grass juice in there. Carrot juice has a lot of vitamin A, which is good for the bladder lining."

J. Keith Benedict, D.V.M., once pointed out that a liquid diet, which of course the above is, "allows the system to clean itself out."

Dr. Benedict also used the herb stinging nettle to treat cystitis. You may want to ask your holistic veterinarian about this herb. (It, or another herb that has the same effects, may be in some of the herbal combinations these doctors are using today.) "This herb makes the cat feel warm," Dr. Benedict said. If you've ever had cystitis, you may know that a feeling of "freezing to death" can be one of the most frightening symptoms. "Stinging nettle also gives the cat a feeling of well-being, and it helps tame the bladder spasms," the veterinarian added.

Bladder and Kidney Stones

Both Dr. Basko and Dr. Weiner say that they use the same therapies for stones as they do for cystitis, covered above. However, the first step now must be to flush out the bladder or kidney by giving a large amount of liquid intravenously. Dr. Basko states that instead of putting painkillers in the liquid, as orthodox veterinarians do, he uses acupuncture and massages the area. Acupuncture and massage are well-proven techniques to help pain without dangerous side effects.

Vitamin C (in the form of ascorbic acid) helps keep the urine acidic. And an acidic urine can actually dissolve stones, which are alkaline. Keeping the cat on a small amount of ascorbic acid after recovery—that is, keeping the urine acidic—is one reason holistic veterinarians don't have the recurrence of stones that is so common with drug therapy.

Urinary Blockage

Complete urinary blockage is an emergency situation. The retention of urine, and its waste products, causes poisoning throughout the body that results in death in forty-eight hours *or less*. The bladder can be so swollen with trapped urine that it is as hard as a stone—and as large as a big orange. (Imagine how much space that would take up in a diminutive body.) A badly swollen bladder can rupture.

The preceding explains why I said earlier that you must have a solid diagnosis of cystitis before you try a simple home treatment. If what you are really dealing with is urinary blockage, you will have a dead cat within two days.

The first step in treating urinary blockage, as with stones, is to flush out the bladder. This removes the "sand" collected in the urethra (the canal that carries urine out of the body) and allows the urine to flow again. This release of the urine also relieves pressure on the kidneys, which is a problem with urinary blockage. The "sand," by the way, is caused by bits of bladder stones passing out of the bladder.

Dr. Weiner says that when he is dealing with *complete* urinary blockage, "I have a cat with an immediately life-threatening situation. So I unblock him the fastest way possible—which is surgery." Once the surgery has released the stored-up urine and debris from the body, "Then I try to convince the owners to put the cat on a fresh-food diet, and I give the animal vitamin C and cod-liver oil. I add Sea Meal for minerals. And then I'll test the cat's body. Depending on what I find the individual animal's body needs, I may use the herbal combination Nonijuice or the herbal formula Rentean. And I'll use whatever homeopathic remedies the cat needs."

Dr. Basko offers a special diet for a cat recovering from urinary blockage: It includes fresh raw beef liver, kidney, or heart several times a week. Also included are cooked chicken, cottage cheese, raw egg yolks (no whites), and whole grain cereals. Do not give dry food, milk, or any food containing fish. Sharp-eyed readers will see a bit of a difference here (*no* fish, and *cooked* chicken) from the recommendations made in chapter 2, but remember that the diet covered in that chapter is to prevent disease. When a disease has developed, holistic doctors may have to modify the preventive diet according to the new needs of the cat's body.

Ask your cat's doctor if you should give your recovering pet distilled water. A number of holistic veterinarians have told me it can help leach out of the body the harmful debris that may be clogging up the bladder. Others have pointed out that it also is free of the impurities in tap water, which can cause even further harm to an already weakened animal. I ask you to question a holistic veterinarian before using distilled water because several doctors have warned me that if it is used too early in the treatment of a highly toxic animal, its leaching effect may create stone formation as the body rids itself—perhaps too fast—of toxic wastes.

The following case history recently given me of a cat with FUS is representative of a fact I mention often in this book: that sometimes natural therapy works so well and so easily that even seasoned holistic veterinarians are amazed. It is also representative of another fact I mention often: that holistic veterinarians prefer to "tamper" as little as possible—even using natural, nontoxic remedies—with an animal's innate healing powers, if the cat or dog's body regains its own healing powers after only a primitive, initial therapy.

Fernando came to the offices of John Fudens, D.V.M., in March 1996. He's a male, altered tabby cat who was seven and a half years old at the time. "He had quite a long history of FUS," Dr. Fudens told me, including the serious problem of urinary blockage. Fernando's body was also highly toxic due to vaccines and numerous drugs given him in an attempt to treat the FUS. Because of the long-standing disease, and the history of toxic drugs, "I thought Fernando and I would have a lot more problems than we did," Dr. Fudens told me.

The veterinarian continued: "The only thing I did with Fernando was to put him on a natural diet and my usual regimen to detoxify animals of a heavy use of vaccines and drugs." (That regimen consists of a homeopathic remedy: liver and immune extracts, lotus seed, and bioflavanoid.) Usually, once the detoxification is accomplished, Dr. Fudens goes on to treat the cat's disorder (FUS, in this case) more directly.

"But," the veterinarian told me, "in Fernando's case, the initial detoxification has been all he has needed. I mean, the cat has been absolutely perfect for over two years now."

Kidney Problems: Chronic Interstitial Nephritis, Uremia, and Renal Failure

Chronic interstitial nephritis, a serious kidney inflammation, is common among older cats not raised on natural diets. It is so common that many veterinarians believe that testing for kidney function should be run routinely on the older animal.

The most common symptom is that the pet drinks increasingly more water and excretes increasingly more pale or colorless urine. As the disease progresses, the animal may have bouts of vomiting, constipation, or diarrhea. When these latter signs appear, your pet may have uremia and may be struggling to get along with only 30 percent kidney function. Uremia is poisoning of the entire body caused by accumulation in the bloodstream of waste products that are normally helped out of the body by healthy kidneys.

Drs. Basko and Weiner recommend the following basic diet to treat kidney inflammation: a low-residual diet with less animal protein than the cat should have when he is healthy. Dr. Weiner stresses, though, that a cat still needs a lot of protein. "While a cat in normal health should get 60 percent to 70 percent of his diet in the form of protein, for a cat with kidney inflammation, I might reduce it to 50 percent."

Richard J. Kearns, D.V.M., once explained that the reason for the two dietary changes (less protein and less residue) in an animal with kidney inflammation is that you now must give the animal food that will take as much strain as possible off the kidney. "You have to help the body produce as little waste as possible, so that the kidney is asked to do the minimum of work to reduce that waste." He added that in cutting down the protein, you must make sure that the protein you do give is of very high quality. (Remember that most, if not all, commercial pet foods have very low-quality protein.)

Dr. Kearns also explained that a low-residual diet includes such foods as chicken and turkey, well-ground and well-cooked grains, rice, squash, and greens.

In a recent interview, Dr. Weiner gave his therapy for chronic interstitial nephritis: "I use a homeopathic remedy, nux vomica, that helps detoxify and cleanse the kidneys. I also give cats a product called Renafood, made by Standard Process, which is a glandular extract that goes in and helps not only to detoxify, but to rebuild, the kidneys. The cats get one tablet a day." Dr. Weiner added that he also uses a product called Rentean, "an herbal formula that helps rebuild and strengthen the kidneys." Or, according to the particular needs of the individual cat, he may use the herbal formula Nonijuice.

"We usually have the owners administer fluids underneath the skin two to three times a week at home," Dr. Weiner added, "to help the kidneys flush out the toxins. We give them an intravenous set with lactated Ringer's, and we teach them how to use it." (Dr. Weiner was talking about that bottle of clear liquid you often see attached to the arm of patients.)

For animals who already have the often fatal uremia when brought to them, Drs. Robert and Marty Goldstein told me in 1981 a few details of what they used, including orthodox therapy and kidney extract, a form of glandular therapy. When a diuretic was necessary, they used herbal diuretics rather than drugs. Dr. Basko said that he uses the same technique today, but would add "intravenous fluids, vitamin C, B complex, and acupuncture."

For uremia, Dr. Weiner says, "I use the same treatment as for chronic interstitial nephritis, except that I administer fluids more frequently."

I asked Dr. Weiner for a case history of a cat with uremia that he treated with holistic therapy. Please keep in mind here that uremia is often fatal when treated by orthodox means. Instead of talking about a specific cat, Dr. Weiner said, "The case histories of these animals are almost always the same, because usually, with uremia, we find that three-quarters of both kidneys are no longer functioning. The cats come in to us on the brink of death, but we can get them comfortable and happy again and give them six months to a year and a half of an extended life—and a nice one."

Robert J. Silver, D.V.M., gave me a case history of a cat with decompensated renal (kidney) failure. The words *kidney failure* certainly give us an indication that, by almost all rights, this cat should have died.

"This is Fluffy," Dr. Silver told me, "a nineteen-year-old domestic longhaired female cat who had been relatively healthy throughout her life." Already she had beaten the odds—right?—so you wouldn't expect her to beat the odds once again when finally stricken with a life-threatening disease at her ancient age. "In the last year or two," Dr. Silver continued, "she had started drinking and urinating more. When I ran the requisite blood tests and urinalyses, I found that Fluffy had decompensated renal failure. We treated this aggressively with herbs, diet, acupuncture, and subcutaneous fluids—and we were able to bring Fluffy back from death's doorstep, so to speak. She was now doing quite well, active, eating well, drinking and urinating normally."

What happened to Fluffy after she "miraculously" survived kidney failure? Did she go on to die soon afterward, as we might expect—if for no other reason than her very advanced age of nineteen? No, Fluffy lived on to provide a successful case history in the chapter on crippling disorders when her owners became concerned that she couldn't leap easily anymore onto her favorite perch on the windowsill. If you have ever had the misfortune—and I hope you haven't—of losing your cat to an almost always fatal problem, I know you would have loved to have had the luxury of later being concerned about a small problem such as Fluffy eventually developed.

Worms and Other Problems of the Intestines

As we will see in this section, an exciting new type of natural products called probiotics has made the treatment of intestinal problems—as well as disorders that we may not think of as stemming from something wrong in the intestines—much easier to treat successfully. This is true not only for our beloved cats but for ourselves. And the reason these products work so well makes supreme common sense medically.

Intestinal Worms

Intestinal worms sap your pet's strength by gobbling up his food and thereby robbing his body of nutrients. These worms also feed on your cat's blood and can damage intestinal tissue. A heavily infested cat can die.

An animal can become infected by intestinal worms through the mouth or through the skin. He may swallow a worm egg, or he may eat a transport host, such as a mouse, that is carrying worms. Worms can enter the skin by way of bloodsucking insects such as mosquitoes or ticks. A kitten can be born with worms passed on by his mother, or he may become infected by her while he is nursing. (If you are owned by a pregnant cat as you read this, see chapter 4 for information on how to help prevent her from passing on worms to her babies.)

SYMPTOMS OF WORMS. It is imperative that you have your veterinarian make regular fecal checks, since the most dangerous worms cannot be seen by the eye. However, you can also take a look at the feces every several days. If you see squiggly things moving around, or if you see what looks like grains of rice, those are roundworms or tapeworms. (Of course, if you have recently fed your cat rice, which we recommend in the early chapters as a healthy food, those things that look like grains of rice may actually *be* grains of rice. So, in order not to give yourself an unnecessary scare, make your inspection some days after Princess has had rice.)

You will not be able to see hookworms or whipworms in the stool. These two types are the most dangerous. Dr. Ralston warns that hookworms can kill very quickly. *So if you see any of the FOLLOWING symptoms—and don't see the signs of worms in the feces—take a sample of the feces to your veterinarian immediately for microscopic testing.*

In kittens, a common symptom of worms is a skeletonlike little body accompanied, peculiarly enough, by a potbelly sticking out of the skeleton. The entity is a skeleton because the worms have been gobbling up his nutrients. The potbelly comes from the direct damage the worms do physically, which causes weak muscles, gas, and fluid buildup.

A kitten or adult cat with worms may also suffer from diarrhea and/or convulsions. There may be loss of appetite, or there may be a huge increase in appetite.

A cat with worms may drag his "behind" along the floor, trying to get rid of the worms around his anus. (Carvel G. Tiekert, D.V.M., once pointed out that dragging the anal area is much more often the result of an anal sac problem than the result of worms. But the latter problem, too, requires the attention of a veterinarian.) Or the animal may try to achieve the same result by licking excessively at the anal area.

WHAT YOU SHOULD *NOT* DO FOR YOUR CAT WITH WORMS. Don't buy a chemical dewormer and use it yourself. If you give your cat such a dewormer, let it be at least by prescription of a veterinarian who supervises its administration. Even then, Dr. Ralston has warned, "please be sure you inform the doctor if you have been giving your pet any medication whatsoever—for worms or for any other problem. Because what your veterinarian might give your pet for worms, in combination with whatever drug you may have been giving him, might kill him."

To give a specific tragic example regarding a kitten: A wild mother cat once chose my friend Nick as an adoptive parent for her children, whom she apparently had no intention of settling down long enough to raise. While pregnant, she was, it seems, casing Nick for his suitability to raise her prospective kittens; she was often seen loitering at safe distances from the house while he ministered to the numerous pets he already had.

Then, one midnight, a wild clamoring was struck up in Nick's basement. When Nick ran down, he saw the cat hanging tenaciously on to a screen door. Using her entire body with all her might, she was swinging the door back and forth to make a loud banging.

Having in this unique manner caught Nick's attention, the wild mother leaped off the door and disappeared—never to be seen again. She had left, at the foot of the door where Nick would be sure not to overlook them, her six tiny kittens.

No adoptive parent ever took better care of his charges. One kitten seemed dead shortly after birth; Nick resuscitated her—at a time when virtually nobody knew how to do that—and eventually nursed her to a healthy adulthood.

But another kitten developed worms. Nick did what at the time all of us had been led to believe, through advertising, was the proper thing to do. He got a dewormer at the supermarket.

For years afterward, Nick would periodically agonize, interrupting conversations about something completely different: "She died right in my hand. I swear I did exactly what the instructions said. But she died right in my hand."

Dr. Ralston once told me, "I have seen many similar tragic cases."

Until now, we have been talking about your using chemical dewormers yourself. Are the chemical dewormers used by orthodox veterinarians also dangerous? Yes. They are poisons, too. And any poison strong enough to kill a lot of healthy worms is strong enough to kill a cat whose health has been weakened by those worms. (However, your veterinarian's individualized prescription and follow-up should help decrease the risks of treating your cat on your own.)

You can help your cat's body detoxify itself of the poisons in standard dewormers by giving him vitamin C before, during, and for two or more weeks after the deworming, according to some holistic veterinarians. Pancreatic enzymes can also be very important.

One veterinarian said he thought the chemical dewormers have become less poisonous in recent years, but a poison is still a poison. These days, I have had trouble finding chemical dewormers in supermarkets. Maybe one reason they have become less poisonous is that they have become less available for the public to administer without the advice of a veterinarian? I much more easily find herbal dewormers in health food stores, but even they might cause a problem for your cat unless you at least call a holistic veterinarian and discuss your individual cat.

Now let's see how holistic veterinarians get rid of worms without poisoning them—and therefore without risking the poisoning of your cat.

Therapy for Worms

Dr. Weiner told me he has in recent years found a natural product, a probiotic called Nature's Biotics, "that works to get rid of all types of intestinal worms."*

If you're extremely skeptical of natural medicine, you may be saying right now: "Oh, sure, a miracle product." As I say often in this book, although the results of nutritional medicine may often *seem* like miracles because they are results we have been led not to expect, they are based on solid medical knowledge.

Dr. Weiner began our interview with an accepted medical fact: "A healthy intestinal tract has a certain known balance of the proper bacteria and flora and fauna." The idea of *proper* bacteria may seem jolting, because all we ever hear about are "bad" bacteria. But if you took a course in biology in high school, you may remember that there are some bacteria, called "friendly" bacteria, that are necessary for good health.

"The only way worms can get into the intestinal tract," Dr. Weiner continued, "is when these bacteria and other organisms are out of balance." So how do probiotics like Nature's Biotics get all these or-

---

* Dr. Basko adds that veterinarians can obtain a Chinese herbal formula, Aquillaria, from Health Concerns Co. that "can be used long-term to treat and control worms of all types."

ganisms to be balanced in the intestines? Very quickly, very simply, and by way of supreme common sense: This product *is* the organisms in proper balance—combined with, as Dr. Weiner said, "all the right trace minerals and vitamins needed to make these organisms grow properly."

Dr. Weiner continued: "When you get the intestinal flora working properly, the worms just get flushed out—no matter what type of worm they are." Actually, since this natural product gets rid of the underlying *cause* of the problem (which, as I've often pointed out, is always the goal of holistic medicine), it can rid the cat not only of intestinal worms but of other intestinal problems as well, as we discuss a bit later.

When Dr. Weiner first described this product to me, I had a fleeting bizarre vision of having to deal with a bunch of horrible wiggly entities and trying somehow to get them into my dogs' intestines. If you had the same fleeting thought, you may have realized quickly that these organisms are microscopic, so you don't even know you're looking at them. And, of course, all food goes through the intestines. So, as Dr. Weiner explained, owners simply put a certain amount of the product on the cat's food once a day.

Other Intestinal Problems—and Beyond

As I mentioned, since Nature's Biotics and other probiotics restore the natural balance of organisms to the intestines, they can take care of other intestinal problems besides worms. Also, as Dr. Weiner pointed out, "There's a basic holistic belief that the *overall* health of a cat, a dog, or a human is very dependent upon a properly functioning intestinal tract. And if you get the proper balance of organisms back in the intestines, many health problems will be eliminated, and a lot of time and money can be saved by not using other therapies that now become unnecessary."

Dr. Weiner shared the case history of Sandra, a tabby cat who was brought to him with several health problems, including diarrhea and vomiting that had plagued her a long time. "I chose Sandra to talk to your readers about," the veterinarian said, "because she is typical of how my treatment commonly goes with cats with problems like this. Kinesiological testing told me that Sandra had chemical toxicity and weakness in her large intestines. It also told me which vitamins and minerals she was deficient in. So I gave her a homeopathic remedy to detoxify the chemical toxicity. In this case I used nux vomica, as I often do. But, according to the needs of the individual cat, I may use the herbal combination called Nonijuice." These products are discussed earlier in the chapter. He chose Sandra's nutritional supplements, of course, according to what his testing had revealed she needed.

"We found that the weakness in Sandra's large intestines was due to the fact that she was on a commercial cat food. So we recommended a more natural diet, adding digestive enzymes and probiotics. Often, we find that cats' symptoms can be traced, at least in part, to a sensitivity to the standard vaccines they've been given. But in Sandra's case, this didn't turn out to be true. If it had, I would have given her a homeopathic remedy that can detoxify these effects." (For more on vaccines, see chapter 3.)

"Sandra's long-standing bout with vomiting typically occurred very shortly after she ate," Dr. Weiner continued, "a fact that made me strongly suspect that the cat was allergic to something she was commonly being fed. We found that Sandra was allergic to a couple of common allergens, and we changed her diet to one that didn't contain them.

"So, after my testing, I gave Sandra's people my recommendations for the treatments they could give her themselves at home, and Sandra was on her way out of my office. As is typical, Sandra's owners called me six months later, saying, 'God! Her hair coat is shiny, and she's more alert and active than she's been in years.' " Since I have spent several decades working closely with holistic doctors and using holistic therapy for myself, my husband, and our animal companions, I was not at all surprised to hear that Sandra's people were reporting resolution of problems they didn't even ask Dr. Weiner to treat. After all, Sandra had been sick for so long with vomiting and diarrhea when they took her to Dr. Weiner that they weren't worried about "little" problems like an unhealthy-looking coat and a lack of joy of life.

I knew what Dr. Weiner's answer would be, but to give you an official answer, I asked him anyway: "But what about the long-standing diarrhea and vomiting?"

"Oh, that, too, of course," Dr. Weiner answered. "They said that Sandra's been free of those problems for quite some time now."

Dr. Long recently wrote me that he, too, uses probiotics—although, unlike Dr. Weiner, he didn't stress any specific product. He did add the information that plain yogurt can provide probiotics, but that powdered preparations are more concentrated. In other words, a small amount is likely to work better and faster. He suggested mixing the powdered form into food at a dose of ⅛ to ¼ a teaspoon twice a day, depending on whether you have a small or large cat.

Dr. Long also provided further details on how and why probiotics help many health problems, not only those of the intestines: "Probiotic (or 'friendly') bacteria produce enzymes that help digest food material and kill pathologic bacteria and viruses, which might otherwise be absorbed from the intestines into the body as a whole," he said.

"I have found probiotic supplements to be helpful in inflammatory conditions of the intestinal tract, such as inflammatory bowel disease and colitis," Dr. Long commented.

He will give supplementary enzymes and dietary fiber along with probiotics.

Dr. Weiner pointed out that, like many of the "really powerful health-promoting products," probiotics work well for both animals and humans. He mentioned chronic fatigue syndrome in humans, for instance. "When you get the intestines back to a normal balance, the person no longer has the puzzling array of symptoms known as chronic fatigue syndrome."

Chapter 10

Heart Problems and Hypertension

"I estimate that, using natural therapies, I successfully treat cats with early to moderate heart disease 97 to 98 percent of the time.

"In treating hypertension, I have almost complete success."

—*Norman C. Ralston, D.V.M.*

"I've had cases of heart disease that were absolutely given up on by other veterinarians, because the cardiograms indicated there was no hope. Natural therapy has improved the animals' health greatly and has given them years more of life."

—*Michael W. Lemmon, D.V.M.*

"Natural therapy has much greater success with heartworms than orthodox therapy—at least it surely does for me. It's so much more satisfying when you get successful results, and the cat doesn't have toxic side effects."

—*S. Allen Price, D.V.M.*

Heart Problems

Norman C. Ralston, D.V.M., who worked closely with me for this chapter—and who reports some 97 to 98 percent success in treating early to moderate heart disease in cats and dogs—gave himself as an example of the success natural therapy can have with the *late stages* of the type of heart disease that has traditionally been common in cats. "In 1976," he said, "I was so ill with congestive heart failure that I couldn't walk across the street and back without sitting down to rest. Now I can work in my clinic, standing up, for twelve hours without stopping." Dr. Ralston talked to me about this some twenty-two years after he probably "should have" died. When we talked, he was seventy-eight.

Traditionally, cats have most commonly been stricken with cardiomyopathy, a thickening of the muscles of the heart. The animals are usually born with this condition, and it keeps getting worse and worse. As Jan Bellows, D.V.M., once explained to me, "This congenital problem can develop into a congestive type of heart failure, where fluids are retained in the body. Or the heart muscles can become dilated—which is a *very* serious condition."

One veterinarian told me that cardiomyopathy has vastly declined in cats in recent years. Dr. Price said that the disease was being caused by the processed foods most people feed their cats. As covered in chapter 1, these commercial foods are cooked, which removes many essential nutrients. One essential nutrient that was always lost was taurine, an amino acid that was discovered only recently. The cardiomyopathy was being caused by a taurine deficiency. The decline in this disease comes from the fact that the amino acid is now being added back to processed foods.

However, Dr. Ralston recently warned of another heart problem that he said affects virtually every cat he sees in his clinic: "Their hearts are pulsing at 30, 37, 40," he told me. "They should be pulsing at 12." (As we'll detail, the heart's pulse is not to be confused with its beat.) "I'd say that 90 percent of the cats I see are pulsing at 20 or above," he said. "I had a cat the other day whose heart was pulsing at 42. That told me he was close to having a convulsion."

What makes a heart's pulse race? "The heart takes over when something is not functioning somewhere else," Dr. Ralston explains. "Say the thyroid gland or the adrenal gland isn't working right. When the heart takes over the pulse effect, that increases the blood pressure, which of course can cause a stroke."

The veterinarian stressed that, unlike the *beats* of a heart, the *pulses* cannot be picked up by listening through a stethoscope. "You have to find some other way to detect the pulsing. I use kinesiology." This technique is relied upon heavily by a number of holistic veterinarians for analyzing the body's health.

Dr. Ralston adds that "all cats' and dogs' hearts should pulse at 12. So should yours and mine." While speeding heart pulses especially strike cats, they are not uncommon in dogs and in people, Dr. Ralston says.

Symptoms of Heart Problems

Even if your cat seems healthy, he should have periodic examinations. Heart problems can't always be properly diagnosed without sophisticated diagnostic tools. But trouble can develop between examinations. So that you will know when you should report any possible problems to your veterinarian, this section discusses some symptoms you can watch out for.

Check your cat's legs. Swelling may indicate a heart problem, the swelling being a sign of accumulation of fluids. You might listen to your cat's heart for signs of trouble. (Again, the following information is not to be used as a substitute for periodic examinations by your pet's doctor.)

Just put your head on her chest and listen. Or make yourself a sort of stethoscope by putting a drinking glass over your cat's heart area and listening through the open end—if this strange device doesn't freak her out. If her heart skips a bit around the fifth or sixth beat, don't panic. Cats and dogs are naturally prone to irregular rhythms (although cats less so than dogs). As a matter of fact, if your pet's heart rhythm is completely regular, you should bring this to your veterinarian's attention. At the same time, if the heart seems to be skipping an entire beat, you should tell the doctor about that.

Is the heartbeat confined to the immediate heart area? Good. (Sounds that can be heard all over the chest area may mean an enlarged heart.) Do you feel a buzzing or vibration over the heart? This may be due to a narrowed valve or a hole in the heart. Do you hear a hissing sound? This may be due to a leaky valve. Does the heartbeat sound muffled? This also should be brought to your veterinarian's attention.

Dr. Bellows once vividly described the progressive stages of congestive heart failure:

- The cat is coughing and has a slight decrease in exercise tolerance.
- The cat's gums start to become blue. Exercise tolerance becomes even less.
- The cat comes into the office puffing. If he takes more than several steps, he coughs hoarsely.
- In the last stage of congestive heart failure, the cat can't walk into the office at all. He is carried in on his side.

"In this last stage of congestive heart failure," Dr. Bellows said, "the animal is literally drowning in the excess fluids accumulated in his lungs. Even at this stage, we can save a few animals, but they have to be put on oxygen and given drugs." Nutrients were used only as supportive therapy, to help increase the pet's chances of surviving.

Remember that the above information from Dr. Bellows referred to congestive heart failure, which is the final stage of cardiomyopathy.

Treatment for Heart Problems

What can be done to get those speeding heart pulses Dr. Ralston talked about earlier down to the normal rate of 12? "You have to find out what malfunctioning organ the heart has taken over the pulsing effect for," Dr. Ralston told me. "Usually you'll find it's the thyroid gland. That gland provides energy for the brain, heart, kidneys, and the adrenal gland." The latter gland pumps fluids through the body.

Dr. Ralston added that "a malfunctioning thyroid gland is the single most common problem in cats."

Some Basics of Treatment for Heart Problems

These are some of the basics of treatment shared by the holistic doctors who have worked with me over many years. See the text for important additional details.

- **Vitamin A.** Depending on the size of the animal and the severity of his condition, up to 400,000 IU a day of the water-soluble form of the vitamin may be used. (This form does not accumulate in the body the way the "usual," fat-soluble form does, and so it can be used in much higher amounts without causing toxicity.)
- **Vitamin C.** As you may know, drugs called diuretics are routinely used in the orthodox treatment of heart problems, both for people and for animals, to rid the body of accumulated excess fluids. Vitamin C is a natural diuretic, with no side effects when used properly. (Up to 20 to 25 grams a day may be used, again depending on the size of the dog or cat and the severity of the illness.)

- **Vitamin E.** Up to 4,000–6,000 IU a day of the water-soluble form may be used. This is another natural diuretic. It also enhances circulation; a damaged heart has trouble fulfilling its major function of circulating blood through the body. Vitamin E also has been well proven to strengthen all the muscles of the body—and the heart is a muscle. (Some holistic veterinarians have warned me that while vitamin E is quite safe for less serious heart problems, it can be very dangerous if used indiscriminately on a very weak heart. They recommend that an animal with a serious heart problem be stabilized first before adding vitamin E, and that it be prescribed for a pet with a very weak heart only by holistic veterinarians.)
- **The elimination of salt (sodium).**
- **Moderate exercise.**
- **Weight reduction in an overweight animal.**
- **And, as with any disorder, a natural diet as detailed in chapter 2 (or chapter 4, depending on the cat's age).**

To the basic regimen sketched in the boxed material, holistic veterinarians will add other natural substances. We'll cover those additional aids after a closer look at some of the recommendations mentioned in the box.

VITAMIN C. We say elsewhere in this book that holistic veterinarians often use the sodium ascorbate form of vitamin C, rather than the more widely known ascorbic acid form. But for heart problems, they use ascorbic acid. They don't use sodium ascorbate because it contains sodium, more commonly known as salt. As we cover in this chapter, the elimination of salt is very important in treating heart disease.

VITAMIN E. As stated in the boxed material, vitamin E can strengthen a weakened heart and can function as a diuretic, helping the body to remove dangerous excess fluid. (Let me reemphasize that in congestive heart failure and in animals with very weak hearts, vitamin E must be used only under the supervision of a holistic veterinarian.) This vitamin also reduces the body's need for oxygen. Oxygen starvation is a major problem in heart disorders.

Richard J. Kearns, D.V.M., as long ago as 1981 said of vitamin E, "This vitamin will cure many heart problems without using the drug digitalis at all. When the animal is in really bad shape, you may have to use a little digitalis." Even in those very advanced cases, however, "if you use enough vitamin E, you can cut the drug down to about 10 percent of what you'd have to use normally."

In the first edition, I cited a number of studies going back as far as 1945 that showed that undersupplying animals with vitamin E produced abnormal electrocardiograms and heart degeneration. I also cited studies from the same era that found that people who had already had heart attacks showed improved electrocardiograms and more regular pulses after taking vitamin E. I think that in this new era of enlightened knowledge about nutrition, I don't have to prove that E helps the heart by citing individual studies.

I will, though, mention again very early research on vitamin E used directly on more than twelve hundred cats and dogs with heart problems. Dr. N. H. Lambert began his work in 1945 and published it ten years later.[1] He had good results with everything from angina to valvular murmur to congestive heart failure. Dr. Lambert's very first case was a nine-year-old dog who was dying; previous treatment had not helped her. With vitamin E, the "dying" dog lived another six years, to the ripe old age of fifteen.

Keep in mind here something you should always remember if you read of studies involving only one nutrient. Vitamins and minerals act synergistically, so the effects found for one nutrient may well be strengthened when other nutrients are added.

THE QUESTION OF EXERCISE. While vigorous, *regular* exercise is a good preventive for heart trouble, once the heart is damaged, you must take a middle-of-the-road approach to your pet's exercise. (Of course, if your cat is in an emergency situation, you won't try to exercise him at all.) Holistic veterinarians have told me that if you just let your cat sit around all day, he will tend to get worse. If you try to get him to do vigorous exercising, he will get worse, too.

LOW-SALT DIET. A low-salt diet is so important in treating heart disease that some veterinarians have informed me that in the early stages of a heart problem, simply cutting out salt alone can sometimes dramatically help the animal.

Low-salt foods include corn grits or farina, oatmeal, lima beans, squash, dried beans, sweet potato, black-eyed peas, egg yolks (not whites), beef, chicken, turkey, lamb, corn kernels, and white rice. (We have said in this book that white rice has fewer nutrients than brown rice. That's true, but it also has less salt.) Feed your cat these meat foods, vegetables, and grains in the proportions given in chapters 2 and 4.

Dr. Bellows once told me that many well-meaning people keep their pets on a special low-salt diet, then—perhaps feeling sorry that the animal isn't getting any treats—give them beef jerky or bologna, both saturated with salt. "Such foods," Dr. Bellows said, "totally defeat everything." Some other *not*-permitted foods are cornflakes, wheat flakes, cheese, margarine, cottage cheese, frankfurters, canned stew, bacon. "Foods like these," Dr. Bellows said emphatically, "can get the animal into *big* trouble."

We do not have the space here to list all the permitted and not-permitted foods on a low-salt diet. So check with your veterinarian before adding a food the doctor has not already recommended. In this instance, a small detail that you don't know might kill your pet. Many packaged and canned foods, for instance, are loaded with salt. And even tuna fish, recommended in chapter 2 as an occasional good food for a healthy cat, weighs in at a stupendous 700 milligrams of sodium (salt) per 3 ounces! So you see, even the addition of an apparently "safe" food might be lethal to your pet. Again, always check with your veterinarian before adding any food to the low-salt diet the doctor has already recommended.

VASCULIN AND CARDIO-PLUS. I asked Dr. Ralston if these two natural products, used in 1981, were still used for heart disease. "You'd better believe it," he said. "Those are very good products." He found a bottle of one of the products and enthusiastically began reading me the list of ingredients, which included bovine heart extract, bovine liver powder, choline, calcium lactate, and numerous other natural factors that can help the heart.

Dr. Lemmon was just as enthusiastic about Vasculin and Cardio-Plus in 1981. "I've had cases that were absolutely given up on by other veterinarians," he told me, "because the cardiograms indicated there was no hope. These two products, though, improved the animals greatly and are giving them years more of life."

Dr. Ralston more recently added that in giving products such as Cardio-Plus, "I have the clients mash the pill up in the cat's food, so he can feel he is still in control of what's going on in his life. I don't want the person he has come to love and depend on grabbing him and shoving things down his throat."

MAGNESIUM AND ENZYMES. H. H. Robertson, D.V.M., once told me that "one major cause of heart problems—in cats and in dogs—is that proteins don't get broken down by the body into amino acids. Therefore, it is complex proteins that are circulating in the system. And of course the body cannot utilize complex proteins.

"When these complex proteins reach too high a level in the circulatory system, the heart rate is increased. Eventually, the heart wears itself out." When testing revealed that the proteins were indeed not being broken down, Dr. Robertson gave magnesium to the animal. "Magnesium will cause the desired release of the nonprotein nitrogen in the body." In other words, it will help the body to get rid of the undigested protein.

Dr. Robertson and Dr. Kearns reported that they also used pancreatic enzymes to help improve the breakdown of protein. Dr. Robertson added that "pepsin and trypsin are particularly important."

LECITHIN. This is a natural substance occurring in some foods, such as soybeans and eggs. Holistic doctors may add lecithin to their therapy for heart problems. Lecithin emulsifies—that is, cuts through—fats. By emulsifying the plaques of fats adhering to the walls of blood vessels, lecithin also helps improve the animal's circulation.

COENZYME Q10. A new weapon to fight heart disease is coenzyme Q10, which, Dr. Price said, "I use for any and all heart problems." He uses 1 mg per pound of body weight.

What is this newly discovered and studied nutrient with the strange name? I researched it before starting work on this book and was so convinced of its helpful effects that I added it to the basic supplementation regimen for myself and my husband, Joe. Because this book has a strong practical focus, I won't go into the textbook facts I found involving lipids, mitochondria, the collection of hydrogen atoms removed during cellular oxidations, and oxidative phosphorylation that describe the biochemical processes by which this coenzyme works.

The long and the short of it is that cells require energy to live, and coenzyme Q10 supplies that energy. Research has found deficiencies of this nutrient in human patients with heart disease such as congestive heart failure and angina and in older people with high blood pressure, subjects covered in this chapter. And, not surprisingly, supplements of the nutrient have been found to help people with these problems. Coenzyme Q10 has also been found to bolster the immune system and in that way to help people undergoing standard cancer therapy to fight the side effects of radiation and chemotherapy. The nutrient has been used in Europe for patients with soft tissue cancer, including breast cancer.

As is true of nutrients in general, no side effects have been found when used as recommended.

SOME SPECIAL WORDS ABOUT THE LAST STAGES OF CONGESTIVE HEART DISEASE. As hopeless as this problem sounds, all of the holistic veterinarians I have talked to over many years say they can save some of these seemingly doomed animals.

Dr. Ralston recently added information I found very interesting. When I asked if his therapy for this end-stage heart problem differed from his therapy for milder cases of heart disease, he answered, "Yes." I expected to hear him tell me of a more intensive nutritional therapy or that he might have to use drugs as well as natural substances. Instead, he said, "You have to be even more careful than ever to avoid stressing this already traumatized animal. For instance, most cats, even when healthy, get absolutely terrified when you try to draw blood from them."

Dr. Ralston stated that the medical facts a veterinarian needs to know at this point "show up in the blood last. Also," he said, "the more stressed a cat is when you're trying to examine her, the more she can change her blood count." So this holistic veterinarian asked rhetorically, "If a blood test is not that accurate at this point, why don't you try to look for something else—and be kind and be gentle?"

Heartworms

Heartworms are worms that congregate in the heart. They can damage not only that organ but also the lungs, kidneys, and liver, and can eventually cause death.

Since heartworms are transmitted by mosquitoes, to prevent heartworms, you must protect your cat from these insects. Dr. Price says that brewer's yeast and garlic are used to repel mosquitoes, and he will sometimes use Advantage, a product employed by orthodox veterinarians. "As much as I hate to say I use a chemical," Dr. Price told me, "this is not a chemical that's absorbed into the skin." Repeating the thoughts of veterinarians who spoke about this product for the chapter on skin and hair problems, Dr. Price commented that to date he hasn't found any side effects, but some may start occurring as the product has been in use longer.

What about the drugs out to prevent heartworms? "I haven't used them," Dr. Price says. "I might consider recommending them for a cat living in a swamp area or a part of the country where there's a tremendous amount of heartworm at the time."

For the first edition, I was unable to find a holistic veterinarian who treated heartworms without some use of a drug along with nutritional therapy. Now Dr. Price is able to "just put cats on antioxidants and natural substances that stimulate the immune system. That way they can live comfortably with the worms until the cats digest them, and the worms leave the body that way."

The antioxidants Dr. Price uses include coenzyme Q10 and vitamins A, C, and E. He also uses "a minute amount" of selenium because in recent years it has been found that this nutrient helps the
action of vitamin E. "I may add supportive treatment," he says, "such
as the vitamin B complex and liver extract."

When I asked if he felt that in general natural therapy had a much
greater success with heartworms than orthodox therapy, he said, "It
sure does—for me, anyway." He added that, "It's just a lot more fun
when you get good results, and the cat doesn't have any side effects."

Going into more detail, Dr. Price said, "If you treat heartworms
with drugs, the animals generally die. But if you leave them alone
and just support their systems with natural substances, they'll digest
the worms and will be free of them in a year or two. In the mean-
time, the worst that might happen is that some of them have a little
vomiting or coughing."

Dr. Price gave as a representative case history the story of Tinkerbell, a four-year-old female cat who was brought to him with heartworms a year ago. "We put her on coenzyme Q10," he said, "and
since then she's been doing fine. She hasn't shown any symptoms
other than an occasional cough." The veterinarian added that he's
giving Tinkerbell only 10 mg of coenzyme Q10 a day, "which is not
much, just about 1 mg per pound of her body weight."

Hypertension

Discussing symptoms of hypertension, Dr. Price said that the external symptoms he looks for include extreme nervousness, "often to
the point where the cat has ceased to be a good pet." Indeed, the
hypertensive pet can sometimes be so nervous that he makes his
owner a nervous wreck. "Also, animals with high blood pressure
have about two or three times the amount of skin problems that
other pets do," he said. "If the animal has a painful condition, the
pain is three times worse than it would be for another pet. In short,
nothing seems to go right for the poor animal with hypertension."

Therapy for Hypertension

Dr. Ralston commented that hypertension is often basically due to a malfunctioning thyroid gland. "Treating hypertension more as hyperthyroidism than as pure hypertension," he said, "I can almost always successfully treat high blood pressure."

Dr. Price told me that scientific tests find that "most of these animals have an extremely high level of sodium." We have previously established that sodium (salt) is a primary cause of high blood pressure. So, of course, he puts the animal on a low-salt diet as detailed earlier in this chapter.

The veterinarian relies heavily on the nutrient coenzyme Q10, also discussed earlier. And of course, he will, as all holistic veterinarians do in treating any disorder, try to persuade the cat's person to put her on a natural diet.

As a matter of fact, Dr. Price stated strongly: "Almost all—if not, indeed, all—cases of hypertension can be traced, I believe, to the processed foods, most particularly those 'meaty-looking' products." He added a poignant fact: "Sometimes you can even see a courageous little cat or dog who has heart and/or circulatory problems, but whose body is managing to compensate for the problems so that the animal has no symptoms. Then the owner puts him on one of those fake meat products, and in three weeks' time the little fellow has dropsy."

Dr. Price added that he may also use Aspertate, "something I've used down through the years on any circulatory problem." Aspertate is in part a combination of magnesium and potassium. "Magnesium is a very mild natural tranquilizer and helps the nervous hypertensive calm down naturally, without the side effects of drug tranquilizers," the veterinarian said. "It also is an excellent support for producing enzymes that digest blood clots." The possibility of blood clots is one of the major dangers of high blood pressure. (Dr. Robertson once stated that, while potassium should always be used for hypertension, magnesium should be used only if the nonprotein nitrogen in the blood tests out to be too high.)

"Potassium," Dr. Price explained, "balances the high sodium level present in the hypertensive." Sodium and potassium work together in a crucial balance in the body. Most people and animals upset this balance by taking in much more sodium than potassium. This overload of sodium tends, in turn, to rob the body of much of the potassium it does take in.

Animals in the wild, of course, don't know about the decades of research on the body's need for a balance between potassium and salt. As nutritionist Adelle Davis once pointed out, when an animal in the wild "overdoses" on eating leaves and grass—which contain high amounts of potassium and no salt—he'll walk hundreds of miles, if he has to, to find the nearest salt lick. This is an instance of something we say often in the book: An animal in the wild instinctively eats what is best for his body. And of course he never eats the fake foods the ads tell us are best for him.

Reference

1. N. H. Lambert, "Clinical Experiences with Vitamin E in Dogs and Cats," *Proceedings of the Third International Congress on Vitamin E,* September 1955, pp. 611–617.

Chapter 11

Cancer: Terminal *Often Doesn't Mean Terminal Any Longer*

"When we get a cat or dog with a prognosis of living only six months because of cancer diagnosed as terminal, we have a 50 to 60 percent chance of restoring that animal to good health. When the animal is diagnosed as being only two or three months away from 'certain' death, our success rate drops, but we still save about a third of these animals."
—*Robert Goldstein, V.M.D.*

"I've been dealing with feline leukemia for years; and I get disgusted with most veterinarians who advocate 'Test and Slaughter'—that is, if the cat tests positive, it's best to kill it. We've had cats who have been able to climb trees and look normal in less than ten weeks. And I'm talking about cats who were brought in to us when they were too weak even to stand up."
—*S. Allen Price, D.V.M. (in 1981)*

"Since there is still no conventional treatment to help feline leukemia, the typical handling of cats who test out to be carrying this disease is to euthanize them, in order to control the virus from spreading to other cats. Treating cats with this disease holistically, I have found that 60 to 70 percent of those who are already ill with leukemia become healthy again."
—*Jack Long, V.M.D. (17 years later)*

"In treating cancer, the number one thing I do is to suggest that the cat or dog doesn't get any more vaccines. The number two thing I do is to try to get the owner to put the animal on a natural diet. Then I find the holistic therapy that seems best for the individual pet."
—*Michael W. Lemmon, D.V.M.*

Cubby Caruso *is* a nine-year-old domestic shorthair tabby cat who was struck by malignant lymphoma. This form of cancer is "the deadliest disease to strike cats," said Robert Goldstein, V.M.D., who told me about Cubby. "It's considered a terminal disease." When Dr. Goldstein started to treat him, the cat had been through surgery and chemotherapy but he certainly wasn't cured. He had several bouts of vomiting and high fever, which required medical maintenance during each crisis. He was anorexic, losing weight, and depressed.

Dr. Goldstein tested Cubby with Bio Nutritional Analysis, a technique he developed, which told him that the cat had weaknesses in the kidneys, adrenal glands, and liver. He also had a clogged lymph system, and his body lacked digestive enzymes. "I put Cubby on homeopathic, glandular, and herbal (Essiac tea) support," Dr. Goldstein said. When the veterinarian and I talked, Cubby had been off all chemotherapy for just about a year.

I asked Dr. Goldstein how the cat's health had been in all those months. "Normal," he said.*

As you'll see from the statements by Drs. Goldstein and Long on the opening page of this chapter, we now have some holistic veterinarians reporting 60 to 70 percent success with animals that orthodox medicine thinks of as hopeless. Since, like orthodox medicine,

---

* It was Bio Nutritional Analysis that saved my miniature poodle when she was diagnosed with terminal cancer, as detailed in the Introduction.

holistic medicine continually seeks and finds new answers to treating diseases, those statistics will hopefully be even higher by the time you read this.

Why do holistic veterinarians have such better results than orthodox veterinarians? Because they use natural substances that restore the pet's body—most importantly, the pet's immune system—to its natural balance. When this can be accomplished, the cat's own immune system fights off the cancer—just as a strong immune system fights off cancer that invades all our bodies every day of our lives. (By the way, surgery, radiation, and chemotherapy *weaken* the all-important immune system, rather than building it up. Might that be a reason orthodox medicine doesn't have a lot of success in treating cancer?)

As a matter of fact, over the years many holistic veterinarians and M.D.s have stressed to me the following idea, as expressed by veterinarian Dr. Robertson: "*I* don't cure the cancer. Actually, I don't cure *anything*. All I do is run tests to see where the animal's body chemistry is and then bring the chemistry back to where it should be. It's the animal's body that actually does the healing."

I have stressed that in treating cancer the immune system must be strengthened. The therapy used by the doctors Goldstein actually injects a total cancer-fighting immune system *into* the body. That sounds like magic, doesn't it? Trust me that it won't sound at all mystical when I explain it to you a little later on.

You probably won't ever need the information in this chapter if you are starting off with a kitten who is brand-new to the world and raise him as holistic veterinarians have detailed in chapters 2 through 4. (See, for instance, this chapter's covering quote from Dr. Lemmon. This same statement was volunteered to me by many holistic veterinarians in reference not only to cancer but to other disorders.) The cancer rampage did not exist among our pets' ancestors, as it did not exist among our own ancestors, when we all ate non-poisonous foods and didn't vaccinate. Indeed, cancer is still virtually unknown in the wild. Dr. Robertson, who has a rural practice and treats animals roaming free, once told me: "I have seen noncancerous tumors in deer, in coyotes, and in foxes—but even these are rare."

The initial diagnosis of cancer is very often a much more defini-
tive death sentence for cats than it is for humans. Why? For one
thing, traditional therapy is very expensive.

The orthodox centers I recently contacted were loath to give estimated costs, saying so much depended on the type of cancer, the
stage, and so on. Let's assume, though, that the top estimate is
$2,000 a week (as it was in 1981), even though we know that as-
sumption is probably wrong. And let's compare that to today's costs
for the very sophisticated natural therapy used today by the brothers
Goldstein. That nontoxic therapy—which saves up to 60 percent of
cats and dogs deemed terminal by orthodox medicine—has a top
estimated cost of $2,000, not for a *week* of therapy, but for *three
months*. And often animals who respond positively to the therapy
don't need to be in treatment that long.

Not only is traditional therapy expensive, it can be extremely
painful and traumatic for the pet. And it often doesn't work. As
John E. Craige, V.M.D., once pointed out, all of this often results in
owners opting, sorrowfully, for putting the animal to sleep once the
word *cancer* is pronounced by the doctor. "The orthodox approach
to cancer is seldom even used in veterinary medicine," he said. The
veterinarian added that "the fact that orthodox cancer treatment is
often not even tried by owners should give [conventional] veterinarians more of a rationale for trying alternative therapy than many
[conventional] M.D.s may feel they have."

Dr. Robert Goldstein, who told me he became a holistic cancer
specialist "out of necessity," once worked for one of this country's
most prestigious orthodox veterinary centers, where he used standard treatments for cancer, including the new orthodox treatment,
chemical immunotherapy. "These therapies—when they worked—
prolonged the animal's life but didn't induce a remission," he said.
"Commonly, we told the pet owner that the prognosis without treatment was that their cat had two to three months to live. With
chemotherapy, the owner could expect six months to a year."

Two Basic Problems in Treating Cancer Holistically: Neither One Lies in the Cancer Itself

The two basic problems reported by holistic veterinarians come from owner skepticism.

Problem number one, as Dr. Kearns once expressed it, is that "we almost always get the animals after they've been through everything else—the surgery, the radiation, the chemotherapy." As mentioned earlier, all these undermine the immune system, rather than build it up. "When everything else has failed, when the cancer has had time to spread, when the animal is terminal, *then* we get a chance to help it," he said.

Problem number two was expressed by S. Allen Price, D.V.M. (who echoed that he seldom gets to use natural therapy on a pet "until the owners realize it's either try natural therapy, or the pet will *surely* die"). Dr. Price stated: "Even once they've agreed to try natural therapy, all they have to do is read somewhere in a newspaper that no natural therapy can possibly work for cancer; and they're on the phone saying, 'Absolutely. I see it here, right here in the newspaper: Only drugs and surgery can help cancer.' And the totally frustrating thing is that so often these are people whose pets were given up to die because the drugs and surgery couldn't work; and they can see that their pets are doing well on the natural therapy. But they read a paragraph in a newspaper . . ."

Dr. Price summarized: "The disease of cancer worries me to death—not because of the cancer itself but because so often you can't fight the owner's skepticism so you can cure the animal."

One basic misunderstanding some people have is that if they choose an alternative therapy for cancer, they will have to deprive their animal (or themselves) of orthodox therapy. As we have just covered, most holistic veterinarians don't get to see a cat until orthodox therapy has been tried and has failed.

Also, remember that, as I said in the introduction, holistic veterinarians have received the same degrees in orthodox veterinary medicine as have strictly orthodox veterinarians. And they will use conventional techniques when it is to the patient's advantage. For instance, holistic doctors tell me that if the tumor is pressing on a vital part of the animal's body, or is in any other way impeding the functioning of the body, they will remove it surgically. In this way, the animal can be functioning again while the more natural, metabolic approach has time to rebuild the immune system. In the same way, holistic veterinarians will sometimes use a drug to help the cat with cancer. However, they never use conventional techniques as the only therapy. The major treatment is always a metabolic approach, which can help do away with the usual side effects of drugs and surgery while at the same time getting at the actual cause of the cancer: a damaged immune system.

Injecting Your Cat with a New Immune System Designed Specifically to Fight Cancer

Although the above heading sounds like something from a science fiction novel, it is accurate. And these new immune systems have been given successfully to cats and dogs for seventeen years (as of 1998) by holistic veterinarians Robert Goldstein, V.M.D., and his brother, Marty Goldstein, D.V.M. This treatment, called Immuno-Augmentative Therapy (IAT), has also been used for even more years by human cancer victims lucky enough to have learned about it. The doctors Goldstein quoted in this section have worked closely with the original researcher for close to two decades to develop the same kind of success for cats that the therapy has shown for humans with cancer.

In a nutshell (we'll go into detail later), IAT uses a new technique to isolate components of the immune system designed by nature specifically to kill cancer. These components, isolated from the serum of healthy donors, are then given by injection to the cancer-stricken animal. Thus, the cat almost instantly has within his body a complete *strong* immune system designed specifically to kill cancer.

In an interview, Dr. Robert Goldstein told me that he and his brother, Marty, have treated approximately three thousand cats and dogs with the IAT treatment. All the animals had been diagnosed (most of them by other veterinarians) as having terminal cancer: three to six months to live.

"When we get them early in the terminal stage—when they are supposed to have six months left—we save 50 to 60 percent of them," Dr. Goldstein told me. "Our success drops below that for those in the late terminal stage, although we can save about a third of those animals." The veterinarian specifies that the 50 to 60 percent success rate means that those animals go into remission and stay in remission until they eventually die of natural causes ("old age"), an accident, or another disease unsuccessfully treated.

Since the diagnosis of terminal cancer is supposed to mean that nothing in the world can save the animal, you can see why Dr. Goldstein commented that he thought those results were "pretty good." (He doesn't consider them nearly good enough, however. As I write this, he is close to concluding further research to *prevent* cancer, which I will talk about soon.)

I pointed out parenthetically above that most of the cats and dogs treated by the Drs. Goldstein were not diagnosed by *them* as having terminal cancer, or as having cancer at all. I wanted to point that out early because there has been a tradition of staunchly orthodox doctors feeling they can discredit doctors with a natural cancer therapy by saying: "These quacks just *told* the patients they had cancer so they could bilk them of their money." Although there certainly may be quackery in treating cancer, I've researched several major natural cancer therapies over more than three decades, and I haven't found one of the doctors whose patients weren't diagnosed by orthodox physicians. I also don't happen to have found any doctor leading a major natural cancer therapy who didn't charge a lot less than the going rate for conventional therapy.

Dr. Goldstein told me, "Sometimes we'll diagnose the cat or dog in our own clinic, but usually another veterinarian—often from the other end of the country—calls me on the phone for help. The animal has been diagnosed by traditional methods: X ray and biopsy. Most often, we never even see the animal. I guide the nutritional support program by phone, using the blood samples and test results that have been sent me by the cooperating veterinarian."

As you can see from that, if you and your cat don't live near Dr. Goldstein, or the very few other veterinarians who use this cutting-edge therapy, you certainly don't need to despair of getting this treatment for your cat.

Immuno-Augmentative Therapy, since it naturally restores the immune system's ability to do what nature intended it to do, has no toxic effects. Another plus of IAT is that pet owners can usually administer it at home.

How expensive is IAT? We have already said that, as of late 1997, if the animal needed the maximum three months on the IAT program the cost was about $1,200. "The *complete* program," Dr. Goldstein said, "including IAT, nutritional supplements, and the Bio Nutritional Analysis (BNA) that tells us specifically what each cat needs in the way of nutrients, will run $1,500 to $2,000 over three months." He added that "when the program is successful, it usually brings the cat into remission in three months or less."

Dr. Goldstein stressed to me that BNA is an integral part of his therapy for cancer. "While the IAT augments the immune system's proteins by injection, the BNA balances the glands of the immune system and tells us what nutrients the animal needs."

Can IAT work for all *forms* of cancer? "Yes," Dr. Goldstein said. "Although, like any other cancer therapy, orthodox or holistic, IAT has a higher success rate with some forms of cancer than with others. Also, not all animals are candidates for the therapy." (The veterinarian adds that one common form of cancer in cats is "vaccine-induced fibrosarcoma.")

By the way, Dr. Goldstein has been working with animal cancer since the early 1970s, when he developed a freezing technique (cryosurgery) to treat malignancies in animals who couldn't be helped by drugs or surgery. In particular, cryosurgery saves many animals with oral tumors from being euthanized, as they would have been before Dr. Goldstein developed cryosurgery. The technique kills tumors through a sort of controlled frostbite, while most of the nearby healthy tissue is unharmed.

Dr. Goldstein sent me the case history of Butch, a domestic short-hair cat, who was ten years old when he was diagnosed with terminal cancer (specifically, meningioma) of the brain. The diagnosis was given by probably the most respected orthodox veterinary center in the country. The owners were not given surgery as an option: There are parts of the brain you can't cut into without killing the patient. The drug cortisone was tried, but it didn't help.

When Butch started IAT, he had recently had poor vision and difficulty in urinating and defecating. Sometimes Butch seemed to be in a coma, with his eyeballs rolling up into his head. Physical examination revealed nonresponsive, dilated pupils and density of lens: Butch was blind. Within only days of starting IAT, the cat was showing improvement. Butch lived in good health for over three years before he died. So, you may ask, he was saved from dying of cancer for more than three years? No, Butch didn't die from cancer. He died a natural death—from old age.*

Technical Information about How and Why IAT Works

If you tend to blanch when faced with technical medical information, you can skip over this section entirely without missing any *practical* information that can help your cat. I write the following mainly for medical professionals who want to learn a bit more about IAT and for lay readers who might like to believe that this therapy can help their cat but are skeptical because I haven't given much of a biochemical rationale as to how IAT works.

Antibodies in the immune system are the "fellows" responsible for identifying and destroying invaders (antigens) that threaten the body they must protect. Specific antibodies are responsible for the "search-and-destroy mission" of specific antigens. Thus, if a measles virus enters your body, the "measles virus antibody" goes into action, while other antibodies relax and take it easy. About forty years ago, Lawrence Burton, Ph.D., stated that an antibody existed that defended the body against cancer cells. Even though his theory was

---

* As I said earlier, IAT was originally developed for humans, and it continues to help people diagnosed as having terminal cancer. For more information on IAT for humans, call 242-352-7455.

consistent with the accepted antibody-antigen relationships of the time, his idea was not accepted by mainstream medicine—as many new ideas (such as penicillin) have historically not been accepted for many years. As Dr. Goldstein pointed out, "More recent developments related to the well-publicized 'monoclonal antibody' theory seem to affirm" Dr. Burton's discovery from four decades ago.

Although Dr. Burton's therapy is not in use in mainstream medicine, the U.S. Patent and Trademark Office supported the theories and progress of his research by granting him a series of patents for his techniques. Dr. Goldstein also points out that Dr. Burton and his staff of M.D.s well proved both the effectiveness and the safety of IAT in animals (mice) before using it with humans.

To get back to the immune system: Let's assume that cancer cells are trying to overwhelm a *healthy* immune system. The tumor antibodies (IgA, IgG, and IgM) learn of the presence of tumor cells by a protein produced by the cancer cells themselves. These traitors are known as tumor complement factor, or TCF.

So right now we have the TCF traitors telling the body's tumor antibodies of their own invasion, and the immune system's tumor antibodies take up the challenge. But if the antibodies do their job too well and destroy too many cancer cells at a time, the person's liver may become overburdened. The liver is the major organ through which all poisons leaving the body must be filtered. If this organ receives too many poisons all at once, the person will die.

So the healthy immune system protects the body by producing blocking protein factors that lessen the rate at which the antibodies can kill the tumors.

The important balance of tumor kill rate is also maintained by another component of blood, called deblocking protein factor, which neutralizes the blocking protein factor if it goes overboard in its job of preventing tumor antibodies of overkill.

When the immune system is *not* healthy, however, it may have an oversupply of blocking protein factor, along with undersupplies of deblocking protein factors and tumor complement factors. In other words, the tumor-fighting antibodies are being prevented from doing their job when they *shouldn't* be prevented, and they aren't getting strong enough information in the first place that they have a job to do. The immune system of the cat, dog, or human is now helpless to stop the cancer from advancing uncontrolled throughout the body. We are now talking about an animal, or a person, who is sure to die from cancer. Sure to die, that is, if we can't find a way to get all those cancer-fighting factors of the immune system working naturally again.

Immuno-Augmentative Therapy has found a way to do just that. The methods of isolating these factors and extracting them from the serum are detailed in U.S. patents officially granted to Dr. Burton and his research team. The tumor antibodies and the factor that neutralizes the blocking protein that prevents antibodies from doing their job fully are extracted from the serum of animals with an immune system that is well equipped to fight cancer and are given to afflicted animals by injection.

The tumor complement factor is extracted from the serum of patients with cancer. Why put blood from someone with cancer into the body of an animal already diagnosed as dying from the disease? Isn't that like giving a blood transfusion tainted with the HIV virus to a person already dying from AIDS? First of all, you're not putting whole blood into the sick animal; you're giving him only the extracted immune factors. Second, this specific immune factor, which alerts the antibodies that they have a battle to fight, enters the body "on the back of " cancer cells—so this factor is not found in animals who don't have cancer.

If any readers who aren't medical professionals are still with me, you must have been following very closely. So you may see that we have a fourth factor that I haven't yet mentioned sharing with the sick cat. That's the blocking protein factor, the one that prevents the antibodies from killing too many cancer cells all at once. While this factor, too, can be isolated and extracted from serum, it's obviously not the first substance that a cat very ill with cancer needs.

With IAT, every time the animal is tested to determine improvement, measurements are made (by spectrophotometry) from blood samples to determine not only the combined "readings" of the four immune system factors we've been talking about, but also the "readings" of each individual factor. Further therapy is modified accordingly. Thus—fulfilling a major goal of holistic veterinarians—each animal's therapy is tailored specifically to what the individual cat or dog's body needs at any given time.

The results of these measurements are combined with conventional measurements of tumor regression, such as biopsy and X rays.

What May Be on the Horizon for Truly *Conquering Cancer?*

When I talked to Dr. Goldstein in late 1997, he was in the process of setting up research grants at universities to study, along stringent scientific lines, work he has developed to *prevent* cancer. Despite the work he has already done to cure so many animals diagnosed as "incurable," he remains dissatisfied: "I don't want to keep battling this disease once it has taken over the animal," he told me, "and I don't want other doctors to have to keep battling it in humans."

Saying that he wished he could tell me more about his research—"because I think it's very exciting"—he added that, as a man of science, he couldn't overstep himself before his work was scientifically well proven. "But," he said, "you can quote me on this: I believe we are very close to *the* answer on cancer—and it is in prevention. And, although you certainly can help prevent cancer with good diet, genetics plays a gigantic role."

Giving a bit more of a hint about his research, Dr. Goldstein commented that "there are specific animal breeds like golden retrievers that are number one for getting cancer. Now, why are they number one? Because we've overbred them, and we've bred them wrong." Dr. Goldstein isn't advocating that we stop breeding golden retrievers, of course. "But let's find out what the specific genetic problem is—and we can breed cancer *out* of the line, just as we bred it *into* the line." He adds that "knowledgeable breeders have already bred hip dysplasia out of the golden retriever line."

Since there may be a long interval between my writing of this book and your reading of it, you might want to keep an eye out for a book by Dr. Marty Goldstein, who as I write this chapter is preparing a book that will cover IAT. (Dr. Robert Goldstein is writing a veterinary book on nutritional therapies.)

Nutritional Therapies for Cancer

As I write this, I know of only four veterinarians who use the cutting-edge Immuno-Augmentative Therapy directly, although other holistic veterinarians will often consult with those four and use this therapy under their guidance. Far more commonly used at this point are a variety of nutrients as well as certain acupuncture and homeopathic techniques that are known to help give strength to the immune system. As always, the specific therapy will be tailored to the individual cat, but you can get a good idea of some of the nutrients commonly used by looking at other sections of this chapter. The section following the one on feline leukemia also tells *why* some of the nutrients strengthen the immune system.

Dr. Lemmon's statement on the covering page of this chapter indicated the first two concerns he has in treating any case of cancer: stopping the use of excess conventional vaccines, as covered in chapter 3, and changing the diet to the cat's natural raw-food diet as detailed in chapters 2 and 4. When an owner can't or won't follow that diet, Dr. Lemmon urges at least a top-grade prepared food (again, see chapter 2) and prescribes enzymes because only raw foods contain these nutrients, which are essential for every biochemical reaction in the body. Dr. Lemmon has the owner give the enzymes with meals, to help the cat digest the food, as well as between meals.

If the cat is on a natural diet, the veterinarian prescribes enzymes to be taken only between meals. "I use Intenzyme from a company called Biotics, or S22 from Tyler." Dr. Lemmon says: "I've seen results with either one of those in reducing tumors of various different types of cancers." For a cat, he will give one or two of these pills every six hours between meals.

Dr. Robertson once told me about his use of the enzyme brome-lain, which helps dissolve the fibrous coating that forms around a long-standing tumor. This "coat" acts as a protective shield for the tumor so that the immune system, even as it gains health with other nutritional therapy, cannot get at the tumor to dissolve it.

Dr. Lemmon told me that he uses bromelain by itself "if it's a good-quality bromelain." Bromelain is also in the Intenzyme prod-uct he mentioned a bit earlier.

Dr. Lemmon added: "One of the things that I've been using for the last six months that has been helpful for some of the cancers we've been working with, and for immune problems including leu-kemia, is a probiotic by the name of Nature's Biotics."

Dr. Lemmon, as well as other holistic veterinarians, will also sometimes use raw glandular extracts corresponding to the organ system that's affected with the cancer. Obviously, if a glandular sys-tem is hit by cancer, it is weakened; and the raw extracts of that par-ticular system can help to strengthen it.

If you give your cat the natural diet that her holistic veterinarian will almost certainly (if not certainly) recommend, you will not only increase her chances of successfully battling the cancer, you will lessen her suffering from pain. How so? There is very little salt in the cat's natural diet. As Dr. Price once explained, "Excessive sodium [salt] attaches with water around cells, forming sodium hydroxide, a very irritating substance."

As you might expect, holistic veterinarians will vary their therapy depending on the stage and the type of the cancer. "For instance," Dr. Lemmon said, "if the tumor is very large, I might suggest surgery to go along with holistic therapy."

A Warning against a Therapy That Works Very Fast to Get Rid of Tumors

On occasion, a natural therapy for cancer can work *too* well, if administered by a doctor who is not very experienced in that par-ticular therapy. In 1981, when I researched the first edition, some holistic veterinarians were reporting very good results with laetrile (otherwise known as vitamin B_{17} or amygdalin). Drs. Robert and Marty Goldstein reported, however, that they had found that laetrile in heavily toxic patients can cause "depression, vomiting, and a downhill course." They felt that these effects might be due to "too rapid [a] breakdown of tumor cells, further overloading the body with toxins." They stressed that in treating cancer, one should not become involved solely in watching tumors shrink, but should keep a close check on what changes may be occurring in the animal's overall body chemistry. "It is possible to have a shrunken tumor and a dead animal." (Earlier, we discussed how the Immuno-Augmentative Therapy, which the doctors Goldstein now use, protects against this problem.)

On the other hand, the doctors pointed out that "it is very common initially in treatment for the tumor to increase in size due to an accumulation of toxin from the detoxifying process."

If your veterinarian is not highly experienced in treating cancer holistically, discuss the previous two points with the doctor.

Feline Leukemia Virus

Feline leukemia is cancer of the blood. The leukemia virus is, sadly, very common. Although not all cats who carry the virus in their bodies ever develop symptoms, far too many of them do. The disease is contagious and can be transmitted from cat to cat and from a mother to her unborn kittens. Dr. Long says that, "as far as we know," feline leukemia can't be transmitted to dogs, so if you have both a cat and a dog as companions, you apparently don't have to panic about your dog if your cat is found to carry the virus. It is also believed that this virus can't be transmitted to humans.

As indicated in part by the quotes on the covering page of this chapter, conventional medicine mainly treats feline leukemia with despair rather than therapy. In sharp contrast, Dr. Long reports that 60 to 70 percent of cats already clinically ill—not just *carrying* the virus—become healthy after receiving the therapy he reports in this section. Dr. Lemmon, who also is experienced in treating feline leukemia, says: "If the cat is on his back, gasping for breath, when he is first brought to me, I don't have much chance of getting him back to health. But otherwise, even if the cat has full-blown symptoms when I first see him, the chances of turning him around are very good."

Reading Dr. Long's description of the disease, it is easy to see why orthodox veterinarians pretty much despair of treating it. Dr. Long tells us that this virus is "very similar to the HIV virus in humans, and it has the potential for producing a variety of health problems very much like those that occur in humans stricken with AIDS." Like AIDS, the feline leukemia virus has as its primary "mission" the destruction of the immune system, the body's crucial line of defense against bacteria, viruses, and cancer.

There are two basic forms of feline leukemia. The form that causes lymphosarcoma cancer to grow in the body, Dr. Long says, does not tend to respond to the therapy he uses.* Much more common is the form of leukemia that causes various blood diseases. "Symptoms often include fever, decreased appetite, lethargy, pale mucous membranes, and weight loss," Dr. Long states. He points out that "this form of leukemia usually produces symptoms after the cat has carried the feline leukemia virus in his body for an average of two to three years."

That last fact may have posed a question for you: If your cat has tested positive for leukemia but has no symptoms, can holistic veterinarians prevent your companion from ever coming down with the disease? "Yes," says Dr. Lemmon. "We just work to improve their immune systems, so that they never develop any of the symptoms."

Before we get into detail about treatment, I'll give one specific example of the differing ways orthodox and holistic veterinarians look at feline leukemia. The high fever that often strikes cats with

---

* If your cat has this form, you might look into BNA therapy. Cubby Caruso, who led off this chapter, had feline leukemia with lymphosarcoma.

symptomatic leukemia frightens orthodox veterinarians, but Dr. Lemmon sees that symptom as a hopeful sign. "The fever is an indication that the cat's vital force is still fighting," he says. Fever is one of the body's natural ways of knocking a disease out of the body, and its presence means that the cat's body and spirit both still have strength. "Also," he points out, "we have a number of natural ways to bring a high fever down if it gets *too* high."

As mentioned previously, saving cats with feline leukemia is nothing new for holistic veterinarians. For instance, back in 1981 animal nutritionist Pat Widmer told me that she had seen "many hundreds of symptomatic cats" recover with the use of a product called Mega C Plus.

In a recent interview, Dr. Lemmon told me that he, too, often used Mega C Plus but has stopped in recent years. "I think it's a good product, but my area of the country [Renton, Washington] is very damp, and Mega C Plus would always clot up, or ball up. Also, I sometimes had a problem with palatability." Dr. Lemmon said, "Today, I use just plain sodium ascorbate [the form of vitamin C used in Mega C Plus] for fever, or not eating. I'll give 500 mg every four to eight hours, depending on the cat. In some cases, even more often, unless that causes excessive loosening of the stool." That reaction means the cat is getting more vitamin C than her body needs at that point in time to fight the leukemia. "Then I'll add other things, such as various types of chlorophyll products. Just putting cats on things like a good-quality spirulina or super blue-green algae can help many of them with leukemia." (Spirulina, for instance, contains a lot of iron, which can increase the red blood cell count that may fall dangerously low in leukemia.) The veterinarian adds that "raw thymus is important. Or from Standard Process I'll use their Thymex or their Immunuplex."

Let me add something important here: the value of loving nursing care. Back in 1981, animal nutritionist Pat Widmer was reporting substantially better success using Mega C Plus for cats with symptomatic leukemia than was the veterinarian who formulated the product. She attributed that to the fact that she did not keep the cats in her clinic but sent them home, where they could feel safe, and where owners might get up "every one or two hours, if need be, to hold the cat in their lap, stroke it, groom it, give it love."

Today, Dr. Lemmon tells me that he agrees wholeheartedly, and that he has most of his patients cared for at home.

S. Allen Price, D.V.M., has also emphasized vitamin C to treat feline leukemia, but didn't use the specific formulation of Mega C Plus. Instead, he added vitamin A, various other vitamins and minerals, laetrile, and a digestive enzyme called Viokase. He would also, according to the needs of the individual cat, sometimes use chlorophyll from fresh green plants, or iron, liver, and vitamin B_{12} to increase the red blood cell count. "And," he told me, "except for the really far advanced cases, most of them recover. We've had cats who came to us without even enough strength left in them to stand up. And in less than ten weeks they've been scampering around, climbing trees, totally normal."

Dr. Price once told me about Rupert, one of several cats belonging to a well-known author, who came down with leukemia. Dr. Price gave him 100 milligrams of laetrile daily, vitamins and minerals mixed with liquid vitamin C, and Viokase. When the veterinarian saw Rupert again later in the year, the cat was free of symptoms. The last report I had—one and a half years after Rupert's bout with this "hopeless" disease—he was still free of symptoms. Not only that, Dr. Price told me, "he now has more energy than all the other cats living with him."

You have seen that holistic veterinarians have various therapies from which to choose to treat feline leukemia, according to what the specific cat most needs. Dr. Lemmon, who earlier gave a few specifics of the way he often treats feline leukemia, states that he sees good response with several different therapies for leukemia. The following boxed material gives some basic information on the highly successful therapy for feline leukemia referred to earlier as used by Dr. Long.

Basics of a Holistic Therapy for Feline Leukemia

- **Natural diet***
- **Megavitamin supplements**
- **Glandular extracts**
- **Cleansers of toxins:**
  - *—Nutrients known to prevent the addition of more toxins to the body by way of foods, and vitamins known to enhance the excretion of toxins*
  - *—Kyolic-purified garlic extract, known to enhance excretion of toxins*
  - *—The herb ginseng, a body cleanser and blood purifier*
- **Acupuncture**
- **Homeopathy**

The call for a natural diet is a universal call from every holistic veterinarian I've worked with over the years—both for preventing disease and as the first step in curing an existing problem. But I realize that some of you may have just come upon this book in a state of panic (an emotion I understand only too well) and are reading only this section. If the recommendations for a natural diet and megavitamin therapy puzzle you, start by looking at chapter 1, which tells of all the harm an *unnatural* diet can do to our cats. To get an idea of what megavitamin therapy can do, just glance through any of the previous chapters on disorders.

The glandular extracts mentioned in the boxed material may, however, need a bit more explaining for many readers. Dr. Long details that "certain amino acids, hormones, and peptides found in extracts of thymus gland have been shown to improve immunity apparently by stimulating thymic activity. The thymus gland is the major governing organ of the immune system." Remember we've said that feline leukemia is very close to human AIDS. You may know that a major factor orthodox doctors worry about in people

---

* In checking the manuscript, Dr. Long reminded me that a truly natural diet includes *raw* meat and vegetables.

with AIDS is keeping the T-cell count up.* Those cells are produced by the thymus gland.

Maybe for many readers the use of acupuncture needs a little more explanation, too. I cover this therapy in the chapter on crippling disorders. More relevant for this present section, Dr. Long specifies that acupuncture has "well-documented immune-stimulating effects such as increasing antibody levels, increasing white blood cell count, increasing bactericidal activity of the serum, and increasing phagocytic activity of blood cells." Phagocytic? I like the way my favorite orthodox medical reference (the *Signet Mosby Medical Encyclopedia*) defines a phagocyte: a cell that "is able to surround, eat, and digest small living things, such as bacteria." We certainly would want phagocytes in our cats' blood to gobble up this virus that is commonly thought to be indestructible.

Homeopathy is used because it is another nontoxic technique to enhance immune function.

Dr. Long adds that, in addition to the therapy as summarized in the boxed material, he will individualize treatment as dictated by the cat's specific symptoms, "whatever expression the body is having of its imbalances due to the virus."

Since feline leukemia has traditionally been such a devastating disease, you might wonder if your cat will have to be hospitalized for ages while receiving holistic treatment. Dr. Long usually keeps these cats in the hospital for only two or three days so that he can "give them their megavitamins and minerals intravenously, rather than orally, to make sure their bodies optimally utilize the nutrients." While they're with him, he also gives several acupuncture treatments. After that, nutritional therapy is given at home by the owners.

For a while, the cat returns once a week for an acupuncture treatment. Blood tests are repeated every three or four weeks, to give solid scientific evidence of how well the cat is responding—and what needs to be changed in the cat's specific therapy.

* Dr. Long presently uses Thymogen, put out by the Allergy Research Group.

What about *keeping* the cat well once he recovers? When the cat's blood test for the virus becomes negative, the owner may be afraid that the cat will become infected again and will ask Dr. Long to vaccinate. "But I think vaccinations at this point are unnecessary," the veterinarian says. "If the cat had the virus and recovered, he now probably has a durable, *natural* immunity." Dr. Long refers to the fact that once an immune system successfully fights off a viral or bacterial invader, it has developed an effective antibody against that specific invader. That's why human adults tend to get significantly fewer colds than children do: We have built up antibodies against many different types of cold viruses. "But," the veterinarian says, "if the owner is still worried that his cat will catch the virus again, I recommend homeopathic nosodes, not the standard vaccinations."

What Dr. Long does recommend to keep the now-healthy cat free of disease is that the owners keep up the high-quality diet and the nutritional supplements.

Some 30 percent of the cats who recover still test out to have the virus in their blood, which means that they are "carriers" and, although they themselves are well, they may infect other cats. For those cats, Dr. Long does not recommend vaccinations. "Vaccines are a stress that might tip the balance for a cat who carries the virus."

Preventing Leukemia in Your Other Cats

I know that many of you have more than one cat, and the previous sentence may have left you wondering if I'm recommending you risk letting your recovered cat who is still a carrier infect your other cats. No, homeopathic vaccinations and a natural diet will guard them against catching the virus.* Check with a holistic veterinarian about keeping your recovered cat separate for a while until the diet and vaccination have had time to take effect.

Holistic veterinarians also point to drug therapy and, as mentioned, the overuse of standard vaccinations as major factors behind

---

* Dr. Lemmon adds that you should also give 500 mg of vitamin C a day to your other cats.

feline leukemia. Another cause is radiation. Drs. Robert and Marty Goldstein once told me that they practiced seven miles from a nuclear reactor, and that they saw "so many leukemic cats and dogs that it is becoming an epidemic."

Dr. Price once reported an interesting observation: "The only leukemic dogs that I've seen have been dogs who have a habit of lying near the television." Television emits a lot of radiation. Dr. Price pointed out that many cats not only often lie near the TV, but even on it. Keep your cat, your dog—and yourself—more than six feet away from the television set.

Some Technical Information on Why Certain Nutrients Are Used to Fight Cancer

I said in the introduction that I would occasionally interrupt the basically practical thrust of this book to point out that holistic veterinarians haven't built their therapies out of thin air, or even just empiric evidence. If you're not interested in technical information, go ahead and skip this section. You won't miss anything of practical help for your cat.

Dr. Long sent me short summaries of some of the biochemical reasons a number of the vitamins and minerals are used to treat feline leukemia. I'll give just a sampling of that information here. In all cases, Dr. Long's references are to effects of the nutrients on workings of the immune system. However, these nutrients have other benefits, too. For instance, the four nutrients mentioned below after vitamin A are B vitamins. As Dr. Kearns has stressed, "The B vitamins enhance appetite, increase the feeling of well-being, detoxify the liver, protect the nervous system, *plus*."

- Thymus extracts: As long ago as 1975, it was shown that crude extracts of thymus increased cell-mediated immunity in children. Since then, more effective extracts of thymus have been developed, and doctors specializing in holistic medicine have kept up with the new developments.

- Vitamin A helps to prevent abnormal atrophy of the thymus gland.
- Animals denied B_2 have a smaller thymus and fewer antibodies.
- Vitamin B_6 is necessary for antibodies and cell-mediated responses.
- People with folic acid deficiencies have an impaired ability to form white blood cells.
- Pantothenic acid helps produce antibodies.
- Vitamin C increases the ability of white blood cells to get to, engulf, and destroy antigens. It also increases the production of Interferon, and the thymus needs vitamin C to produce its hormones.
- At lower levels of intake, vitamin E assists healthy immune responses. At higher levels, it fights inappropriate immune responses.
- The mineral calcium is essential for the destruction of foreign substances after they are engulfed by white blood cells.
- Cobalt helps the white blood cells to swallow and destroy the toxins.
- Manganese serves the same function as cobalt.
- Selenium in modest excess of what a healthy body needs stimulates antibody production.
- As reported by the Memorial Sloan-Kettering Cancer Center (a world-famous *orthodox* cancer center), zinc is essential for maintaining normal T-lymphocytes and other functions of the immune system.

Steps You Can Take Yourself to Help Your Cat Beat Cancer

I am definitely *not* telling you that you can use the suggestions in this section to cure your cat of cancer by yourself. You can use them primarily to give him a nutritional support that will help strengthen his immune system while at the same time offsetting some of the harmful effects of conventional cancer therapy. If your cat is being treated directly by a holistic veterinarian, show the suggestions in the rest of this chapter to your cat's doctor before proceeding to follow them on your own. This will serve two important purposes: First, the veterinarian may see that certain factors will duplicate or even overload your cat with something he or she is prescribing. Second, if the veterinarian doesn't have the extensive experience in treating cancer that Dr. Robert Goldstein does, he or she may look into something new that will help other cats in the future, or may opt to consult with Dr. Goldstein to get further details to help your cat.

Dr. Goldstein sent me the following nutritional cocktail as printed in *Love of Animals*, a newsletter he puts out with his wife, Susan, who edits it.* (Dr. Goldstein, who started out as an orthodox veterinarian, readily admits that Susan was ahead of him in pursuing alternative cancer therapies for humans, and it was at her urging that he started seeking alternative cancer therapies for cats and dogs.)

This nutritional cocktail, Dr. Goldstein writes, "is a helpful adjunct to treatment for just about any debilitating, degenerative, or chronic disease or condition. You can use it for any of the following diseases: cancer, liver and kidney disease, arthritis, skin problems, lupus, Lyme disease, inflammatory bowel disease, degenerative conditions of the pancreas, feline leukemia, feline AIDS."

Dr. Goldstein stresses that the ingredients in the cocktail must be organic: free of pesticides and other chemicals. "You certainly don't want a sick animal to get any more of these chemicals!" Organic foods are most easily obtained in health food stores. But thanks to the public's new awareness, many supermarkets are carrying organic food sections.

Dr. Goldstein calls the following "the radiation cocktail," perhaps because it does naturally what radiation therapy for cancer should do. He explains that the recipe "provides ample digestible proteins,

---

* You may subscribe by calling 1-800-711-2292.

which help the body to manufacture more of the immunoproteins necessary to fight disease. The beta-carotene gives the cocktail anticancer properties. Chlorophyll purifies the body. Aloe vera and vitamin E are renowned healers. Plus, this drink is teeming with life-force enzymes."

The Radiation Cocktail

In a blender, gently mix the following on the lowest speed possible. Because only the fresh drink with freshly extracted juices gives you the live enzymes, make a couple days' supply of the base and add the fresh juices just before feeding. Force-feed animals who are off their feed, but don't overfeed and cause vomiting. The ingredients are available at any good health food store.

Base:
¼ cup distilled or filtered pure water
1 tbsp. aloe vera juice
1 tbsp. powdered dulse or kelp
1 tbsp. nutritional yeast (unprocessed yeast containing the B vitamins)
1 tsp. organic apple cider vinegar (detoxifies the body)
½ tsp. ground rosemary (a natural preservative)
400 IU vitamin E (open a capsule and add its contents)
You can make up to a week's worth of this base at a time and keep it refrigerated.

Fresh Juices:
½ cup organic carrot juice (freshly extracted)
½ cup raw organic calves liver (fresh and blended) or 2 organic, raw egg yolks (no whites)
1 tbsp. parsley juice (freshly extracted)
These should be made fresh daily and added to the base just before feeding. Blend together on the lowest speed.
Dosage: For a cat 1 to 12 pounds: 2–3 tbsp. two to three times daily

You have already read that stopping vaccinations is a major concern of Dr. Lemmon in battling cancer. Dr. Goldstein states that "vaccination-induced weakness of the immune system can lay the groundwork for cancer." He further states that he has treated "scores of cats and dogs with cancer who I know had had their immune systems weakened by annual vaccinations."

Dr. Goldstein adds that once a cat is diagnosed with cancer, "he should *never* be vaccinated. I have seen cats go out of remission after getting a vaccine."

As I write in chapter 3, holistic doctors have a homeopathic remedy to do away with the negative effects of standard vaccinations. Dr. Goldstein says that "the homeopathic remedy Thuya occidentallis 30C removes the immune-suppressing effects of vaccinations." You can call a holistic veterinarian from the list at the back of this book, and he or she will send this remedy to you. Dr. Goldstein advises: "Crush three tablets and put the powder directly on the tongue one hour before or one hour after a meal. Do not repeat this therapy." (I know it's tempting to think that if three pills can help your cat, six or nine might help him even more. But medically, things don't work that way. Please heed Dr. Goldstein.)

The veterinarian recommends a product called Essiac, which contains a number of herbs combined synergistically to be "a potent tonic and detoxifier." He states that he never uses Essiac by itself for cancer patients, but that it works beautifully in combination with other remedies.

(Dr. Goldstein says that you can find Essiac at human health food stores, or you can call Essiac International at 1-800-668-4559 for further information. He advises: "Follow the instructions closely for how to make up the remedy. After the tea is made and the herbs strained out, dilute the Essiac with equal parts of distilled water and give your cat 1 teaspoon twice a day, either one hour before or after food.")

Dr. Goldstein reminds us that vitamin C works directly on strengthening the immune system. In a late note, the veterinarian wrote me that he prefers the newer Ester-C over both sodium ascorbate and ascorbic acid, two forms of vitamin C more traditionally used. "It is pH balanced and generally will not cause diarrhea," he noted. (It has been common to recommend giving C to the point of bowel tolerance, to avoid diarrhea. Dr. Goldstein stated that this may not be necessary with Ester-C; "just give it by dose," he recommends.)

The following boxed information gives Dr. Goldstein's further recommendations for nutritional support for your cat with cancer.

Additional Nutritional Support for Cancer Patients

Give all supplements at mealtimes unless otherwise noted. The AOX/PLX mentioned later is a high-dose antioxidant formula in an herbal base. Dr. Goldstein states: "I love this product, but it is hard to find." You can order it from the Animal Health Line at 203-222-0260.

- **Vitamin E (the mixed tocopherols form):** 400 IU daily
- **Daily Health Nuggets:*** Follow package directions.
- **Beta-carotene:** 5,000 IU daily
- **Garlic tablets (Garlicin):** one tablet twice daily
- **Selenium:** 50 *mcg* daily. Don't confuse this with 50 *mg*, a much higher amount that can cause a lot more harm than good.
- **Pancreatin:** one tablet daily
- **Coenzyme Q10:** 10–20 mg daily
- **Astragalus capsules:** half a pill twice daily
- **AOX/PLX:** one tablet twice daily

Whenever you give your cat supplements, the liquid or powdered form should be used, rather than tablets. If those forms are hard to

---

* Available by calling 1-800-711-2292. These are Dr. Goldstein's own formulas.

find, the tablets should be crushed (making them, of course, into a powder). Cats have a short digestive system, and as Dr. Price warns, a whole tablet sometimes goes through the cat's body so fast that "it comes out still a whole tablet." Obviously, the animal's body has not been able to utilize any nutrients in the tablet. Other veterinarians have warned that a cat can choke on a whole tablet.

If you're working with a holistic veterinarian, remember to discuss all of Dr. Goldstein's recommendations to avoid duplication or overloading.

The Story of Stevie from the Bronx

I'm concluding with the story of Stevie from the Bronx. It tells of a cat with terminal cancer whose owner saved him with the more typical holistic therapies detailed above combined with the newer IAT technique covered early in this chapter.

Steve, Stevie's owner, called me as I was beginning work on this edition to thank me for the information in the first book. Stevie's tumors had begun to shrink soon after Steve followed the nutritional therapies detailed in that edition. Steve, the owner, also consulted with Dr. Pitcairn on homeopathy—and Stevie, the cat, got even better. When Steve called me, I said I was researching IAT, which I felt might offer even more help for his cat.

But Steve didn't live near either Dr. Robert Goldstein or Dr. Marty Goldstein. "What if they ask me to travel to them?" Steve asked me. "Stevie has always been terrified of travel. Even when he didn't have this awful cancer, he would be sick for days if he rode in a car for an hour."

I said that very possibly what needed to be done could be accomplished through phone calls and the mail. (We saw earlier in the discussion on IAT that this is indeed true.) Drawing on my knowledge of the concern holistic veterinarians have for cats' psyches, I told Steve that maybe Dr. Marty Goldstein could give him pointers to calm Stevie's spirit if he did have to travel. (At the time, Dr. Robert Goldstein was dedicating himself exclusively to research.)

Several weeks later, Steve was kind enough to call me once again. "Stevie's cancer no longer shows up on any standard tests—or any of the more sophisticated tests of holistic veterinarians!"

So Stevie hadn't had to travel to Dr. Goldstein? "Well, he thought it best to see Stevie personally. But Dr. Goldstein gave me some pointers on how to travel with him. And now Stevie loves to travel! You should see him glow as soon as he sees he's going to go in the car!"

Summary

I hope the information in this chapter gives your cat years more to enjoy her life with you (and vice versa)—and that she gets to leave this world peaceably and without any suffering after a very long life. Or, as many holistic veterinarians have expressed to me as their goal, "when the cat herself has chosen to move on."

As mentioned, I have personal experience with return to full health from diagnosed terminal cancer in my little poodle, Shiki. My husband is alive and well a quarter of a century later than he "should be," according to orthodox specialists, of a disorder still classified as terminal even if found early. So I have been where you are now. Believe me, I know what you're feeling. And I wish you the same luck with alternative medicine as I have had.

But we have to face the fact that no doctor has yet found the secret to eternal life. If your cat doesn't respond to holistic therapy, you can comfort yourself that you tried the most advanced medical techniques to save her—and that maybe *she* made the choice.

National List of Holistic Veterinarians

The following list gives addresses and phone numbers not only of the veterinarians who worked on this book but also of many others throughout the country. I am indebted to Carvel G. Tiekert, director of the American Holistic Veterinary Medical Association (Bel Air, Maryland), who supplied the majority of these names.

Dr. Tiekert warns that a listing such as this changes frequently.

This directory is organized by the states in which the veterinarians presently practice. Each listing is followed by initials in capital letters that indicate the modalities each veterinarian uses. The code follows.

MODALITIES

AC - Acupuncture
AC(IVAS) - Acupuncture (International Veterinary Acupuncture Society certified)
AK - Applied Kinesiology
BF - Bach Flower Remedies
BI - Biotron II
CH - Chinese Herbs
CM - Conventional Medicine
CN - Clinical Nutrition
CR - Chiropractic
CT - Color Therapy
EAV - Electroacupuncture (Voll)
GT - Glandular Therapy
H - Homeopathy
HC - Homeopathy Classical
HO - Homeopathy Other
IN - Interro
MT - Magnetic Therapy
NU - Nutrition
PMT - Pulsating Magnetic Therapy
WH - Western Herbs

ALABAMA

Mary Battistella, DVM
2630 Dadeville Road
Alexander City, AL 35010
205-329-9900
AC(IVAS), CM

S. Allen Price, DVM
1444 Montgomery Highway
Birmingham, AL 35216
205-822-0210
Small Animal
AC, BF, CN, HC, NU

ALASKA

Jeanne Olson, DVM
1684 Palomino Drive
North Pole, AK 99705
907-488-2906
FAX: 907-488-2906
AC(IVAS), CR, CN, CM, EAV, H,
HC, NU

ARIZONA

James C. Armer, DVM
2085 Mountain Road, Suite 1
Sedona, AZ 86336
520-204-1034
Small Animal
AC(IVAS), BF, CH, CR, CN, CM,
HO, NU, WH

Holly R. Keppel, DVM
2641 E. 9th Street
Tucson, AZ 85716
520-297-3593
Small Animal, Exotic
CN, CM, HC

Deborah C. Mallu, DVM
215 Disney Lane
Sedona, AZ 86336
520-282-5651
FAX: 520-282-3586
AC(IVAS), BF, CH, CN, CT, CM,
GT, BI, NU, WH, Hands-on
Healing, Animal
Communication

Judith A. Stolz, DVM
67422 E. Avalon, Suite 3
Scottsdale, AZ 85251
602-899-1624
AC(IVAS), BF, CH, CN, CT, CM,
EAV, GT, HO, IN, NU, MT, WH

Norman Ward, DVM
7030 E. Fifth Avenue, Suite 3
Scottsdale, AZ 85251
602-946-0663
Small Animal, Exotic
AC(IVAS), BF, CH, CN, CM, GT,
HC, HO, NU, MT, WH,
Homotoxicology

ARKANSAS

Pat Bradley, DVM
Joy R. Dunn, DVM
#65 Sunny Gap Road
Conway, AR 72032
501-329-7727
FAX: 501-329-7727
Small Animal, Equine
HC, NU

CALIFORNIA

Manjit S. Nagi, DVM
2335 "F" Street
Livingston, CA 95334
209-394-8556
FAX: 209-394-8250
Small Animal
H, HC, HO

J. Lauren De Rock, DVM
16311 Gustafson Avenue, #331
Patterson, CA 95363
209-664-1764
Equine, AC(IVAS)

Linda C. Boggie, DVM
Village Veterinary Hospital
3125 W. Benjamin Holt
Stockton, CA 95219
209-951-5180
FAX: 209-951-0732
AC, NU, CR, WH, CH

Marc Bittan, DVM
11673 National Boulevard
Los Angeles, CA 90064
310-231-4415
FAX: 310-231-4418
Small Animal, Equine
AC, BF, CH, GT, HC, HO, NU

Roger W. Valentine, DVM
1637 Sixteenth Street
Santa Monica, CA 90404-3801
310-450-CATS
FAX: 310-392-7369
Feline
AC, AK, BF, CH, CR, CN, CM,
EAV, HO, NU, Allergy
Elimination Technique, House
Calls, Cat Products and Foods

Kathleen M. Carson, DVM
2103 Arlington Avenue
Hermosa Beach, CA 90501
310-372-8881
Small Animal
AC(IVAS), BF, CT, CM, HO,
Crystals, Therapeutic Touch

Richard Palmquist, DVM
721 Centinela Avenue
Inglewood, CA 90302
310-673-1910
Small Animal
AC, CM, GT, HO, NU

William L. Farber, DVM
2106 S. Sepulveda Boulevard
West Los Angeles, CA 91384
310-477-6735
Small Animal, Avian, Exotic
AC(IVAS), CH, CN, EAV, NU

Henry Pasternak, DVM
526 Palisades Drive
Pacific Palisades, CA 90272
310-454-2917
AC(IVAS), CH, CN, CM, GT, NU,
WH, Ozone

Beth Wildermann, DVM
17333 Bear Creek Road
Boulder Creek, CA 95006
408-354-1576
CM, GT, H, HC, NU, Reiki

Darren Hawks, DVM, DACVIM
1360 So. DeAnza Boulevard
San Jose, CA 95129
408-996-1155
FAX: 408-996-9434
Small Animal, Equine
BF, CR, CM, HC, HO, NU, WH,
Reiki

Pamela Bouchard, DVM
39 Crestview Drive
San Rafael, CA 94903-2880
415-499-0909
AC(IVAS), BF, CH, CN, CM,
NU, WH

Stanley Goldfarb, DVM
P.O. Box 150149
San Rafael, CA 94915-0149
415-459-2195
BF, CH, CR, CN, CT, EAV, GT,
HC, IN, BI, NU, WH

David W. Penney, DVM
Irving Street Veterinary
1434 Irving Street
San Francisco, CA 94122
415-664-0191
FAX: 415-664-6708
510-652-1003
Small Animal, Avian, Exotic
AC(IVAS), BF, CH, CR, CN,
CM, GT, HC, NU

Cheryl Schwartz, DVM
3619 California Street
San Francisco, CA 94118
415-387-6844
Small Animal
AC(IVAS), H

Kevin M. Fenton, DVM
78-359 Highway 111
La Quinta, CA 92253
619-564-1154
Small Animal, Equine, Exotic
AC, CH, CR

Adrienne Moore, DVM
Fallbrook, CA 92028
619-723-6633
BF, H

Robert Smatt, DVM
5621 Balboa Avenue
San Diego, CA 92111
619-278-1575
AC(IVAS), BF, CH, CR, CN
CM, GT, H, NU, MT, WH

Jack M. Long, VMD
5033 Gravenstein Highway No.
Sebastopal, CA 95472
707-823-7312
AC, CR, CN, CM, GT, H, HC,
NU, WH

Kerry Parker, DVM
Vallejo, CA
707-426-2174

Douglas Coward, DVM
25290 Marguerite Parkway
Mission Viejo, CA 92692
714-768-3651
Avian
CH, CN, CM, NU, WH

Don E. Lundholm, DVM
10130 Adams Avenue
Huntington Beach, CA 92646
714-964-1605
AC, CN, CM, EAV, H, HC, BI

David A. Gordon, DVM
22421 El Toro Road, Suite B
Lake Forest, CA 92630
714-770-1808
FAX: 714-770-8984
Small Animal
AC, CH, CR, CN, CM, NU, WH

Douglas Lemire, VMD
P.O. Box 40521
Santa Barbara, CA 93140
805-565-3985
AC(IVAS), BF, CH, CN, GT, HO,
NU, WH

Margaret M. Larned, DVM
3433 State Street, Suite D
Santa Barbara, CA 93105
805-569-5997
FAX: 805-569-5728
Small Animal, Avian
WH, CM, HO, Intuitive
Diagnostics Pendulum Dowsing

Ken Ninomiya, DVM
3624 Via Pacifica Walk
Oxnard, CA 93035
805-984-6293
FAX: 805-984-6293
Small Animal
AC(IVAS), CN, CM, HC, NU,
Network Chiropractic

John B. Limehouse, DVM
Priscilla A. Taylor, DVM
10742 Riverside Drive
No. Hollywood, CA 91602
818-761-0787
AC(IVAS), BF, CH, CR, CN, CT,
CM, EAV, GT, H, HC, HO, BI,
IN, NU, PMT, WH

Nancy Scanlan, DVM
13624 Moorpark Street
Sherman Oaks, CA 91423
818-784-9977
FAX: 909-597-8933
Small Animal
AC(IVAS), BF, CH, CR, CN,
CM, HO, NU, WH

Thomas Van Cise, DVM
1560 Hamner Avenue
Norco, CA 91760
909-737-1242
Small Animal, Avian, Exotic
AC(IVAS), CH, CR, CT, CM,
HO, WH, Acuscope, Reiki,
Auricular Medicine, Low Level
Laser Therapy

Robert A. Anderson, DVM
1695 Clara Avenue
Fortuna, CA 95540
916-944-3749
BF, CM, H, HC

Henry W. Kostecki, DVM
964 Rubicon Trail
South Lake Tahoe, CA 96150
916-541-3551
AC, BF, CH, CR, CN, CM, GT,
H, HC, NU, WH

Neal K. Weiner, DVM
P.O. Box 628
316 Texas Avenue
Lewiston, CA 96052
916-778-3109
Small Animal
BF, CR, CN, CM, GT, HO, NU,
WH, Reflexology

Monica A. Laflin, DVM
2159 San Elijo Avenue
Cardiff, CA 92007
760-436-3215
FAX: 760-436-4126
Small Animal, Avian, Exotics
AC(IVAS), CH, WH, CR, AVCA
certified, CN, NU, AK

COLORADO

Robert J. Silver, DVM
4660 Table Mesa Drive
Boulder, CO 80303
303-494-7877
FAX: 303-494-4496
Small Animal
AC(IVAS), BF, CH, CR,
CN, GT, HO, NU, MT, WH,
Therapeutic Touch, Crystal
Healing, Human Animal Bond

Rhonda L. Rodman, DVM
7910 W. 20th Avenue
Lakewood, CO 80215
303-202-0420
FAX: 303-202-0420
Small Animal, Equine
AC(IVAS), BF, CR, CN, HC,
MT, PMT

Jan Facinelli, DVM
5015 Raleigh
Denver, CO 80212
303-458-5428
AC(IVAS), BF, CH, CR, CN, GT,
CM, H, HC, NU, WH

David H. Jaggar, MRCVS, DC
5139 Sugar Loaf Road
Boulder, CO 80302-9217
303-682-1167
FAX: 303-682-7168
Small Animal, Equine, Farm
Animal
AC(IVAS), CH, CR, NU

H.C. Gurney, Jr. DVM
26497 Conifer Road
Conifer, CO 80433
303-674-0280
AC, BF, CH, CN, CT, CM, EAV,
GT, H, NU, MT, WH,
Immunology

David McCluggage, DVM
9390 Rogers Road
Longmont, CO 80503
303-702-1986
FAX: 303-702-9602
Small Animal, Avian, Exotic
AC(IVAS), BF, CH, CN, GT, HC,
NU, WH, Reiki

Linda East, DVM
311 S. Pennsylvania
Denver, CO 80209
303-733-2728
BF, CN, HC

Jay Clapper, DVM
7700 W. 101st Avenue
Broomfield, CO 80021
303-469-7387
H, NU

David Fong, DVM
P.O. Box 440410
Aurora, CO 80044
303-693-9314
AC, H, NU, BF, Contact Reflex
Analysis, House Call, CR, Reiki

Holly S. Foster, DVM
7187 E. Wyoming Place
Denver, CO 80224
303-759-4540
AC, BF, House Call Only

Jean Hofve, DVM
334 S. Pennsylvania Street
Denver, CO 80209
303-733-2728
303-733-3466
FAX: 303-733-2858
Small Animal (Feline)
BF, HC, NU

Judith Miller Shoemaker, DVM
2002-B West 120th Avenue
Westminster, CO 80234
303-438-0439
FAX: 303-460-7622
H, NU, (Clinical)

Barbara S. Shor, DVM
30884 Kings Valley Drive
Conifer, CO 80403
303-838-3419
FAX: 303-838-4244
BF

Rachel Blackmer, DVM
P.O. Box 841
Conifer, CO 80433
303-838-7698
FAX: 303-838-7698
Small Animal, Equine, Exotic
AC(IVAS), BF, CR, CT, HC,
Reiki, Pranamonics

Ron Carsten, DVM
1602 Grand Avenue
Glenwood Springs, CO 81601
970-945-0125
AC, H, NU, Osteopathic Manip,
Meridian Therapy

Elayne Williams, DVM
2633 S. College
Ft. Collins, CO 80525
970-226-4620
Small Animal, Avian, Exotic
BF, CH, CN, GT, HC

CONNECTICUT

Theresa M. Digiulio, VMD
356 Talcott Hill Road
Coventry, CT 06238
860-677-4638
AC, CM

Marcie Fallek, DVM
248 Alden Street
Fairfield, CT 06430
203-254-8642
Small Animal
AC(IVAS), BF, CM, GT, HC,
NU, WH

Jeff Feinman, DVM
73 Lyons Plain Road
Weston, CT 06883-2901
203-222-7979
FAX: 203-227-3231
Small Animal
AC, BF, CH, CR, CN, CM, GT,
HO, IN, BI, WH

Robert S. Goldstein, VMD
606 Post Road East
Northern Skies Animal Clinic
Westport, CT 06880
203-222-0260
FAX: 203-227-8094
Small Animal
AC, BF, CH, CR, CN, GT, HO,
NU, MT, WH, Immuno-
Augmentative Therapy (IAT) for
Cancer, Bio Nutritional Analysis
of Blood

Allen M. Schoen, DVM
15 Sunset Terrace
Sherman, CT 06784
860-354-2287
FAX: 860-350-3482
AC(IVAS), CH, CR, CN, CM,
GT, H, HC, HO, BI, NU, MT,
WH

Neil C. Wolff, DVM
530 E. Putnam Avenue
Greenwich, CT 06830
203-869-7755
AC(IVAS), BF, CH, CM, H, HC,
HO, NU, Laser AC

Stephen Tobin, DVM
26 Pleasant Street
Meriden, CT 06450
203-238-9863
FAX: 203-237-2334
CN, H, HC, WH

DELAWARE

Greig Howie, DVM
21 Muirfield Court
Dover, DE 19901
302-734-8425
FAX: 302-674-3099
Telephone Consultations
AC(IVAS), BF, CH, CN, CM,
GT, H, HC, WH

Lorraine Parris, DVM
Wilmington DE 19804
302-998-8851
AC(IVAS)

Shelley R. Epstein, VMD
828 Philadelphia Pike
Wilmington, DE 19809
302-762-2694
FAX: 302-762-1620
Small Animal, Exotic
CN, CM, HC

FLORIDA

Larry A. Bernstein, VMD
751 Northeast 168th Street
North Miami Beach, FL 33162-2427
305-652-5372(DAY)
305-653-7244(FAX)
Small Animal, Equine, Exotic
AC(IVAS), BF, CH, CR, CN, HC,
NU, WH

Russell Swift, DVM
7154 N. University Drive
Suite 720
Tamarac, FL 33321
954-720-0794
Small Animal, Avian, Exotic
BF, GT, HC, NU, WH,
Telephone Consultations,
Product Development,
Marketing

Peggy Fleming, DVM
21412 Field of Dreams Lane
Dade City, FL 33525
352-583-2400
FAX: 352-583-4007
Equine
AC(IVAS), BF, CH, CR, CN,
EAV, GT, HC, HO, NU, MT,
PMT, WH

Gerald A. Wessner, VMD
Belleview Holistic Veterinary Clinic
11409 S.E. US Highway 301
Belleview, FL 34420
352-245-2025
Small Animal, Equine
CN, EAV, GT, HO, NU

Brenda J. Ernest, DVM
1795 10th Avenue
Vero Beach, FL 32960
561-562-0666
CM, H, HC, NU, WH

Robert Katz, DVM
Arthur Young, DVM
3003 S. Federal Highway
Stuart, FL 34994
561-287-2242
FAX: 561-287-0089
Small Animal, Exotic, Avian
AC(IVAS), BF, CH, CM, CN,
EAV, GT, HC, NU, WH

Pamela Wood-Krzeminski, DVM
5142 Glencove Lane
West Palm Beach, FL 33415
561-964-8553
AC(IVAS), CR, CM, H, HC, HO,
NU, WH

Joseph Demers, DVM
496 N. Harbor City Boulevard
Melbourne, FL 32935
407-752-0140
FAX: 407-752-0150
Small Animal
AC(IVAS), BF, CH, CN, GT, HC

Lisa R. Edwards, DVM
545 Gus Hipp Boulevard
Rockledge, FL 32955
407-632-3800
FAX: 407-632-2366
Small Animal, Equine
AC(IVAS), BF, CR, CN, CM,
GT, HC, NU, Neuroemotional
Technique

Laura Earle, DVM
545 Gus Hipp Boulevard
Rockledge, FL 32955
407-632-3800
FAX: 407-632-2366
Small Animal, Avian, Exotic
CR, CN, CM, HC, NU

John Fudens, DVM
1171 Lakeview Road
Clearwater, FL 34616
813-446-3603
AC, HC, MT, NU, WH
Small Animals, Equine
Also Gemmotherapy,
Organotherapy, Radionics

Lucille Kohut, DVM
6465 142nd Avenue, N., #BB104
Clearwater, FL 34620
813-524-1190
FAX: 813-524-1190
Small Animal, Equine, Avian,
Exotic
HC, NU

Anne Lampru, DVM
9409 Tillotson Court
Odessa, FL 33556
813-933-6609
FAX: 813-933-1103
Small Animal, Avian, Exotic
AC(IVAS), BF, CH, CN, CM,
GT, HO, NU

Jeff Saunders, DVM
7200 US Highway 27 N
Sebring, FL 33870
813-382-9400
Small Animal, Equine, Exotic
AC, CH, CN, CM, HC, NU, WH

Betsy Coville, DVM
510 Stratfield Drive
Lutz, FL 33549
813-949-1818
Small Animal, Farm Animal,
Avian, Exotic
AC(IVAS), BF, CH, WH, HC

Mary Foster, DVM
Alachua, FL 32615
904-462-7017
AC(IVAS)

Maurice F. Casey III, DVM
Marianna Animal Hospital
Marianna, FL 32446-3445
904-482-3520
AC(IVAS)

Beth Brown, DVM
Braden River Animal Hospital
5012 State Road 64 East
Bradenton, FL 34208
941-366-4623
FAX: 941-746-0515
Small Animal, Equine
AC(IVAS), BF, CH, CR, CN,
CM, GT, HC, HO

John C. Haromy, DVM
3631 Highway 60 E.
Lake Wales, FL 33853
944-676-5922
FAX: 941-676-7342
Small Animal
AC(IVAS), CN, CT, CM, HC,
NU, MT

Ronald A. Johnson, DVM
680 Tennis Club Drive
Fort Lauderdale, FL 33311
954-731-2000
Small Animal
CH, CN, CM, HO, MT, WH

GEORGIA

Mary Brennan, DVM
965 Bobcat Court
Marietta, GA 30067
770-612-0318
FAX: 770-916-9809
AC(IVAS), BF, CH, CR, CN, CT,
GT, H, HC, HO, MT, WH,
Physical Exercise Therapy

Howard L. Rand, DVM
2000 Bill Murdock Road
Marietta, GA 30062
770-973-4133
AC(IVAS), CM, EAV, H, HO

Susan Wynn, DVM
1080 North Cobb Parkway
Marietta, GA 30062
770-424-6303
FAX: 770-426-4257
*AC(IVAS), BF, CH, CN, CM,
HC, HO, NU, WH*

Michelle Tilghman, DVM
1975 Glenn Club Drive
Stone Mountain, GA 30087
770-498-5956
FAX: 770-498-3458
*AC(IVAS), BF, CN, CM, GT, H,
HO, BI, NU, WH*

Heidi S. Newell, DVM
3270 Summer View Drive
Alpharetta, GA 30202
779-752-7237
*Small Animal
BF, CN, CM, NU, WH*

HAWAII

Ihor John Basko, DVM
P.O. Box 159
Kapaa, HI 96746
808-828-1330
FAX: 808-822-2452
*Small Animal, Equine, Farm
Animal, Avian
AC(IVAS), BF, CH, CR, CN, CT,
CM, GT, HC, HO, NU, PMT, WH,
Laser Therapy Massage*
*Does phone consultations worldwide at
above phone number or E-mail at
drbwavevet@hawaiian.net

IDAHO

Ronald L. Hamm, DVM
Grace, ID 83241
208-427-6233
801-750-7610
AC(IVAS)

Heather K. Mack, VMD
P.O.Box 597
Mountain Home, ID 83647
208-366-7992
*Small Animal, Equine
AC, BF, CH, CR, CM, HC, WH*

Debra J. Mack, DVM
3660 Flint Drive
Eagle, ID 83616-4534
208-322-4449
FAX: 208-322-4612
*Small Animal
AC, BF, CN, CM, HO, NU, MT, WH*

ILLINOIS

Ellen M. Paul, DVM
908 E. Main
Urbana, IL 61801
217-344-1017
FAX: 217-344-0654
AC(IVAS), BF, CH, CM, GT, NU, WH

Sharon L. Willoughby, DVM
P.O. Box 249
Port Byron, IL 61275
309-658-2920
FAX: 309-658-2622
*Equine, Canine
CR*

Judith Rae Swanson, DVM
1465 W. Catalpa Avenue
Chicago, IL 60640
773-561-4526
*AC(IVAS), BF, CN, CM, H, HC
(rare), HO (acute), NU*

Deborah M. Mitchell, DVM
2237 W. Schaumburg Road
Schaumburg, IL 60172
847-891-8944
FAX: 847-891-9040
Small Animal
AC(IVAS), BF, CH, CN, CM,
GT, H, HO, HC, NU, WH,
Massage/Touch Therapy

Herbert W. Preiser, DVM
2975 Milwaukee Avenue
Northbrook, IL 60062
847-827-5218
FAX: 847-827-7176
Small Animal
AC, BF, CR, CN, CM, HC, NU, WH

Annie Logan, DVM
34W 856 Country Club Road
St. Charles, IL 60174
630-513-7199
FAX: 630-377-8898
Small Animal, Equine
AC(IVAS), AK, CH, CR, EAV

Ray Sytek, DVM
1211-11th Street
Rockford, IL 61104
815-963-9685
FAX: 815-963-8192
CR(AVCA), EAV,
Orthomolecular Medicine

INDIANA

Carolyn S. Blakey, DVM
1821 W. Main Street
Richmond, IN 47374
317-966-0015
FAX: 317-935-9043
Small Animal, Exotic
AC(IVAS), BF, CN, CM, GT, HO,
NU, WH

Mark P. Haverkos, DVM
Box 119
Oldenburg, IN 47036
812-934-2410
AC, CH, CR, CM, EAV, H, HC,
NU, WH, Network Chiropractic

IOWA

Richard J. Holliday, DVM
3 Allamakee Street
Waukon, IA 52172
319-568-3401
AC(IVAS), Dairy Cattle
Specialist, Colostrum Therapy

Charles L. McDaniel, DVM
2804 68th Street
Des Moines, IA 50322-3469
515-278-9032
Small Animal, Equine, Farm
Animal
AC(IVAS), CR

William Pollak, DVM
1115 East Madison Avenue
Fairfield, IA 52556
515-472-6983
CH, CR, CN, CM, NU, WH,
Ayurvedic Medicine

KANSAS

Jeffrey F. Van Petten, DVM
RR 1 Box 98
Meriden, KS 66512
913-484-3358
FAX: 913-484-3230
Small Animal, Equine, Farm
Animal
AC(IVAS), CR, CM, EAC, MT

Yashema, DVM
Box 206
Neodesha, KS 66757-0206
316-325-2758
Small Animal, Equine, Farm
Animal, Avian, Exotic
Communication with Animals

KENTUCKY

Elizabeth (Betty) Boswell, DVM
5607 Oxford Court, #862
Louisville, KY 40291
502-459-4506
AC, CH, CN, CM, EAV, NU,
Physical Therapy

Earl Sutherland, DVM
P.O. Box 12009
Lexington, KY 40579
606-281-1183
AC(IVAS), CR

Frances E. Baker, DVM
303 Stoner Avenue
Paris, KY 40361
606-987-0856
FAX: 606-987-1971
Small Animal
AC(IVAS), BF, CM, EAV, WH

LOUISIANA

Casey Lestrade, DVM
P.O. Box 339
#4 Western Expressway
Westwego, LA 70094
504-436-7911
FAX: 504-436-7911
Small Animal, Avian, Exotic
AC, AC(IVAS)

Mary Finley, DVM
P.O. Box 234
Leonville, LA 70551
318-879-2020
Small Animal, Avian, Exotic
AC(IVAS), CH, CM, WH

Adriana Sagrera, DVM
802 Octavia Street
New Orleans, LA 70115
504-899-9510
FAX: 504-529-7183
Small Animal, Avian, Exotic
BF, CR, HO, MT

Lowell K. Roger, DVM
539 Bonnabel Boulevard
Metairie, LA 70005
504-832-5113
FAX: 504-832-5115
Equine
AC(IVAS), HC

MAINE

Lynda J. R. Bond, DVM
Vet Centre of Cape Elizabeth
207 Ocean House Road
Cape Elizabeth, ME 04107
207-799-2162
FAX: 207-799-1794
Small Animal, Exotic
AC, CH, EAC, MT

Sandra Haggett, VMD
21 Federal Street
Bar Harbor, ME 04609
207-288-5733
FAX: 207-288-5147
Small Animal
AC(IVAS), CH

Mary Orff, DVM
Limerick Mills Animal Hospital
Route 11, P.O. Box 537
Limerick, ME 04048
207-793-4493
FAX: 207-793-2968
Small Animal
BF, CH, WH, CM, HO, NU

MARYLAND

F. L. Earl, DVM
2613 Hughes Road
Adelphi, MD 20783
301-434-1811
CN, CM, NU

Monique Maniet, DVM
4820 Moorland Lane
Bethesda, MD 20814
301-656-2882
FAX: 301-656-5033
Small Animal
AC(IVAS), BF, CH, CR, CN,
CM, GT, H, HC, NU, WH

Christina B. Chambreau, DVM
908 Cold Bottom Road
Sparks, MD 21152
410-771-4968
F, H, HC, NU

John A. Eagling, DVM
11843 Ocean Gateway
Ocean City, MD 21842
410-213-1170
AC, CM

Linda Gray, DVM
1200 W. Old Liberty Road
Eldersburg, MD 21784
410-795-6106
*Small Animal, Equine, Avian,
Exotic*
AC, NU, HC, Reiki, Massage,
CH, Chiro, Magnets, WH, CM

Wendy Jensen, DVM
7764 Chatfield Lane
Ellicott City, MD 21043
410-379-0671
*Small Animal, Farm Animal,
Avian, Exotic*
GT, HC, NU, Reiki

Francine K. Rattner, VMD
85 West Central Avenue
Edgewater, MD 21037
410-956-2932
FAX: 410-956-3755
Small Animal, Exotic
BF, CM, HC, NU

Carvel G. Tiekert DVM
2214 Old Emmorton Road
Bel Air, MD 21015
410-569-7777
FAX: 569-2346
*Small Animal, Equine
(Acupuncture, Chiropractic)*
AC(IVAS), BF, CR, CN, CM, GL,
H, HC, BI, PMT, NU, AK

Grace L. Calabrese, DVM
P.O. Box 245
Phoenix, MD 21131-0245
410-557-6040
Small Animal, Equine
AC, BF, CH, CN, HC, NU, Reiki

Shearon C. Smith, DVM
3217 Henson Avenue
Annapolis, MD 21403
410-571-9661
301-261-8488
Small Animal
CH, CN, CM, HC, NU, WH,
Grief Counseling

Cindy Dahle, DVM
150 Kent Landing
Stevensville, MD 21666
410-643-7888
FAX: 410-604-0081
Small Animal
AC(IVAS), CH, WH, CN, CM

MASSACHUSETTS

Walter C. Jaworski, DVM
87 Old Wendell Road
Northfield, MA 01360
413-498-0174
Small Animal
GT, HC, NU

Jeffrey Levy, DVM
RR 01 Box 178-G
Williamsburg, MA 01096
413-268-3000
H, HC, NU

Robert G. Sidorsky, DVM
Rt. 2
Shelburne Falls, MA 01370
413-625-9517
CN, CM, H, NU, WH

Brian Corwin, DVM
96 Inverness Lane
Longmeadow, MA 01106
413-565-5104
FAX: 413-565-5104
1-888-567-3840
Small Animal
AC(IVAS), BF, CH, CN, CM,
GT, HC, NU, WH,
Homotoxicology, Dr. Reckewee

Bud Allen, M.S., DVM
99 Main Street
Haydenville, MA 01039
413-268-8387
FAX: 413-268-3899
Small Animal, Equine, Avian,
Exotic
AC(IVAS), AK, CR

Robin Karlin, DVM
99 Main Street
Haydenville, MA 01039
413-268-8387
FAX: 413-268-3899
Small Animal, Equine, Avian,
Exotic
BF, CM, HC, HO

Sarah L. Cochran, DVM
75 Locust Street
Uxbridge, MA 01569
508-278-6511
FAX: 508-278-7356
Equine
AC(IVAS)

Constance Breese, DVM
P.O. Box 1709
Edgartown, MA 02539
508-627-3623

Randy Caviness, DVM, CVA
35 Militia Circle
Stow, MA 01775
508-733-1337
Small Animal, Equine
AC(IVAS), CH, CN, CM, EAV,
GT, NU, WH

Nancy Crowley, DVM
120 Canal Street
Salem, MA 01970
508-741-2300
FAX: 508-744-4578
Small Animal
BF, CN, CM, HC, H, NU

MICHIGAN

Michael H. Stajich, DVM
Ann Arbor, MI 49404
313-434-5800
AC(IVAS)

H.D. Sheridan, DVM
16025 68th Avenue
Coopersville, MI 49404
616-837-8151
AC(IVAS), CM, H, HO

Lynne Friday, DVM
5346 Main Street
Lexington, MI 48450
810-359-8828
AC, CR, CM, HO, AK

John M. Simon, DVM
410 N. Woodward
Royal Oak, MI 48067
810-545-6630
*AC, BF, CH, CR, CN, CM, EAV,
GL, HO, MT, NU, AK, Mega
Therapy*

Albert W. Lynch, DVM
7966 U.S. 31 S.
Grawn, MI 49637
616-276-6361
*Small Animal
CN, CM, NU, WH, Super Blue-
Green Algae*

Russell W. Wagner, DVM
7045 Traverse Avenue
P.O. Box 242
Benzonia, MI 49616
616-882-9906
FAX: 616-882-4434
AC, CR, HO, Energy Sensory

Grace Chang, DVM
20158 Maplewood Street
Livonia, MI 48152-2021
248-356-0822
FAX: 248-356-0826
*Small Animal
AC*

MINNESOTA

Roger DeHaan, DVM
RR 1, Box 47A
Frazee, MN 56544
218-846-9112(MWF 9–12)
*Small Animal, Equine, Farm
AC(IVAS), BF, CH, CR, CN,
CM, GT, H, HC, HO, NU, MT,
WH, Telephone Consultation,
Neuro-muscular Release,
Proliferative Therapy, Neural
Therapy, Applied Kinesiology,
Laser Therapy*

Catherine Sayler, DVM
2400 Stevens Avenue, South
Minneapolis, MN 55404
612-870-4778
*AC(IVAS), BF, CH, CN, CM,
EAV, GT, H, HO, NU, WH*

William G. Winter, DVM
3131 Hennepin Avenue S
Minneapolis, MN 55408
612-825-6859
FAX: 612-824-6436
*AC, BF, CH, CN, CM, GL, H,
HC, HO, NU, WH, Massage
Therapy, Behavior Therapy*

Fred Pomeroy, DVM
185 E. 7th
St. Paul, MN 55101
612-224-4815
*Small Animal
GT, Cont Reflex Analysis, AK*

Charlie Westman, DVM
2620 Kenzie Terrace, #228
St. Anthony, MN 55418
612-464-8542
Small Animal, Equine
AC, CR, CN, MT

MISSISSIPPI

John R. Adams, DVM
5854 Canton Park Drive
Jackson, MS 39211
601-977-9327
Small Animal, Avian, Exotic
CH, CN, CM, WH

MISSOURI

Robert Schaeffer, Jr., DVM
7001 Hampton Avenue
St. Louis, MO 63109
314-353-3444
Small Animal, Equine, Avian,
Exotic
AC(IVAS), BF, CH, CN, CM,
HC, NU, WH

Randy Kidd, DVM
911 W. 33rd Street
Kansas City, MO 64111
816-561-9011
FAX: 816-561-9011
Small Animal, Equine, Farm
Animal, Avian, Exotic
AC, BF, CR, CN, CM, HC, NU,
WH, Network CHIRO

Christine J. Crosley, DVM
2615 S. Big Bend Boulevard
St. Louis, MO 63143
314-781-1738
FAX: 314-781-1702
Small Animal
BF, CN, CM, HC, WH

MONTANA

John K. Harshman, DVM
P.O Box 371
Chinook, MT 59523
406-357-2936
FAX: 406-357-3367
Small Animal, Equine, Farm
Animal, Avian, Exotic
BF, GT, HO, NU

NEBRASKA

Joseph E. Landholm, DVM
Lincoln, NE 68510-4972
402-483-4862
AC(IVAS)

Diane Simmons, DVM
707 Tara Plaza
Papillion, NE 68046
402-593-6556
FAX: 402-593-8810
Small Animal, Equine
AC(IVAS), CH, CR, CN, EAC,
HO, NU, WH

NEVADA

Joanne Stefanatos, DVM
1325 Vegas Valley Drive
Las Vegas, NV 89109
702-735-7184
FAX: 702-732-4266
AC(IVAS), BF, CH, CR, CN, CT,
CM, EAV, GL, H, HO, IN, NU,
MT, PMT, WH, Chelation
Therapy, Neural Therapy

Amy K. Mason, DVM
P.O. Box 20283
Carson City, NV 89721
702-884-4362
Small Animal, Equine, Farm
Animal
AC, BF, CR, CN, CM, NU

NEW HAMPSHIRE

Katherine Evans, DVM
38 Ham Road
Raymond, NH 03077
603-225-9680
AC(IVAS), CH, CM, WH

Gretchen E. Ham, DVM
Derry, NH 03038-1949
603-329-6689
AC(IVAS)

George Tarkleson, DVM
123 Main
Colebrook, NH 03576
603-237-8871
FAX: 603-237-8248
Small Animal, Equine, Farm Animal
HC, NU

NEW JERSEY

Gerald Buchoff, DVM
9018 Kennedy Boulevard
North Bergen, NJ 07047
201-868-3753
Fax: 201-868-0453
Small Animal
AC(IVAS), BF, CH, CR, CN, GT, HC, WH

Brian T. Voynick, DVM
1202 Sussex Turnpike
Randolph, NJ 07869
201-895-4999
FAX: 973-895-4948
Small Animal
AC(IVAS), WH, EAV, Moxabustion

Gloria B. Weintrub, VMD
190 Rt. 70
Medford, NJ 08055
609-953-3502
FAX: 609-953-5907
Small Animal
AC(IVAS), BF, CH, CR, CN, CM, GT, HO, IN

Mark D. Newkirk, DVM
9200 Ventnor Avenue
Margate, NJ 08402
609-823-3031
FAX: 609-822-9152
Small Animal, Avian, Exotic
AC(IVAS), BF, WH, CR, Immuno-Augmentative Therapy for Cancer, Metabolic Nutrition Analysis

Charles T. Schenck, DVM
777 Helmetta Boulevard
East Brunswick, NJ 08816
908-257-8882
AC(IVAS), BF, CN, CM, HO, IT

NEW MEXICO

B. Dee Blanco, DVM
P.O. Box 5865
Santa Fe, NM 87502-5865
505-473-1012
Small Animal
AC(IVAS), BF, CN, GT, HC, NU, WH

Mona Ann Boudreaux, DVM
3200 Coors Suite D
Albuquerque, NM 87107
505-836-1736
FAX: 505-836-1736
Small Animal
AC(IVAS), BF, CH, CR, CM, GT, HO, NU

Annet L. Sheffield, DVM
8200 Montgomery NE #230
Albuquerque, NM 87109
505-292-3666
FAX: 505-332-8187
Small Animal

Gigi Gaulin, DVM
Rt. 2, Box 135
San Juan Pueble, NM 87566
505-852-0213
Small Animal
AC, BF, CH, HC, NU

Sharon Reamer, DVM
2501 E. 20th, Suite A6
Farmington, NM 87401
505-327-2031
Small Animal, Avian, Exotic
BF, CN, CM, EAV, HC

Jody Kincaid, DVM
901 E. Franklin
Anthony, NM 88021
915-886-4558
Small Animal, Equine
AC, CH, CM, HO, NU, WH,
35% H₂O₂ Therapy

NEW YORK

Michele A. Yasson, DVM
1101 Rt. 32
Rosendale, NY 12472
914-658-3923
Has office in New York City
Tuesdays at 47 E. 30th
AC(IVAS), BF, CN, HC, NU

Steven Kasanofsky, DVM
250 West 100th Street
New York, NY 10025
212-865-2224
FAX: 212-787-1993
Small Animal
AC, CN

Richard J. Joseph, DVM
Animal Medical Center
New York, NY 10021
212-838-8100
AC(IVAS) Neurology

Phillip Racyln, DVM
219 West 79th Street
New York, NY 10024
212-787-1993
FAX: 212-787-1397
Small Animal
AC, BF, CH, CN, CM, GT, HO,
NU, WH

Marcie Fallek, DVM
451 E. 83 Street, Apt. 5B
New York, NY 10028
212-330-7061
Small Animal
AC(IVAS), BF, CM, GT, HC,
NU, WH

Peter L. Brown, DVM
112 W. Lake Road
Penn Yan, NY 14527
315-536-2771
Small Animal, Equine, Exotic
AC, BF, CH, CN, CM, HC, HO,
NU, MT, WH

Ron Scharf, DVM
2764 Troy Schenectady Road
Niskayuna, NY 12309
518-785-9731
AC(IVAS), CM

Lisa G. Potkewitz, DVM
Foothills Veterinary Services
P.O. Box 3040
Saratoga Springs, NY 12866
518-587-5228
Small Animal, Farm Animal
WH, CN, NU, Anthroposophy,
Biodynamic Farming
Preservation of Rare Farm
Breeds

Craig H. Russell, DVM
P.O. Box 396 Pleasant Street
Westport, NY 12993
518-962-8228
FAX: 518-962-8308
Small Animal
WH, CN, CM, NU

Margaret B. Ohlinger, DVM
3800 County Route 6
Alpine, NY 14805
607-274-8090
Small Animal, Equine, Farm
AC, CR, CM, HC

Iris Prestas, DVM
90 Main Street
Candor, NY 13743
607-659-4220
CM, H, HC, NU, WH

Cynthia Lankenau, DVM
3380 Maple Road
Wilson, NY 14172
716-751-3885
Small Animal, Equine, Farm
Animal, Avian
AC(IVAS), BF, CH, CR, GT, HC,
HO, WH, NU, Reiki

Patrick Tersigni, VMD
Hemmer Road, RD 1
Wayland, NY 14572
716-728-5562
CR, Radiance Technique (AKA-
Real Reiki)

John A. Ober, DVM
West Main Street
Westfield, NY 14787
716-326-3933
Small Animal (Split shift)
AC(IVAS), CH, CR, HO, WH

Alisa Sheade-Koenig, DVM
653 South Street
E. Aurora, NY 14052
716-687-1808
Small Animal, Equine
HC, NU, WH

Mark E. Haimann, DVM
1 Bay Club Drive, Apt. W19J
Bayside, NY 11360
718-631-1396
CH, CN, H, HC, NU, WH

John F. Sangiorgio, DVM
12930 Clove Road
Staten Island, NY 10301
718-720-4211
FAX: 718-720-4212
Small Animal, Equine
CH, CR, CN, CM, HC, NU, MT,
PMT, WH

Ivan Szilvassy, DVM
98 Norman Avenue
Brooklyn, NY 11222
718-389-8866
CH, CN, H, HC, NU, MT, WH,
Reflexology

Beverly Cappel-King, DVM
11 S. Main Street
Chestnut Ridge, NY 10977
914-356-3838
Immuno-Augmentative Therapy
(Cancer)

Mary Finger, DVM
East Village Vet
241 Eldridge Street
New York, NY 10002
212-674-8640
CN, CM, H, NU, WH

Martin Goldstein, DVM
Rob Witel, DVM
400 Smithridge Road
South Salem, NY 10590
914-533-6066
AC(IVAS), BF, CH, CR, CN,
CM, GT, H, HC, HO, NU, MT,
WH, Immuno-Augmentative
Therapy (Cancer), Ozone
Therapy, Metabolic Nutritional
Analysis (MNA)

Diane C. Abbysinian, DVM
250 Central Park Avenue
White Plains, NY 10606-1218
914-949-8860
FAX: 914-949-3478
Small Animal
AC, CH, CR, CN, CT, NU, MT,
Acupressure, Reiki

NORTH CAROLINA

William M. Martin, DVM
6795 Hendersonville Road
Fletcher, NC 28732
704-684-4244
AC(IVAS), CM

James Miller, DVM
493 Warrior Mountain Road
Saluda, NC 28773
704-749-2233
AC, BF, IN, MT

James E. Schacht, DVM
6400 E. Independence Boulevard
Charlotte, NC 28212
704-535-6688
Avian, Exotic
AC(IVAS), BF, CH, HC

Kim V. Hombs, DVM
6520 McMahon Drive
Charlotte, NC 28226
704-542-2000
FAX: 704-542-2000
Small Animal
AC, AC(IVAS), BF, CH, CN,
CM, HO

John H. Koontz, DVM
4306 Roxboro Road
Durham, NC 27704
919-471-1579
Equine
AC, CN, CT, HC

Charles E. Loops, DVM
Route 2, Box 568
Pittsboro, NC 27312
919-542-0442
H, HC, Telephone Consultations

Adele C. Monroe, DVM
4122 Pecan Drive
Stem, NC 27581
919-693-0442
Small Animal
CR, CN, HC, NU, WH, Flower
Essence Therapy, Reiki

Ann Davis, DVM
3741 High Point Road
Greensboro, NC 27407
910-299-5431
FAX: 910-299-5441
Small Animal
BF, CH, WH, HC, NU

Kathy Radford, DVM
4740 High Point Road
Greensboro, NC 27407
910-294-1944
FAX: 910-297-1040
Small Animal
BF, CH, WH, CN, CM, HC, NU

OHIO

Pamela Fisher, DVM
5250 Pinedrive Circle NW
North Canton, OH 44720
330-494-7387
FAX: 330-494-8179
Small Animal
CH, CN, CM, GT, HO, NU, WH

Ronald L. McNutt, DVM
Lima, OH 45805
419-331-1456
AC(IVAS)

George D. Norris, DVM
5756 North High Street
Worthington, OH 43085
614-885-0333
AC(IVAS), BF, CN, CM, H, HC,
NU, MT, PMT

Donn W. Griffith, DVM
3859 W. Dublin-Granville Road
Dublin, OH 43017
614-889-2556
FAX: 614-761-3623
AC(IVAS), BF, CH, CR, CN, CT,
CM, EAV, GT, H, HC, HO, NU,
BI, MT, WH, Osteopathic,
Radionics, Counseling,
Prepurchase Exotic Animals

OKLAHOMA

Nita McNeill, DVM
130 E. Highway 152
Mustang, OK 73064
405-376-4556
AC, BF, CR, CN, CM, EAV,
NU, Bio Acidative Medicine

George A. Carley, DVM
Hunters Glen Vet Hosp
9150 South Braden
Tulsa, OK 74137
918-493-3332
Small Animal, Exotic
AC(IVAS), CN, CM, HC, N, WH

OREGON

R. H. Anderson, DVM
1590 E. Ellendale
Dallas, OR 97338
503-623-8318
AC(IVAS), CR, CN, CM, EAV,
H, IN, NU, MT

Jeffrey Judkins, DVM
Bob Ulbrich, VMD
1431 SE 23rd
Portland, OR 97214
503-233-2332
Small Animal, Avian, Exotic
AC(IVAS), BF, CH, CN, CM,
GT, HC, WH

Jim Simpson, DVM
19073 Beavercreek Road
Oregon City, OR 97045
503-650-1667
FAX: 503-650-1667
Small Animal
AC, BF, CH, WH, CR, CN, CM,
GT, HC, HO

Richard Pitcairn, DVM
1283 Lincoln Street
Eugene, OR 97401
541-342-7665
FAX: 503-344-5356
Small Animal
BF, CN, H, HC, NU

Donna Starita Mehan, DVM
27728 SE Haley Road
Boring, OR 97009
503-663-7277
FAX: 503-663-9393
Small Animal, Equine, Farm
Animal
BF, CH, CR, CN, CT, CM, EAV,
GT, HO, NU, MT, WH,
Radionics, Crystal Healing

Bob Ulbrich, VMD
2227 SW Primrose Street
Portland, OR 97219
503-233-2332
Small Animal
BF, CH, GT, HC, NU, Pranic
Healing

PENNSYLVANIA

Deva Kaur Khalsa, VMD
1724 Yardley-Langhorne Road
Yardley, PA 19067-5517
215-493-0621
Small Animal
AC(IVAS), BF, CH, AK, EAV,
CR, CN, CM, GT, HO, IN, NU,
MT, WH, Phone Consultations,
Ozone, NAET, Allergy
Elimination Technique

Michael S. Tierney, VMD
428 Brownsburg Road
Upper Makefield
Newtown, PA 18940
215-598-3951
FAX: 215-598-3746
Small Animal, Equine, Farm
Animal, Avian, Exotic
AC(IVAS), BF, CH, CR, CN,
CM, GT, HC, NU

Susan Yatsky, VMD
341 W. Butler Avenue
New Britain, PA 18901
215-340-0345
AC, CH, CN, CM, GL, HO, NU

Sally Myton, VMD
999 Killarney Drive
Pittsburgh, PA 15234
412-884-2434
FAX: 412-884-5222
Small Animal
BF, CM, H, HO, NU

Douglas E. Knueven, DVM
357 State Street
Beaver, PA 15009
412-774-8047
FAX: 412-774-5774
Small Animal
AC(IVAS), BF, CM, HC

John C. Harthorn, DVM
2176 Brush Run Road
Avella, PA 15312
412-345-3350
FAX: 412-345-3706
Equine
AC(IVAS), WH, CR, HC

Elizabeth E. Burke, DVM
929 Northampton Street
Easton, PA 18042
610-559-0728
Small Animal
BF, HC

Carlos F. Jimenez, DVM
All Creatures Mobile Vet
St. Peters, PA 19470
610-469-1119
AC(IVAS)

Meredith Snader, VMD
2140 Conestoga Road
Chester Springs, PA 19425
610-827-7742
FAX: 610-827-1366
Equine
AC(IVAS), CH, CR, HO

Jeanne F. Wordley, VMD
402 W. 3rd Street
Media, PA 19063-2601
610-566-9019
Small Animal
AC(IVAS), CH, CM, NU

Marjorie M. Lewter, DVM
RR 2, Box 155F
Ulster, PA 18850
717-596-3757
Small Animal, Equine, Farm
Animal
AC, AC(IVAS), BF, CH, CN,
HO, WH

C. Edgar Sheaffer, VMD
47 N. Railroad Street
P.O. Box 353
Palmyra, PA 17078-0353
717-838-9563
FAX: 717-838-0377
Small Animal, Equine, Farm
Animal
CM, HC

Susan Beal, DVM
Glen Dupree, DVM
East Main Street
Big Run, PA 15716
814-427-5004
FAX: 814-427-5929
Small Animal, Equine, Farm
Animal, Avian, Exotic
AC, BF, WH, CR, CN, GT, HO,
NU, MT, Magnetic Therapy

RHODE ISLAND

Elizabeth Campbell, DVM
Wolfrock Animal Health Center
710 South County Trail
Exeter, RI 02822
401-294-0102
Small Animal, Farm Animal,
Exotic
AC, BF, CH, CM, EAV, HO, NU,
WH

SOUTH CAROLINA

Jeanne R. Fowler, DVM
409 Old Buncombe Road
Travelers Rest, SC 29690
864-834-7334
AC, CN, CM, GT, H, HC

Stanley Gorlitsky, DVM
461 Coleman Boulevard
Mt. Pleasant, SC 29464
803-881-9915
AC(IVAS), BF, CH, CN, CM,
GL, H, HC, HO, MT, WH

TENNESSEE

Sandra Priest, DVM
600 Bennington Circle
Knoxville, TN 37909
423-690-3863
FAX: 423-690-3863
Small Animal
BF, CR (AVCA certified), GT,
HC, NU, WH, Reiki

TEXAS

Norman C. Ralston, DVM
12500 Lake June Road
Mesquite, TX 75180
214-286-6407
AC(IVAS), BF, CR, EAV, H, MT,
Proliferant, & Neural Therapy

Thomas L. Granger, DVM
380 North LHS Drive
Lumberton, TX 77656
409-755-7216
Small Animal
AC(IVAS), CH, CM, EAC, WH,
Reiki

Jackie Cole, DVM
3802 Cove View
Galveston, TX 77554
409-740-0808
Small Animal
AC(IVAS), CM, EAV

William Falconer, DVM
8005 N. Madrone Trail
Austin, TX 78737
512-288-5400
FAX: 512-288-5402
Small Animal, Avian
BF, GT, HC, NU

Madalyn Ward, DVM
Rt. 6, Box 47-H
Austin, TX 78737
512-288-0428
Equine
CR, CN, HC

S. J. Gravel, DVM
Rt. 2 Box 140
Lockhart, TX 78644
512-398-3719
Small Animal
AC(IVAS), CH, CM, EAV, WH

Patricia A. Cooper, DVM
1951 Lexington
Houston, TX 77098
713-520-5588
FAX: 713-523-8345
Small Animal
BF, CN, HO, NU

Nancy A. Bozeman, DVM
5721 SW Green Oaks Boulevard
Arlington, TX 76017
817-572-2400
AC(IVAS), BF, CR, CN, CM,
GT, H, HC, HO, NU, WH

Jerry B. Dittrich, DVM
9009 Highway 377 South
Benbrook, TX 76126
817-249-2744
FAX: 817-249-0714
Small Animal, Equine, Farm,
Avian, Exotic
AC(IVAS), CH, CR, CN, CM,
EAC, GT, H, NU

Paul R. Bruton, DVM
1615 E. Southlake Boulevard
Southlake, TX 76092
817-481-1382
Small Animal, Equine
AC(IVAS), CR, CM, EAV, NU

Brian A. Reeves, DVM
2711 University Boulevard
Tyler, TX 75701-7465
903-566-2011
AC(IVAS)

Shawn Messonnier, DVM
2145 W. Park Boulevard
Plano, TX 75075
972-867-8800
FAX: 214-985-9216
Small Animal, Avian, Exotic
AC, CM, NU, Dietary
Supplement, Allergy and
Arthritis Treatment

Anna Maria Scholey, DVM
2922 Mill Trail
Carrollton, TX 75007
972-245-1123
FAX: 972-245-1123
Small Animal
AC(IVAS), BF, EAV, GT, HC,
NU, MT, Reiki

Betsy Walker-Harrison, DVM
100 Park Road S.
Wimberley, TX 78676
210-935-2596
Small Animal
BF, CN, GT, HC, WH,
Telephone Consultations

James K. Bielfeldt, DVM
305 Fawn Drive
San Antonio, TX 78231
210-696-1700, 210-696-3753
Small Animal
AC, EAV

UTAH

Kimberly Henneman, DVM
150 Starview Drive
Park City, UT 84098
801-647-0807
FAX: 801-647-2985
Small Animal, Equine, Exotic
AC(IVAS), BF, CR, CM, ElecAC,
H, MT, N, WH

Shannon Hines, DVM
3305 So. Orchard Drive
Bountiful, UT 84010
801-296-1230
FAX: 801-298-8445
Small Animal
CM, H, MT

VERMONT

David T. Lamb, DVM
Justin Morrill Highway
South Stafford, VT 05070
802-765-4400
AC, CR, CM

George Glanzberg, VMD
RR 1, Box 373
No. Bennington, VT 05257
802-442-8714
CN, CM, H, HC, NU

Alaire Smith-Miller, DVM
RR 1, Box 636
Wilmouth Hill Road
Cuttingsville, VT 05738
802-747-4076
Small Animal, Equine, Avian
AC, BF, CN, CM, HC, NU, MT

William K. Kruesi, DVM
Nickwackett Animal Hospital
RR 3, Box 3113
Pittsford, VT 05763
802-483-9318
Small Animal
WH, CN, CM, HC, NU

VIRGINIA

Cheryl A. Caputo, DVM
P.O. Box 240
430 Roanoke Road
Daleville, VA 24083
540-992-4550
FAX: 540-992-1822
Small Animal
AK, BF, CN, CM, GT, HC, MST,
NU, WH

Joyce C. Harman, MRCVS
P.O. Box 488
Washington, VA 22747-0008
540-675-1855
FAX: 540-675-1447
AC(IVAS), BF, CH, Network
CR, CN, H, HC, HO, NU

Carol A. Lundquist, DVM
P.O. Box 394
Washington, VA 22747
540-675-2273
FAX: 540-675-2040
Equine
AC, AK, BF, CH, CR, CN, HC,
HO, LM, MT, NU, WH

Jordan A. Kocen, DVM
6136 Brandon Avenue
Springfield, VA 22150
703-569-0300
FAX: 703-866-4962
AC(IVAS), CH, HC

Maureen McIntyre, DVM
6540 Megills Court
Clifton, VA 20124
703-449-9144
Small Animal, Equine
AC(IVAS), CR, EAV

Anita Walton, DVM
P.O. Box 488
Locust Grove, VA 22508-0488
703-972-3869
FAX: 703-972-9216
Small Animal
AC(IVAS), BF, CN, CM, GT,
HC, NU, WH

Nino Aloro, DVM
2212 Laskin Road
Virginia Beach, VA 23454
757-340-5040
FAX: 757-340-5043
Small Animal
CH, CN, CM, NU, WH

Stephen Dill, DVM
Rt. 2, Box 156
Barboursville, VA 22923
804-985-4795
Equine
AC(IVAS), CR, CM, HC

Martin Schulman, VMD
RR 1, Box 20
Crozet, VA 22932
804-823-4300
FAX: 804-823-6436
Small Animal
CH, CN, GT, NU, WH

WASHINGTON

Michael W. Lemmon, DVM
P.O. Box 2085
Renton, WA 98056
206-226-8418
AC, BF, CH, CR, CN, CM, GL,
H, HC, NU, MT, PMT, WH

Donna Kelleher, DVM
6741 Beach Drive SW
Seattle, WA 98136
206-935-3041
Small Animal
AC(IVAS), CH, CN, CM, EAV,
GT, WH

Patti Schaefer, DVM
3430 Pacific Avenue, Ste #6355
Olympia, WA 98501
360-923-5759
206-370-1350
Small Animal
AC, BF, CH, CN, CM, HC, NU

Steve Marsden, DVM
7302 NE 43rd Way
Vancouver, WA 98662
503-255-7355
Small Animal, Exotic
AC, BF, CH, CN, CM, EAV, GT,
HC, NU, WH, Naturopathic
Medicine

Pamela Jen, DVM
21416 NE 10th Avenue
Ridgefield, WA 98642-9459
360-887-0714
Small Animal
AC(IVAS), BF, CH, CR Network,
CN, CM, HO, NU, WH, Qi
Gong, Massage TX, Physical
TX

Tevinder Sodhi, DVM
6501-196th Street SW, #F
Lynnwood, WA 98036
Bellevue, WA 98004
206-771-6300
FAX: 206-771-6300
206-455-8900
FAX: 206-455-9946
Small Animal, Exotic
BF, CN, HC, HO, Ayurveda

Eric P. Hartmann, DVM
704 E. Thomas Street, #107
Seattle, WA 98102-5434
206-781-6709
Small Animal
AC(IVAS), BF, CH, CN, GT, HC,
HO, NU, WH

Lee Herzig, DVM
8306 Stringtown Road East
Eatonville, WA 98328
360-832-6500
FAX: 360-832-6252
Small Animal
AC(IVAS), CR, CN, CM, GT, WH

Junia Childs, DVM
Holistic Veterinary Medicine
and Acupuncture
722 16th Avenue West
Kirkland, WA 98033
425-889-9498
Small Animal
Traditional Chinese Medicine
AC, CH, WH, BF, H, NU
Phone Consultations

Larry Siegler, DVM
8015 165th Avenue NE
Redmond, WA 98052
425-885-5400
FAX: 425-869-2304
Small Animal
AC(IVAS), BF, CH, WH, CN,
CM, HC, NU

Douglas R. Yearout, DVM
9004 Vernon Road
Everett, WA 98205
425-334-8171
FAX: 425-334-1136
Small Animal, Avian, Exotic
Wildlife Rehab
AC, AK, AR, AY, BF, CH, CR,
CN, CM, EAV, GT, HC, LM,
MT, PMT, NU, RI, WH

Kerry Fisher, DVM
11901 North Division
Spokane,WA 99218
509-468-0443
FAX: 509-468-0452
Small Animal
AC, CH, WH, CR, CN, MT, Pain
Management

H. Jonathan Wright, DVM
7327 South Cedar Road
Spokane, WA 99224
509-443-0803
Small Animal
BF, GT, H, HO, NU, Reiki
Telephone Consultations
Housecalls

Michael Flaherty, DVM
6741 Beach Drive SW
Seattle, WA 98136
425-745-6745
Small Animal, Exotic
CN, CT, CM, NU, Home
Euthanasia Consultations

WEST VIRGINIA

Jane Laura Doyle, DVM
P.O. Box 568
Berkeley Springs, WV 25411
304-258-5819
AC(IVAS), BF, CH, CR, CN, CM,
EAV, H, HC, HO, NU, WH

WISCONSIN

Maria H. Glinski, DVM
1405 W. Silver Spring Drive
Glendale, WI 53209
414-228-7655
FAX: 414-228-1072
Small Animal
AC(IVAS), BF, CH, CR, CN,
CM, EAV, GT, HC, HO, LM,
MT, PMT, NU, WH

Pedro Luis Rivera, DVM
9824 Durand Avenue
Sturtevant, WI 53177
414-886-1100
FAX: 414-886-6460
Small Animal, Equine, Farm
Animal, Avian, Exotic
BF, CH, CR, CN, CT, CM, GT,
HC, HO, NU, WH, Massage
Therapy, Acupressure

Marta Engel, DVM
Rt. 1, Box 1198
Soldiers Grove, WI 54655
608-734-3711
FAX: 608-734-3306
Small Animal, Equine, Farm Animal
CM, H, HC, NU

Mike Kohn, DVM
1014 Williamson
Madison, WI 53703
608-255-1239
Small Animal
AC(IVAS), BF, HC, NU, WH

Deborah L. Schroeder, DVM
1440 E. Washington Avenue
Madison, WI 53703
608-255-2977
AC(IVAS), BF, CH, CN, CM

WYOMING

Stephen M. Kerr, DVM
Rural Route #2, Box 326
Torrington, WY 82240
307-532-7704
FAX: 307-532-4736
Small Animal, Equine, Farm Animal, Avian, Exotic
AC, BF, CH, CR, CN, CM, EAV, HC, WH

Vicki Burton, DVM
812 S. 13th Street
Laramie, WY 82070
307-742-2488
Small Animal, Equine
AC(IVAS), BF, CH, WH

Index

Notes About My Cat's Diet

_____
_____
_____
_____
_____
_____
_____
_____
_____
_____
_____
_____
_____
_____
_____
_____
_____
_____
_____
_____
_____
_____
_____
_____
_____

Notes About My Cat's Diet

_____
_____
_____
_____
_____
_____
_____
_____
_____
_____
_____
_____
_____
_____
_____
_____
_____
_____
_____
_____
_____
_____
_____
_____
_____

About the Author

PAT LAZARUS has been a respected investigative medical journalist since the late 1970s, publishing some four hundred articles in magazines for the public and in technical publications written for doctors. These articles disseminated little-known successful orthodox and natural treatments for humans. Her first book, *Keep Your Pet Healthy the Natural Way,* one of the very first books written on holistic care for animals, was widely acclaimed, remained in print for almost two decades, and is often considered the classic book in the field of natural care for cats and dogs. This present book greatly expands and completely updates the earlier book and focuses only on cats. As this present book goes to press, the author is finishing its companion book, *Keep Your Dog Healthy the Natural Way.*

A second book, *Healing the Mind the Natural Way,* compiled the work of a number of psychiatrists who use nutritional therapy and other natural techniques to treat emotional and mental disorders in humans.

Pat, who greatly respects orthodox techniques such as drugs and surgery—especially in emergency situations—has come to her particular passion for natural therapies by a personal route. She, her husband, and many of her own animal companions have used nutritional therapy, acupuncture, homeopathy, and/or glandular therapy to recover easily from problems diagnosed by orthodox doctors as needing dangerous major surgery or potent drugs—or as being untreatable or downright terminal.